WHO OWNS DEATH?

WHO OWNS DEATH?

CAPITAL PUNISHMENT, THE AMERICAN CONSCIENCE, AND THE END OF EXECUTIONS

ROBERT JAY LIFTON

AND

GREG MITCHELL

WILLIAM MORROW

An Imprint of HarperCollins*Publishers*

364.6609
L,f

HarperCollins books may be purchased for educational, business, or sales promotional use. For information please write: Special Markets Department, HarperCollins Publishers Inc., 10 East 53rd Street, New York, NY 10022.

FIRST EDITION

Designed by Jam Design

Printed on acid-free paper

Library of Congress Cataloging-in-Publication Data
Lifton, Robert Jay
Who owns death?: capital punishment, the American conscience, and the end of executions / Robert Jay Lifton and Greg Mitchell.—1st ed.
    p.   cm.
Includes index.
ISBN 0-380-97498-3
1. Capital punishment—United States.   I. Mitchell, Greg.   II. Title.
HV8699.U5 L54 2000
364.66'0973—dc21
                                    00-032464

00 01 02 03 04 RRD 10 9 8 7 6 5 4 3 2 1

*To the families of murder victims, and to
advocates of a state that does not kill*

Contents

Acknowledgments

Much wisdom based on extensive experience with the death penalty was conveyed to us by Patricia Barnes, William Bowers, David Bruck, Marie Deans, Kevin Doyle, Norman Mailer, Edwin Mathews, Ron Sievert, and Richard Stetler.

Our greatest source of week-to-week (almost day-to-day) information on developments around the country and opinions on all sides of the issue was provided by Rick Halperin of Amnesty International in Texas.

Dialogs with Charles B. Strozier and Michael Flynn enriched the book, as did responses from members of the Wellfleet Psychohistory Group, to whom many of our ideas were presented.

We would also like to thank the authors of books that proved particularly useful in our work, including Hugo Bedau, John Bessler, Wendy Kaminer, Wendy Lesser, Lewis P. Masur, Stephen Trombley, and others cited in our notes.

Barbara Bedway and Betty Jean Lifton maintained loving support and offered incisive commentary throughout, as did Kenneth and Michelle Lifton, Natasha Karen Lifton, and Daniel Itzkovitz.

From beginning to end Tina Bennett and Sara Lazin provided astute agentry and advice, always with a human face. Rachel Klayman's early enthusiasm was crucial to the project.

Gail Winston, our editor, managed to combine tough-minded criticism with unflagging enthusiasm and a true maestro's sensitivity and coordination.

PREFACE

CAPITAL PUNISHMENT IN AMERICA
Are Its Days Numbered?

CONFLICT, contradiction, and ambivalence surround capital punishment in America. This has been true for centuries, but only now have we reached a state of profound confusion. More inmates were executed in our country in 1999 than in any year since 1952, and the execution rate has soared 800 percent in the past decade. At the same time, opposition to state killing—on moral, practical, and legal grounds—has intensified, as reflected in recent opinion polls, attempts by legislators to abolish or restrict the death penalty, and the refusal of many jurors to sentence killers to death.

From death row one controversy after another has emerged, ranging from whom we kill (a woman, in Texas) to how we kill (the electric chair, in Florida), threatening the institution of capital punishment. Yet the machinery of execution in America grinds ever more efficiently as the appeals process is tightened. Even as debate swirls, the death houses become more densely packed, with more than 3,500 prisoners—an all-time record—now awaiting their fate. Many of them have already dodged the executioner for a decade or more. If the logjam finally breaks, "we're going to be executing people quicker than we can refill the lethal injection syringes," warns a former warden, Donald Cabana.

Executions have become relatively glitch-free, and so common that the news media no longer cover or even mention all of them. Seats set aside for reporters to witness executions often go unclaimed. Public protests dwindle. "After a while, it just gets to be something that people expect," comments an assistant attorney general in Oklahoma.

At the same time, however, the number of new death sentences imposed by juries has declined in recent years, hitting a low in 1999. The public still embraces the death penalty in theory, but in practice they look at it with an increasingly critical eye. Opinion surveys show that a vast majority of Americans endorse the idea of executions, yet support plummets when tough alternative sentencing, such as life without parole, is proposed. Polls also suggest that most people are deeply troubled by revelations of innocent men on death row. Sam Jordan, director of Amnesty International's death penalty project, observes, "The picture around the country is a reexamination of the death penalty in light of weaknesses and defects in its imposition."

Indeed, ambiguity around this issue abounds. Nearly everyone feels that there is *something* wrong about capital punishment, perhaps because it violates our fundamental commitment to life while claiming to uphold it.

A legislator in Nebraska wonders how his state could have 155 men and women imprisoned for first-degree murder, and yet they are not on death row, while ten others convicted of similar crimes face execution. Two bills recently came before the state legislature in New Mexico. One called for speeding executions; the other proposed banning them altogether.

Twelve states continue to outlaw executions, but one abolitionist state, Massachusetts, nearly brought back the death penalty, while conservative states such as Indiana, Kentucky, and Montana considered closing their death chambers. New Hampshire's conservative legislature became the first such body in decades to abolish the death penalty, although the state's governor later vetoed the bill. Even Texas, which has set the execution pace for the nation since the 1970s, finds itself torn between acceleration and moderation. In the aftermath of the execution of Karla Faye Tucker—a woman who gained backing from religious conservatives such as Pat Robertson—support for the death penalty in the state fell off in polls. Legislators for the first time proposed life without parole as an alternative to death. Then, after a horrific racial slaying in Jasper, Texas, lawmakers proposed *expanding* the death penalty, and in 1999 Texas led the nation with thirty-five executions.

Several governors granted clemency to condemned prisoners, but as always it was hard to explain why some killers were saved and others left to die. Fob James, the conservative governor of Alabama, spared a woman (now a born-again Christian) who had abducted a 13-year-old girl from a shopping mall; the child was sexually assaulted, injected with drain cleaner, shot, and thrown into a canyon. The state attorney general, taking issue with the governor, called the spared woman "the worst killer—her crime is the most gruesome—of any on death row, certainly worse than any of the cases where there's been an execution" since he'd been in office.

More governors are granting reprieves, but still there is a sense that the execution regimen has been fine-tuned, with the elimination of multiple appeals and increased reliance on the more "humane" killing method of lethal injection. In the spring of 2000, Tennessee executed its first man since 1960, and Arkansas took the life of its first woman ever. The present move away from the electric chair, in the wake of several botched executions in Florida, means that, in the short run, more will probably die, if less horribly. Brad Thomas, a top policy aide on this issue to Governor Jeb Bush, recently commented that he hoped Florida could "become more like Texas. Bring in the witnesses, put them on a gurney, and let's rock and roll."

The long-term outlook for executions in America, however, remains murky—and, we believe, they will come to an end fairly soon. For, as the *New York Times* declared in February 2000, "America is at last beginning to grapple honestly with the profound flaws of the death penalty system."

Like our previous collaboration, *Hiroshima in America*, this book blends our varied backgrounds in psychology, history, and journalism. We have long been involved with issues of death and life-continuity, with myriad forms of violence, and with their larger meanings for society. And the death penalty, after all, is the only circumstance other than war in which it is legal for us to kill.

One of us (Lifton) is a psychiatrist who has written much about death and its symbolism, and about the psychology of survivors. Studies of mass killing and genocide on the part of governments led him to a strong concern about capital punishment—government killing of *individuals*—and about the complex psychological and ethical reverberations of such killing. The other author (Mitchell) has long been fascinated with the death penalty as represented by the media and popular culture, going back to the Chessman case in the 1950s. He turns to it now, in this book, because of the growing urgency surrounding this issue—given the rising execution rate, with thousands of other lives in the balance.

While we have opposed capital punishment for many years, we felt compelled in writing this book to learn more about those on the other side. Clearly, we hold a minority view on this issue, and public opinion appeared to be changing very little when we turned to this subject four years ago. How could we ever hope to address popular enthusiasm for the death penalty if we did not understand the reasons for America's unyielding support for executions, and the emotions behind it? So we set out to explore the motivations at the very heart of the issue. Indeed, we took a similar approach in our previous book, when we sought to learn why Americans have strongly supported the atomic bombing of Japan for so many decades.

Much has been written about inmates on death row, dedicated defense attorneys, and legal issues surrounding the death penalty. Our book focuses instead on why American society and most of its citizens continue to embrace capital punishment, which has been abandoned by every other developed nation in the West. It explores, from both a psychological and a social perspective, the new waves of pained feelings engulfing this issue. We examine human experience, but rather than emphasize discord between individuals, we focus on the conflicts *within* most of us, and within our society.

We believe that a nuanced psychological perspective, exploring multiple points of view, can yield fresh insights. And so we talked with scholars and activists, prosecutors and defense attorneys, religious figures and prison officials, always emphasizing questions of attitude and motivation—their own and the nation's as a whole. After much reflection, we reached two conclusions that surprised us.

First, we find that the prevailing wisdom—that America is fiercely in favor of executions—is largely wrong. Americans may support executions in the abstract, but they are confused about how capital punishment works and should work, and uneasy about seeing it carried out. In fact, they now prefer another method of punishing the wrongdoer and protecting society. Although few raise their voices loudly in protest, many are uncomfortable with the notion of the state as killer, and this number rises every time an inmate is released from death row when new evidence, often from DNA testing, establishes his innocence. Such doubts led Governor George Ryan to declare a moratorium on executions in Illinois early in 2000.

Our second conclusion also challenges conventional thinking. We believe that even as the execution rate soars, the death penalty's days are numbered. We find ourselves agreeing with Victor Streib, dean of the College of Law at Ohio Northern University, who recently predicted that the death penalty, in most parts of the United States, "will fade out. We will probably get rid of it." Qualms about the rising tide of executions may even be a *cause* of abolition, or the catalyst may be the increasingly strong stand taken by Catholic bishops and other religious leaders against the death penalty—or the growing recognition that viable alternatives to executions exist. Or perhaps unforeseen events will lead to abolition, as they did, many years ago, in England and France. As prominent anti–death penalty attorney Stephen Bright puts it, "There seems to be a growing awareness that the death penalty is just another government program that doesn't work very well."

The famous attorney Clarence Darrow once observed that issues about capital punishment that seem to have been resolved "do not stay settled, for the emotions change as new stimuli are applied to the machine." What we have done in this book is examine the newest "stimuli" with the aim of better understanding the emotions underneath.

It is important to emphasize at the outset that a searching exploration of this subject, from all sides, does not mean that we in any way take lightly the initiating acts in this drama: the cruel slaying of one human being by another. Whenever we mention a condemned prisoner in our narrative, we describe the nature of his crime, if we know it. We believe that we must, as writers and as citizens, face squarely these vicious acts and their impact on the victims' families. And we can well understand how a husband or sister of a murder victim might want to tear the killer limb from limb; we'd probably feel the same way, at least initially.

Yet this does not provide a clear indication about what *society* should do with convicted killers. In his film *Dead Man Walking*, the director Tim Robbins did not shrink from graphically portraying both a murder and an execution. The profound moral question, he explained, is: "Can we kill *anybody?*"

Another way of putting this might be: Who owns death?

Our book opens with a brief examination of how recent events in three very different states—Missouri, Massachusetts, and California—reveal the conflicts and divisions beneath what is generally referred to as America's overwhelming support for capital punishment. Then we step back to explore the history of the death penalty in the United States, not so much to learn how it developed in the legal arena but to understand how it entered into the American psyche and how it established patterns that linger to this day. From there we probe changes in methods of execution, from hanging to lethal injection, considering what this search for more "humane" executions reveals about us as individuals and as a society.

For much of the rest of the book we focus on individual Americans deeply involved in the death penalty process: prosecutors and governors, judges and jurors, murder victims' families, wardens and guards, and witnesses to executions, among others. We try to bring empathy to our explorations of the deeper emotions, moral views and, in some cases, political calculations behind both public attitudes and official behavior. We examine how those who ratify or carry out executions are protected against experiencing what they are actually doing, and how misgivings, nevertheless, often surface. Uncovering the psychological conflicts that complicate capital punishment, we aim to understand *why* executions persist in America, and why they will not endure much longer.

From our study of individuals, we then open out, in our concluding chapter, to society as a whole, and examine the broad effects of capital punishment. What ripples and reverberations do executions send out to society as a whole? Does the death penalty have a brutalizing effect, contributing to both a habit of violence and our psychic numbing to that violence? What does our society have, or lack, that creates what Pope John Paul recently called our "culture of death"? On the other hand, what factors within ourselves nearly cripple capital punishment, preventing the execution of large numbers of convicted killers? We conclude that the state's ownership of death, in the name of eliminating evil, cannot be justified—and cannot be sustained indefinitely.

Although our findings are at times troubling, they are also hopeful, as we explore the possibility that Americans, more divided on this issue than opinion polls seem to indicate, will one day retire execution chambers all over this country. This kind of exploration, we believe, can contribute to further wisdom about the nature of killing—and the value of life.

PART
I

TODAY

AND

YESTERDAY

1

THE POPE'S TRAVEL PLANS

Three States, Three Views of the Death Penalty

NEARLY three decades have passed since the U.S. Supreme Court ruled that the death penalty had been applied capriciously and arbitrarily in America. Justice Byron White declared that "there is no meaningful basis for distinguishing the few cases in which it is imposed from the many cases in which it is not." The court threw out all state and federal laws prescribing capital punishment but did not ban future executions if the system could be made more consistent.

Rather than letting capital punishment go, most states set out to reform their laws to win the Supreme Court's approval so that executions could resume. They might not have gotten very far, except that public opinion, which had briefly turned against state killing, had changed again. The murder rate was soaring and fear of crime—along with increasing anger at the perpetrators—had sent support for executions spiraling upward again.

Reflecting the shift in popular sentiment, the Supreme Court in 1976 ruled that executions could indeed return as states made their capital procedures clearer for all and somewhat fairer for racial minorities. Now events moved swiftly. The following year Gary Gilmore became the first condemned American to die since 1967, shot by a firing squad in a makeshift execution chamber in Utah. By the early 1980s, backing for capital punishment had reached 72 percent in the Gallup poll, and it kept gaining after that. Slowly, the execution rate rose, from a handful a year to several dozen to ninety-eight in 1999—marking a return to the level of the pre-1950s, where it may well remain for some time.

On the surface, then, we are experiencing what might be called a return to the heyday of capital punishment in America. In fact, the upsurge in executions may be sowing the seeds for its demise.

For the death penalty protocol in the United States remains nearly as arbitrary as it was thirty years ago when it was halted, for a time, by the Supreme Court. It could hardly be otherwise, in a country with fifty states, each with its own laws covering executions. Even within the same state, procedures for prosecuting capital cases vary from county to county. And this doesn't even begin to take into account the luck of the lottery—the fact that a prisoner's fate is often determined mainly by the makeup of a jury and the competence of his attorney, not the brutality of his crime.

So the arbitrary nature of capital punishment is nothing new. Indeed, it is inherent. What appears to be changing is that a wide range of Americans—from Catholic bishops to conservative governors—appear increasingly uneasy with its still erratic application. In fact, the latest Gallup poll on this issue, in February 2000, found support for capital punishment at its lowest level in nineteen years—66 percent, down from 80 percent in 1994. In the spring of 2000, a number of conservatives, including evangelist Pat Robertson, endorsed a national moratorium, citing concerns about unjust convictions, or expressed new "skepticism" regarding the death penalty, as columnist George Will put it.

And although the overall execution rate is up, this masks the fact that the majority of executions are carried out by just four states: Texas, Florida, Virginia, and Missouri. Most states rarely, if ever, execute anyone, although laws allowing executions remain on the books; and twelve states continue to ban the practice altogether. Kill one man in Texas, and you lose your life; slaughter a family in Michigan, and you never face the execution chamber.

A look at three widely scattered states, with very different attitudes toward capital punishment, illustrates the volatility of public and official attitudes about the death penalty in America, and how its arbitrary nature causes widespread discomfort, and increasingly, moral or ethical outrage.

Missouri: Who Can We Execute?

In November 1998, the Missouri supreme court ruled that Darrell J. Mease must die by lethal injection at the state penitentiary in Potosi on January 27, 1999. This was, in death row parlance, a "firm date," and further appeals appeared hopeless. Missouri had executed nine men in the past two years, making it the third most active death penalty state in the nation, and few doubted that Mease would soon be added to that list. A state Republican leader called Mease a "poster boy for the death penalty." The prisoner had avoided the death chamber for ten years, but now his luck was running out.

Or was it?

Back in 1988, Darrell Mease, then 42, hid along a gravel path in the Ozark woods near Reeds Spring, Missouri, dressed in camouflage clothes, and ambushed a 69-year-old man (his former drug partner), the man's wife, and their 19-year-old grandson (a paraplegic) as they approached, driving all-terrain vehicles. Then he shot each of them in the face at point-blank range. Mease confessed to the crime. A jury convicted him, and the verdict was upheld on appeal in one court after another during the following decade. The governor of Missouri, a moderate Democrat named Mel Carnahan, was not likely to commute his sentence; this happened only about once a year in the entire nation, and Mease was considered an exceedingly poor candidate for clemency.

But then Darrell Mease, in a sense, became the luckiest man alive. A few days after the state's highest court set a date for his execution, the Vatican announced that Pope John Paul II, an increasingly outspoken opponent of the death penalty, would visit St. Louis on the very day Mease was to take his last breath. In an attempt to avoid a public relations fiasco, the court postponed Mease's execution two weeks, but this only drew more attention to it. A Vatican spokesman called the delay "a mockery," and the pope prepared a speech, to be delivered in Missouri, affirming in his strongest language yet his opposition to capital punishment. He called on America to "resist the culture of death and choose to stand steadfastly on the side of life."

When the pontiff arrived in St. Louis, he met with Carnahan and asked the governor to spare Darrell Mease's life. The pope had made similar appeals in other states in recent years, with little success; in fact, he had once asked Carnahan to spare another inmate, to no avail. Those pleas, however, had come from across the ocean, not in person. Still, Mease seemed doomed. In those previous cases, there was always some element of doubt about the condemned man's guilt, or the fairness of his trial, or his mental balance, and yet the pope's appeals had failed. These mitigating elements were all missing in regard to Mease.

There was this further obstacle for Mease: Carnahan was known as a law-and-order governor who had approved twenty-six executions since taking office in 1993, intervening in just one case (involving a mentally retarded inmate). He had let an execution proceed just twelve days before the papal visit, without apparent concern for the timing. Also, he planned to challenge the incumbent, John Ashcroft, in an upcoming contest for the U.S. Senate, meaning that he was even less likely to buck public opinion to spare a condemned killer. Carnahan wasn't even a Catholic but a southern Baptist, in a largely Protestant state.

Yet Governor Carnahan, perhaps to his own surprise, found himself swayed by the words from the pope's own lips and quickly commuted Mease's sentence, to a storm of criticism.

And no wonder. Carnahan did not claim that he had learned anything new about the condemned man or his case for clemency. He professed no change in his moral view or his opinion of capital punishment. He had spared Mease simply because of "the historical significance" of the pope's visit, and because the pope had *asked*. "I continue to support capital punishment," Carnahan announced, "but after careful consideration of his direct and personal appeal and because of a deep and abiding respect for the pontiff and all he represents, I decided last night to grant his request."

The pope praised Carnahan's "generous decision," but many others were outraged. If the governor was going to spare someone, why Mease? Even one of Mease's lawyers admitted that "this case was probably one of the weaker clemency cases," including some involving men already executed. "I guess timing is everything, huh?" he quipped.

The county prosecutor who had put Mease on trial added sardonically, "God works in mysterious ways." A spokesman for the state Republican party, savoring the expected political repercussions for Democrats, asked, "If we can't execute Darrell Mease, who can we execute?" Senator Ashcroft, preparing for his showdown with Carnahan on the campaign trail, said that the U.S. Congress should prevent acts of clemency, such as the one perpetrated in his state. Then he held a victims' rights hearing in St. Louis and invited as his star witnesses relatives of the three people Mease had killed. Polls showed that Carnahan lost four potential votes for every one he gained by sparing the prisoner.

Members of the murder victims' family were livid. The dead couple's son charged that the governor and the pope "are showing more mercy toward a convicted killer than toward us." One friend of the family said that if he could get close to the pope he would "sock him straight and sure in the mouth."

Most newspaper editorials railed against the governor. The publisher of a daily newspaper in Columbia, Missouri, who supported Carnahan, declared that the governor "should have received the pontiff's admonition and ignored it." But the *Kansas City Star*, charging that the sparing of Darrell Mease showed the inconsistency and arbitrariness of the death penalty, called for its abolition. An unexpected public debate over capital punishment had broken out in Missouri, raising "new possibilities," the newspaper said, "to rethink this barbaric punishment that so many civilized countries have abandoned."

Yet would anything change in Missouri after the Mease case, or was it merely an aberration? With several other executions pending, it wouldn't take long to find out. "A governor who would put him- or herself in this position is facing a real challenge in the next case," commented Mike Johanns, governor of neighboring Nebraska.

Death penalty opponents in Missouri and around the country seized on the Mease case as a shocking example of the unfairness, absurdity, and cruelty of capital punishment. Why should he live and thousands of others on death row still face execution? "Surely some opportunistic lawyer should file suit for these inmates, making that precise point," the *St. Louis Post-Dispatch* editorialized.

In fact, the next prisoner slated to be executed in Missouri had already thought of that. "I think that if you do it for one person, you should do it for all," argued James Edward Rodden, who had stabbed a woman to death in 1983 and then tried to set her on fire. Rodden's lawyer, Kent Gipson, had a more realistic view, observing that his client was probably doomed because Carnahan would now try to prove he was *not* soft on crime. "I knew as soon as the pope's feet left the tarmac, they'd be scurrying to issue death warrants," Gipson observed. "I don't think anyone has much of a chance between now and the Senate race, unless you have a videotape and DNA showing he's innocent—and another visit from the pope."

Indeed, Rodden would die by lethal injection a little more than a month after the pope's visit. Carnahan denied a request for clemency, while affirming that he still had no second thoughts about sparing Mease. Since Rodden had displayed no remorse for his crime, and had few outside supporters, the governor probably lost little sleep over this decision. But another impending execution in Missouri put the capriciousness of this life-or-death issue squarely at center stage.

Roy Roberts had been convicted of killing a prison guard in 1983, but he always maintained his innocence—his alibi was that he was brawling with *another* guard at the time—and he had many supporters who felt that the evidence against him was, at best, contradictory. Roberts had allegedly held a guard down during a prison riot while two other inmates stabbed him to death. Owing to strange twists of fate (no small factor in capital cases), neither of the two actual killers now faced execution. A deadlocked jury led to a sentence of life in prison for one, while the other faced a retrial because of prosecutorial error.

"That kind of discrepancy shows how arbitrary you can get," Roberts's attorney argued. He maintained that Carnahan should at least delay the execution. Pressure built when Roberts passed a lie detector test, but his backers feared the worst anyway. One of Roberts's lawyers charged that his client might have been spared if Mease had died as scheduled. Another called on Carnahan to exhibit "courage."

On March 10, 1999, Missouri executed Roy Roberts. His final words were, "You're killing an innocent man." Governor Carnahan had turned down a last-minute reprieve. A few days later, an editorial in the *Washington Post* declared that "one couldn't ask for a better portrait of the arbitrariness of the death penalty" than the recent events in Missouri. The governor "ended up granting clemency in a case with no significant question of innocence and denying clemency in a case where questions remain about the evidence. Who gets executed should not, in a sane criminal justice system, depend upon the pope's travel schedule."

On the day Roy Roberts died, the Missouri supreme court set an execution date five weeks hence for a man who had killed a Grandview couple in 1988. And so the sparing of Darrell Mease, in the end, had not slowed—and might have even accelerated—the execution assembly line in the state of Missouri.

The pope's dramatic lifesaving effort in Missouri produced wide ripples elsewhere, however. The nation's fifty-five Roman Catholic bishops for the first time made opposition to the death penalty an urgent priority. They released a statement on Good Friday, "a day when we recall our Savior's own execution," asking "all people of goodwill, and especially Catholics, to work to end the death penalty." Polls showed that the country's 60 million Catholics were no more likely to oppose the death penalty than others. The bishops admitted that this was understandable, because of fear of crime, empathy for murder victims, and desire for revenge, but expressed the hope that Catholics "will come to see, as we have, that more violence is not the answer. We cannot teach that killing is wrong by killing. The death penalty offers the tragic illusion that we can defend life by taking life."

In Texas, the nation's leading death penalty state, the bishop of the Austin Diocese issued a separate call, denouncing the injustice of the death penalty, since "only the poor get executed." In Ohio, on the eve of the state's first execution in thirty-five years, the archbishop of Cincinnati called the death penalty "a relic of barbarism in our society."

The explicit statements by the pope and the American bishops put many of the governors in death penalty states, especially those of the Catholic faith, on the spot. In Virginia, second only to Texas in frequency of executions, Walter Sullivan, bishop of the Richmond Diocese, called for a halt, with seven executions planned in coming weeks. "The taking of human life falls within the providence of God alone," he asserted. A few weeks later, Governor Jim Gilmore of Virginia spared a mentally ill prisoner just hours from execution, his first clemency since taking office. Florida's Catholic bishops called on Governor Jeb Bush to spare two condemned killers, contending that "killing people to show that killing is wrong is a piercing contradiction." Although Bush was not swayed, it marked the first time the state's bishops had addressed a governor in an open letter and the first time they had specifically called on one to commute a death sentence.

Mike Johanns, the governor of Nebraska, faced a controversial decision himself in the wake of Missouri's papal controversy. An American Indian named Randy Reeves who had killed two women in 1980 and now faced execution had won wide public support. Reeves was apparently drunk on beer and high on peyote when he stabbed the two women—one of them a Quaker, the other her close friend. The parents of one of the victims, and the husband

and daughter of the other, both lobbied the governor to spare the killer, a lonely struggle in a pro-execution state.

So what would Johanns do? The pope's representative in Washington, D.C., urged him to halt the execution. Several bishops in Nebraska also called for clemency. This was particularly touchy for Johanns, because as a candidate for governor a few months earlier he had asserted that his desire to serve the state was animated by his religious faith. Ultimately, he threw his weight against clemency. "The pope is the leader of the church I belong to," he explained, "but I also am governor of the state of Nebraska and bound by my oath to follow the laws of this state." A short while later, however, Reeves earned relief from another quarter, when the state supreme court granted a stay.

Then, as 1999, and the century, neared its end, Governor Jim Hunt of North Carolina, who had previously turned down all twelve pleas for clemency from death row during his four terms in office, spared a prisoner named Wendell Flowers on the eve of his execution. In the new atmosphere of sensitivity to blatant injustice, Governor Hunt took mercy on this prisoner. Flowers was one of four men who had been charged with killing a prison guard, but none of the other three had ever faced execution, and the evidence against Flowers was far from airtight. Details such as these had rarely spared condemned men in the past. In fact, Flowers's case eerily resembled the Roy Roberts case in Missouri, and Roberts had been executed.

It is revealing that in his statement explaining his move, the governor emphasized that Flowers would "spend the rest of his natural life in prison with absolutely no possibility of parole"—probably sensing that today, in most such cases, the majority of the public is satisfied with that.

The Flowers example, along with the papal intervention in Missouri and official reexamination of execution policy in Illinois, Florida, New Mexico, and several other states, heartened death penalty opponents around the country. "There's a change in the public attitude on the death penalty," exclaimed Steven Hawkins, director of the National Coalition to Abolish the Death Penalty. "We're very encouraged by what we're hearing in the heartland." In time, the pope's visit to Missouri, and his sparing of a single, not particularly worthy prisoner—an act of mercy as arbitrary as the execution of so many others—may be regarded as a turning point in America's history of state killing.

Massachusetts: "Wrong, Morally Evil, and a Sin"

Oddly, one of the most emotional and significant debates over the death penalty in 1999 took place in a state far removed from Missouri on many levels, a state that has not come close to sponsoring an execution in more than half a century. It happened in Massachusetts when Governor Paul Cellucci, recently elected after campaigning strongly for executions, threw his weight behind legislators' attempts to repeal the state's ban on the death penalty.

Pressure for executions had been building in this liberal state since 1997, when a 10-year-old Cambridge boy named Jeffrey Curley was brutally slain and dumped into a river after being sexually molested by two pedophiles. The legislature voted 81–79 to bring back the death penalty, but then one lawmaker, John P. Slattery of Peabody, changed his vote, killing the bill for the moment. The following year, Cellucci made the repeal a centerpiece of his campaign for governor and defeated an anti-death penalty Democrat in November. Republicans quickly drew up a bill allowing capital punishment for sixteen crimes, including killing a policeman or a child under age 14.

Observers predicted another close vote. Polls suggested that a clear majority of the state residents favored capital punishment. Governor Cellucci admitted that capital punishment was not a "panacea" but said it would be worth trying if it saved just one life. "It is one way that society can send a clear and unmistakable message that we're not going to tolerate deadly, horrific violence in our state," he argued. Others pointed out that violent crime was at a thirty-year low in the state despite the absence of the death penalty, and the director of the state ACLU publicized recent events in Illinois involving the near-execution of several innocent men. The *Boston Globe* editorialized that life without parole was an appropriate punishment for killers, and that it protected the public sufficiently; anything more was simply "revenge."

Still, the vote appeared to be a toss-up, until a new element entered the debate. In the wake of Pope John Paul's statements in Missouri, bishops in the overwhelming Catholic state spoke out more forcefully against the death penalty. This was a problem, both politically and personally, for the state's Catholic governor. The influential cardinal of Boston, Bernard Law, testified at a state hearing against capital punishment; then, at a news conference, he challenged Cellucci provocatively. "The teachings of the church are very clear," Law declared. "For a well-informed Catholic to support capital punishment, it would be morally wrong. And if one knowingly rejects the teachings of the church it is wrong, morally evil, and a sin."

Cellucci replied: "Well, I mean, that's his opinion. There's an awful lot of Catholics in Massachusetts and an awful lot of them support the death penalty," which was no doubt true.

Cardinal Law's most dramatic confrontation, however, came not with the governor but with a woman in Peabody named Susan Gove, who also testified at the hearing, speaking in favor of the death penalty for two men who had bludgeoned her daughter to death in 1996. She assailed Cardinal Law, saying that he must understand that he "has only one vote in this state." Then she crossed paths with the cardinal in the lobby at the statehouse. "Don't you feel that the men who destroyed my daughter should deserve a punishment equal to the crime?" she asked him angrily.

"I believe that the crime against your daughter, the crime against her life, is not going to be taken care of by the killing of another person," he replied evenly. They talked awhile longer, quietly, and parted with an embrace, but with no shift in beliefs on either side. Several legislators, however, seemed to shrink from support for executions following Cardinal Law's pronouncements—and ulti-mately the repeal bill was shelved by a wider margin than the pre-vious year's vote.

California: Death Row Bursting at the Seams

So Massachusetts would remain ambivalently abolitionist while Missouri remained shakily committed to capital punishment. But what of the vast majority of states: those with the death penalty on the books but rarely, or never, utilized? Less than twenty states executed anyone even in the high-water year of 1999.

As always, California may be a trendsetter in this regard, or at least it provides tantalizing clues. In the first twenty-one years after the U.S. Supreme Court reinstated the death penalty in 1977, California executed only five prisoners, despite having a number of governors who favored capital punishment. The state has a lurid history of executions, with death row celebrities like Caryl Chessman and Barbara Graham, and its gas chamber at San Quentin has been immortalized, or satirized, in many Hollywood movies. But the population of California also has a strong liberal (anti-death penalty) segment and many abolitionist activists.

By 1999, something had to give. California's death row was practically bursting at the seams, with more than 550 awaiting execution, the most in the nation. More than 100 had been there over *fifteen years*. And California had a new governor, Gray Davis, with something to prove. Davis had come to prominence in the 1970s as chief aide to Governor Jerry Brown, who was opposed to capital punishment. Davis had promoted Brown's views on the issue at that time but, running for governor himself in 1998 against a law-and-order Republican, he emphasized that long ago he had swung over to the pro-execution side. Or, as he put it: "If you take someone else's life, forget it."

Davis had learned his history lessons well. Jerry Brown's father, Governor Edmund G. "Pat" Brown, was defeated for reelection in 1966 by Ronald Reagan at least partly because of his distaste for capital punishment. More than a decade later, Jerry Brown suffered humiliation after voters, in an unprecedented ballot measure, removed three anti–death penalty justices Brown had appointed to the state supreme court. And Jerry Brown's sister, Kathleen, had lost a race for governor in 1994 against the incumbent, Pete Wilson, who highlighted her opposition to executions.

When he took office in January 1999, Gray Davis had campaign promises to uphold. He also had a controversial clemency case before him practically from his first day in office. It involved a former Buddhist monk from Thailand named Jaturun Siripongs, who had killed two people but had gone on to express remorse and become a model prisoner. Davis decided to let that execution proceed, and it did, and normally that would have been the only case a governor of California would have to consider for another year or more, with popular and judicial sentiment divided in his state. But the pace of executions was picking up in California, and within weeks another sticky case attracted national attention.

The inmate this time was Manny Babbitt. He had broken into the apartment of an elderly Sacramento woman named Leah Schendel in 1980, intent on robbery, and had beaten her so severely he split her skull and fractured her dentures; she died of a heart attack. The next night he robbed and attempted to rape another Sacramento woman. Years before, he had assaulted and sodomized a 13-year-old baby-sitter. But he had a few things going for him in the court of public opinion: he was a Vietnam veteran with a Purple Heart and a long and well-documented pattern of mental illness. And, like Theodore Kaczynski, the "Unabomber," he had been turned in by his own brother after the police had assured the brother that this would save Manny from the death chamber.

In campaigning for governor, Gray Davis had not only embraced the death penalty but promised his fellow Vietnam vets that he would speak up for them in office. Now thousands of Vietnam veterans lobbied the governor for clemency in the Babbitt case. Certain details of the murder strongly suggested to them that Babbitt was suffering from posttraumatic effects, and there was little question in any case that he was mentally impaired (he had once been diagnosed as a paranoid schizophrenic, and he had spent time at a hospital for the criminally insane). Perhaps since Governor Davis had let Siripongs die, proving his mettle, he might now spare Babbitt? Davis was a Catholic, as well, and other Catholic governors, as we have seen, seemed troubled in the wake of the pope's recent statements.

At a clemency hearing, among those speaking for Babbitt was a Vietnam vet who said Babbitt had saved his life at Khe Sanh. Two jurors in his original case claimed they wouldn't have sentenced Babbitt to death if they'd known about his mental problems; and his original lawyer admitted having "failed completely in the death penalty phase" of the trial. Weighing in from Massachusetts—Babbitt's home state—Cardinal Law asked Governor Davis to show mercy toward a mentally ill inmate. More surprising, the father of Jeffrey Curley (the boy whose death had instigated the uproar over the death penalty in Massachusetts in 1997) also spoke out for clemency. He said he still supported capital punishment, but "Babbitt sounds like a sick man. . . . I just feel that we're all best served on both sides of the death penalty to work toward preventing this."

Questions of mental competency, as always, raised thorny issues. By some reckonings, Manny Babbitt was too evil to live but too deranged to die. In a word, was he "executable"? The U.S. Supreme Court had long ago ruled that prisoners who are mentally incompetent cannot be put to death, but this is, of course, a subjective area, open to changing standards and practices.

The Babbitt case followed hard on the heels of the Horace Kelly debacle in California. Kelly had been sentenced to die years ago for shooting to death two women and an 11-year-old boy and had been found sane by the jurors. Later, he began to sit in his own feces in his cell and speak gibberish. As he neared execution in the spring of 1998, a court suddenly convened a new panel to decide whether he was now too mentally ill (diagnosed as schizophrenic) to be killed. And if it found him incompetent? The state announced that it would send him to a prison mental hospital for treatment— in hopes of improving his condition enough to execute him.

But what if Kelly refused to cooperate with doctors in their quest for mental improvement? Such cases were ultimate expressions of Catch-22. Indeed, several death row prisoners around the country were now arguing that they had the right to refuse to take the medication that made them mentally stable enough to be executed. "They're sane enough to know that by stopping their medication they will not be executed," quipped Dudley Sharp, an advocate of victims' rights in Texas. "Is that the reasoning of a sane man or an insane man? It sounds very sane to me."

The Catch-22 logic extends to the current phenomenon of many death row inmates' volunteering to drop appeals and speed their executions. In some cases their lawyers now argue (unsuccessfully, so far) that making such a decision only *proves* that these prisoners are insane and therefore cannot be executed.

Horace Kelly remains among the living but, in the end, no legal gyrations could save Manny Babbitt. Governor Davis ruled that Babbitt's "lifelong and violent criminal activities" did not support a plea for clemency. Thousands of others had served in Vietnam and not come home to rape, beat, and kill. The victim's family praised the governor's "strong commitment to justice." On May 4, 1999, Babbitt was laid out on a gurney in the death chamber at San Quentin and put to death by lethal injection. His last words to the warden were: "I forgive you all."

At one point during the normally placid procedure, his body bucked several times and his chest strained against the straps, causing Laura Thompson, his victim's granddaughter, to look away. Babbitt's brother declared that he had "died as a result of state-sanctioned murder, and history will come to realize that fact."

Most chilling to foes of the death penalty in California was the fear that the trickle of executions in the state would soon become a torrent. "We definitely have the potential for being the next Texas, even with support for capital punishment in California polls at a ten-year low," a director of the state's leading abolitionist group, Death Penalty Focus, warned. Of the seven men the state had put to death since 1977, Manuel Babbitt was the first African American. It was as if the state had to prove that it was not racially motivated by first executing five whites and then a foreign national (Siripongs), before killing a black man. Now, having demonstrated impartiality, it was free to kill anyone—and as many as—it wished, or so it seemed.

Yet months passed, and no other death row inmate approached death's door. Appeals continue to clog the California court system. And if a prisoner neared execution—would Gray Davis now feel he was free to offer clemency in a "marginal" death penalty case such as Babbitt's? "He has to have several executions under his belt to establish his credentials," commented a law professor at the University of California, Franklin Zimring. There never was much chance the governor would show mercy to Babbitt, whose timing for approaching the execution chamber "was all wrong," Zimring observed dryly. Even if the pope had come to California instead of Missouri, Zimring added, his plea for mercy would have been denied.

Lucky Darrell Mease. Unlucky Manny Babbitt. But how had the death penalty in America—after 500 years—come to this?

2

EXECUTIONS IN AMERICA
Trends and Beginnings

S0 long as there have been people on earth, those in authority—familial, tribal, or governmental—have executed wrongdoers in their midst. America has embraced the death penalty since colonial times, and probably before that. Of course, much has changed concerning the institution of capital punishment over these centuries, but what is most striking, in pondering this rich if bloody history, is how much remains the same. Methods of execution evolve—we no longer crucify criminals or stone them to death—but almost every theme, argument, and issue surrounding the death penalty today was sounded or debated in the past. To understand why support for executions persists in our country, one must acknowledge the primal, and universal, emotions that have sustained it for so long, while also recognizing that voices of opposition have always been heard.

Consider the first classic debate on capital punishment, which took place in 428 B.C., in the agora of Athens. It was recorded by Thucydides, who may have been present. During the Peloponnesian War, one of the Athenian city-states, Mytilene, cast its lot with Sparta. Athens sent a fleet to quell the rebellion and bring back the instigators, and they were swiftly executed. Yet this did not satisfy the blood thirst. The assembly soon issued an order to put to death the entire male population of Mytilene, and a ship was dispatched for this purpose—an expression of the death penalty as extreme retribution.

The following day, Diodotus, son of Eucrates, introduced a motion to rescind the order. He then engaged in a debate with Cleon, each airing crucial arguments that envelop the death penalty to this day. Cleon ridiculed the softheartedness of those who called for mercy, and he agitated for carrying out the mass execution on grounds of both vengeance and deterrence. "Punish them as they deserve," he advised, "and teach your other allies by a striking example that the penalty of rebellion is death. Let them once understand this and you will not so often have to neglect your enemies while you are fighting with your confederates." This was an extension of the death penalty, collectively applied to an entire population as a deterrent.

Then Diodotus took the floor. He denounced demagoguery and declared that Athens should act in its best interests, not out of revenge.

> All states and individuals are alike prone to err, and there is no law that will prevent them, or why should men have exhausted the list of punishments in search of enactments to protect them from evildoers? . . . Either some means of terror more terrible than this must be discovered, or it must be owned that this restraint is useless.

This must be one of the first assertions of the death penalty failing as a form of deterrence and the argument carried the day by a slim margin. Another ship was sent to Mytilene, arriving barely in time to prevent a slaughter.

The death penalty by then already had a long history. Patriarchs in early tribes condemned wayward family members to death as a human sacrifice to the gods. One can trace capital punishment with certainty as far back as Babylon, where Hammurabi's Code prescribed death for twenty-five crimes, including sorcery and making false accusations of murder. Many of the early legal codes were based on simple retaliation—doing unto others what they had done to you, or *lex talionis*. Mosaic law, which listed several dozen capital offenses, endorsed the idea of proportionality or, as it came to be written in Exodus, "life for life, eye for eye, tooth for tooth, hand for hand, foot for foot, burning for burning, wound for wound." This rule, often cited to defend capital punishment, was actually prescribed to *limit* the offenses that might be punished by death.

In Greece, under the Draconian Code (circa 621 B.C.), "One penalty was assigned to almost all transgressions, namely death," Plutarch wrote, "so that even those convicted of idleness were put to death and those who stole salt or fruit received the same punishment as those who committed sacrilege or murder." Draco explained that simple misdeeds deserved death—and for greater crimes no heavier penalty could be found. This suggests an illusion of total control over society, with the inference that only good people will survive (by adhering to all laws, all social norms).

Yet the Draconian Code was so harsh it could not be enforced for long: opposition swelled, and Solon soon revised it. A pattern that persists to the present day had already appeared: rapid swings in the severity of death penalty statutes based on the temper of the times.

In the Roman republic, the Law of the XII Tablets upheld the death penalty, but with telling class distinctions: a slave could be condemned for killing a freeman, but not the reverse. Slaves were seen as less than human, as death-tainted, so that killing them, and others from the lower classes, was not really killing. (In every society since, the poor have filled the death houses.) Although early Roman law in many ways showed little advance from the Draconian Code, it did call for juveniles to receive lighter punishments than adults who committed the same offense, a principle sustained to this date, although often bitterly disputed.

Subsequently, across Europe, a long catalog of capital offenses included sorcery, counterfeiting, assorted sexual aberrations, and brawling. "Painless" beheadings were favored for members of the upper classes. Men of the lower classes faced hanging, which was sometimes deliberately prolonged; or they were drawn and quartered, disemboweled, dismembered, burned at the stake, or broken at the wheel. Women were simply drowned, although witches might be burned alive—and tens of thousands were.

During the Middle Ages, public executions were the order of the day; and most were well-attended and enjoyed by the crowds. A carnival atmosphere accompanied the event, often preceded by a procession of the condemned through the streets of the village. Church leaders not only blessed executions—citing biblical passages—but often helped ritualize them, establishing "an entire complex of beliefs and practices that constitutes a kind of tradition," as the theologian James Megivern recently observed.

Animals that killed (or had sexual intercourse with) a human being were, for centuries, tried, defended by counsel, and executed in much the same manner as men—burned, hanged, or buried alive. It was a kind of caricature of the execution of a man or woman. Witnesses often felt ashamed, watching the hanging of an animal, because they sensed the unfair incorporation of another species into our criminal justice system. Arthur Koestler would later ask: "Why do we find the hanging of an animal even more revolting and disgusting than the hanging of a human being? The question deserves some reflection . . . We know that hanging pigs won't deter other pigs from attacking babies left carelessly lying around . . . [But] experience also proves that executing the human criminal is also no more effective as a deterrent than penning him up."

During the eighteenth century, sentiment against capital punishment arose in England, but it was muted. At first the argument (which remains prominent today) was offered on purely religious grounds: the power of life and death rested solely with God. When that didn't work, critics advanced two other reasons that also endure: the death penalty does not succeed as a deterrent, and it violates the hope that many criminals can be rehabilitated.

The idea that authority for killing rests solely with God is a recurrent theme throughout the history of capital punishment. One can put the matter of taking a life in human hands only when one claims the ultimate authority of God. Always present, however, is a sense of *hubris*, of man *becoming* God and taking absolute control over life and death: an accusation that advocates of the death penalty can never fully overcome or dismiss.

The American Way: Laying the Groundwork

Why has capital punishment proved so enduring in America? There are myriad reasons, which we will explore throughout this book. One common opinion, however, is offered by the federal judge Alex Kozinski, a prominent advocate of the death penalty. "I think there's some idea in this country that if people are evil enough you're insulting the memory of the victims if you let them live," he explains. A leading capital defense attorney, Kevin Doyle, expressed another widely shared view when he told us that it's "something in the American character, like we've invented something as creative as jazz but also very creative and persistent forms of violence, going back to the frontier days—there's some connection between American dynamism and self-destruction."

In the American colonies British law served as a model, but often a loose one. For one thing, each of the colonies had its own laws; and regarding capital punishment, some were more severe than others. (Little has changed in this regard in the past four centuries.) During an early period in Pennsylvania—founded by William Penn, a Quaker—only murder and treason were punished by death; but in Virginia even petty crimes (such as killing chicken or trading with the Indians) could lead to the gallows. Usually covered in all colonies were arson, robbery, and rape; sexual offenses such as buggery, adultery, and bestiality were included in the more Puritan regions. In the Massachusetts statute, each of the thirteen capital offenses was accompanied by a biblical quotation justifying it.

The extension of the death penalty to minor crimes came to resemble medieval codes in some states but greatly differed from them *in a reluctance to actually carry out* the policy. In that way it resembles America's present approach to the death penalty. From the outset in America, capital punishment was more a need than a practice. Americans apparently want to feel that they are in control of evil and have an answer for it, but that answer becomes less convincing, and certainly less appealing, at the moment of truth.

The first recorded execution in America occurred in 1608. The victim was George Kendall, a Virginian accused of plotting to betray the colony to the Spanish. Hanging was the preferred method of execution in the colonies, although slaves and Indians were sometimes burned at the stake. In other ways, too, the authorities followed the European example, inviting the public to attend the ceremonies, and putting the bodies on display for hours or even days afterward (reflecting what Charles Dickens would later call "the attraction of repulsion"). Anti-witchcraft hysteria also found its way to these shores. The Salem trials of 1692, and the hanging of nineteen people for witchcraft, was hardly an aberration. The killing of witches could seem clear-cut; they were carriers of evil seen as threatening the entire community, much like modern-day mass murderers.

As in Europe, religious authorities played an intimate part in executions; and they often still do today, if in lesser roles. Processions led by preachers often escorted the condemned from the jail to the church to the gallows. Hundreds of onlookers would sing hymns, and a pastor might address the prisoner directly, informing him that he must die "as a spectacle to the world, a warning to the vicious," as one minister in Connecticut put it. The ritualization of the execution rendered it transcendent. All those involved, including the spectators, could feel that they were part of a beneficent religious and historical moment.

Manuals for ministers provided appropriate statements for both pastors and prisoners. It was vital that the prisoner admit guilt, plead for mercy, and repent, for then the minister might announce that he "would this day be in heaven." This helped transform the grisliness of execution into something hopeful, and therefore more socially acceptable. After the condemned man offered his last words, often following a script, a hood might be put over his face and then he would be "launched into eternity." The final confession enabled everyone to imagine the prisoner as finding salvation.

Gallows literature appeared, embellishing or inventing criminals' final statements for maximum effect, and was widely distributed. With their final breath the condemned (or their ghostwriters) warned others, particularly youths, to seek the path of virtue, "to abstain from excess of Liquor, bad company, and lewd women, which have brought me to this untimely end," as one 19-year-old put it. Few suggested that society shared any responsibility for evil behavior; criminals simply were born with a bad streak and did not struggle strongly enough against their inclinations (a view still widely shared). In his book *Rites of Execution*, the historian Louis P. Masur described the significance of this ritual:

> The spectators who gathered on execution day viewed, heard, and read a variety of messages about the culture they lived in and the behavior expected of them. It was a day on which civil and clerical figures appeared in a public ceremony before a congregation of thousands to display their authority and to convey the values they believed most fundamental to the preservation of the moral and social order of the community . . . Execution day served as both a warning and a celebration . . . Civil and clerical figures offered proof that society worked properly and that God saved souls.

Masur depicts execution day as a vast public ceremony affirming the overall rightness and lasting virtue of the executioners—both "warning" and "celebration."

This was particularly crucial in the years after American independence, amid the disorder and confusion (and occasionally, rebellion) in the new society. Executions for treason were seen in a positive light. Samuel Adams, one of the revolutionary heroes once targeted for execution by the British, now declared that treason in a *monarchy* was understandable, "but the man who dares rebel against the laws of a republic ought to suffer death." If one lives in an ideal society, any deviation from its rules has to stem from individual weakness.

After careful study, Louis Masur could find no attempts to rescue criminals at the gallows, no riots, no popular refusal to comply with the rites of execution. Then, as now, there was no constituency for the condemned, who were almost always outsiders, thoroughly isolated prior to their execution. By the very fact of being condemned, such men and women were (and are) divested of their claim to life and designated as distinct and separate from other human beings.

As the eighteenth century neared its end, at least 1,500 executions had already taken place in America. Several important trends were already evident. Many more executions were taking place in the South, per capita, than in the North. In both regions, the percentage of African-Americans executed was well out of proportion to their numbers in society. As in Rome, slaves who attacked their masters were often executed, never the reverse. Today, it is still rare for a white man who has murdered a black to enter the death chamber.

Abolitionist Strivings

Little abolitionist sentiment existed in America until several years after the Revolutionary War, when many intellectuals and some ministers questioned the continuing harshness of punishment. As they do today, Americans wished very devoutly to consider themselves—and be regarded by outsiders—as more decent and humane than others. Believers in Enlightenment principles of proportion and benevolence, they saw in the establishment of a new republic an opportunity for a profound change in the way society treated criminals. As in Europe, the writings of one man served as a catalyst for a social movement.

He was Cesare Beccaria, the Italian jurist, whose *Essay on Crimes and Punishment*, published in 1764 (anonymously at first), had caused a sensation throughout Europe and had led to a shortening of the long list of crimes punishable by death. (Ironically, one of Beccaria's foremost champions in prerevolutionary France was Robespierre, who called the death penalty "fundamentally unjust.") Translated and published in America a few years later, the essay had a powerful impact on influential figures such as Thomas Jefferson, who would later write that Beccaria "had satisfied the reasonable world of the unrightfulness and inefficiency of the punishment of crimes by death." Nevertheless, the Catholic church placed his essay on its index of forbidden books; this meant that Protestants would have to lead the abolition movement.

Borrowing from Enlightenment writers such as Montesquieu, Diderot, and Voltaire, Beccaria concluded that the sole aim of punishment was to deter future crimes, not to serve as vengeance. Capital punishment must be abolished unless its deterrent value could be proved—and Beccaria argued that the death penalty provided only a "momentary spectacle" and did not deter murder, or even lesser crimes. As Voltaire, one of his champions, would observe, "The sword of justice is in our hands; but we must blunt it more often than sharpen it."

Beccaria's related arguments form the bedrock from which abolition rhetoric springs, even to this day: since it is irreversible, capital punishment is different from any other penalty, making belated findings of innocence all the more tragic; *certainty* of punishment is more just and effective than its severity; long-term imprisonment deters just as strongly as execution; and state killing increases the level of violence in society.

Hegel and Kant denounced Beccaria, citing retribution as more than enough reason to maintain capital punishment. "If a man has committed a murder," Kant wrote, "he must die . . . There is no substitute that will satisfy the requirement of legal justice." This had tremendous influence on the Protestant theologians of that time and, in fact, reverberates through every later era. Such a declaration makes contact with primal human emotions that have in no way disappeared. One has removed a life, and therefore one's own life must be ended. Here the psychological and the moral converge, and the force of this argument—of retribution as necessary for so-cial balance—should not be underestimated. It seeks the restoration of a moral universe.

Many trace the founding of the American abolition movement to a lecture on March 9, 1787, in the Philadelphia home of Ben Franklin, when for the first time a prominent public figure declared, with no reservations, that capital punishment must be out-lawed. He was Benjamin Rush, an eccentric 42-year-old physician, essayist, and signer of the Declaration of Independence, also known as the "father of American psychiatry" and the "father of progressive penology"—not to mention the first major American critic of both alcohol and masturbation.

Rush adapted Beccaria's arguments but focused on an area that the Italian had largely avoided—moral objections—and declared that oft-cited biblical support for executions was highly questionable. He explained, for example, that the precept in Genesis, often cited by death penalty proponents—"Whoso sheddeth man's blood, by man shall his blood be shed"—was not an *instruction* but a *prediction*. He observed that God had not killed Cain but sent him to exile—with a mark placed on him to discourage others from executing him. He added that the New Testament represented the "triumph of truth and Christianity over ignorance and Judaism." And, as a pioneering psychiatrist, Rush believed that criminality, at bottom, was an illness.

Rush quickly won some support in New York, Massachusetts, New Jersey, and Ohio, particularly among Quakers and the newly organized Unitarians and Universalists. Pennsylvania in 1794 became the first state to abandon capital punishment except for first-degree murder. This was the first time murder was defined in terms of "degrees," each earning a different penalty.

The excesses of the French Revolution, and the frightening image of the guillotine, promised to promote further curbs on capital punishment in America. Victor Hugo wrote of the new decapitating device in *Les Misérables*: "He who sees it shudders with an inexplicable dismay. All social questions achieve their finality around that blade." This suggests that capital punishment provides a lethal anchor for any society where it exists, and ultimately defines that society. Every individual in such a society (including ours today) is affected by the existence of capital punishment even if law-abiding and not particularly conscious of the policy. Referring to reports of French mobs carrying the heads of former officials on spikes, Thomas Paine, the American patriot, observed,

> They learn it from the governments they live under and retaliate the punishments they have been accustomed to behold . . . It may perhaps be said that it signifies nothing to a man what is done to him after he is dead; but it signifies much to the living. It either tortures their feelings, or it hardens their hearts; and in either case, it instructs them how to punish when power falls into their hands. Lay then the axe at the root, and teach governments humanity. It is their sanguinary punishments which corrupt mankind.

Paine focuses on a terrible duality. If, as a person of conscience, one allows oneself to make psychological contact with the killing, one can experience overwhelming anxiety and guilt. To protect oneself from such unmanageable feelings, most people undergo considerable psychic numbing, and come to feel little or nothing at all.

Following the lead of Pennsylvania, three other states in 1796 shortened the list of capital crimes. "Is it not murder . . . to put a man to death for an offense which does not deserve death?" Benjamin Franklin asked, and many now reflected on this question. Although Franklin did not endorse Benjamin Rush's views on outright abolition, he did support Rush's call for a new type of prison, where criminals would be not just punished but rehabilitated. Three years later, the Walnut Street Jail was constructed in Philadelphia—America's first penitentiary, and a model for a new kind of penal system. But this was as much as Rush achieved. Very few prominent individuals joined him in advocating abolition.

Most ministers argued that the death penalty, too, promised rehabilitation; repenting on the gallows promised a quicker route to salvation than years in a penitentiary.

And when, after a few years, the idealism behind the new penitentiary system was crushed by the reality of unreformable prisoners, the abolition movement was nearly extinguished. Benjamin
Rush despaired of achieving his goal in his lifetime, but declared:
"To you, the unborn generations of the next century, I consecrate
this humble tribute to justice."

The "Thick, Gloomy Veil"

Capital punishment remained widely accepted, but execution as
spectacle soon fell into disfavor.

Religious figures, and the rich and educated, who had once endorsed or even taken part in the ceremonies, now found the celebration distasteful. The crowds had started to get out of hand, and
the well-to-do had never enjoyed rubbing shoulders with the rab-
ble anyway. These pillars of the community began to fear that the
tawdry procedure imperiled the institution of capital punishment.
"Rioting, drunkenness and every species of disorderly conduct"
prevailed, blunting "moral sensibilities . . . and [brutalizing] people by the barbarity of the example," one writer observed. At the
same time, the public display of the condemned at the gallows was
bound to elicit sympathy for them from many observers. After a
public hanging in 1825 a pastor declared that the "object of public justice would be better secured if executions took place in the
jail yard."

Disaffection with the killing spectacle always reflects a decline in
confidence in society's policy of execution. When an execution inspires "revulsion," one can say that it has lost its power to affirm
social mores. Probably the pendulum was always poised to swing in
the direction of hidden executions because of the uneasiness surrounding capital punishment from the beginning.

Pennsylvania, the Quaker state, staged the first private hanging.

A new state law mandated that all executions be held in the prison yard, with witnesses to include at least one doctor, the state attorney general, and twelve "reputable citizens." By the mid-1840s every state in the Northeast and Atlantic Coast regions had passed similar laws. The trend met surprisingly little opposition, but the fears that were expressed were revealing, especially in relation to later developments. Some who favored capital punishment warned that private execution would decrease its value as a deterrent; they also worried that a society ashamed to execute for all to see would soon abolish the death penalty entirely. Some abolitionists agreed that this was a likely scenario—and so they welcomed the move indoors. But other abolitionists feared that it would lead to *more* executions, likening it to the private slaughters carried out by monarchs and dictators throughout history.

In any case, the hope for dignified hangings before a tidy group was not realized. Inevitably, scores of invited guests attended, representing the influential and well-to-do, who now could observe the execution without the distraction of a disorderly mob or the fear that the condemned prisoner might find some favor in the crowd. In his *American Notes*, Charles Dickens in 1842 observed:

> The prison-yard . . . has been the scene of terrible performances. Into this narrow, grave-like place, men are brought out to die . . . The law requires that there be present at this dismal spectacle, the judge, the jury, and citizens to the amount of twenty-five. From the community it is hidden . . . The prison-wall is interposed as a thick gloomy veil.

The veil remains in place today, and witnesses selected, then and now, tend to be people who embody social authority and respectability. Of course, there must be a doctor among them; there is always a medicalized dimension to executions. For many decades no women were permitted, as they were considered too weak to manage the experience—and potentially dangerous as perhaps more likely to oppose it. A newspaper editor in New York asserted that hangings now resembled "a private judicial assassination," but this did not prevent large crowds from gathering outside the prison gates as execution neared, howling their assent or disapproval—a scene still evident today, if with smaller numbers.

As time passed, opponents of executions, sensing a historic turning point, asserted that public hangings obviously had not served to deter, so private executions couldn't possibly serve this function. Horace Greeley, the crusading New York newspaper editor, and a future presidential candidate, declared:

> When I see any business or vocation sneaking and skulking in dark lanes and little by-streets which elude observation, I conclude that those who follow such business feel at least doubtful of its utility and beneficence. They may argue that it is "a necessary evil," but they can hardly put faith in their own logic . . . So, when I see the Gallows, once the denizen of some swelling eminence, the cynosure of ten thousand eyes, "the observed of all observers," skulking and hiding itself from public view in jail-yards, shutting itself up in prisons, I say, "You have taken the right road! Go ahead! One more drive, and your detested, rickety frame is out of the sight of civilized man for ever!"

To offset the mystery, newspaper reporters were allowed to attend, and their first-person accounts at least provided an illusion of openness—just as they do today. Predictions of capital punishment's demise proved premature.

Abolitionists Seek "Mildness"

Allowing reporters to witness hangings, however, was a double-edged sword for the authorities. Journalists were dangerous because they sometimes make the wrong kind of witness—failing to reassert social claims to truth and virtue in their execution narratives. True, their presence suggested that the executioners had nothing to hide, but they also provided the first accounts of hangings that were not tightly controlled by the social establishment, the church, or the publishers of gallows literature.

In previous pageants the condemned man usually admitted guilt, repented, and was delivered up to heaven when he died. Reporters for the new and popular "penny press" presented a more complex picture. Some prisoners were belligerent, or sobbed, or proclaimed their innocence to the end. Hangings were horribly botched. In some cases, medical personnel experimented on the lifeless bodies afterward. "Readers were free to construct their own interpretation rather than receive only an official one," Louis Masur has observed.

Many of them, in fact, were horrified by what they read, inspiring abolitionists to organize a new national movement. Leading ministers and crusading newspaper editors railed against the practice—just as many of the same men (such as William Lloyd Garrison and Horace Greeley) were attacking slavery. There was much overlap between the two abolition movements. Each, after all, had as its chief tenet the basic dignity of every human being. Slavery abolitionists were passionate social reformers and near-fundamentalists (in today's terms), and as such the only people prone to speak out early and absolutely about a particular evil. In the nineteenth century, it required similar people to take a stand against the death penalty as well.

Again we see that core arguments against capital punishment heard today have deep roots. Charging that deterrence was nonexistent, the reformer Edward Livingston issued this challenge:

> Your favorite [method] of death . . . has been fully tried. By your own account, all nations, since the first institution of society, have practiced it, but you yourselves must acknowledge, without success . . . You have made your experiment; it was attended in its operation with an incalculable waste of human life . . . yet there was no diminution of crime; and it never occurred to you that mildness might accomplish that which could not be effected by severity.

Horace Greeley, meanwhile, stressed the dangers of mass brutalization, charging that executions weaken "the natural horror of bloodshed" throughout society, and excite "a pernicious sympathy for the convict." Greeley's arguments were echoed everywhere. The death penalty is always vulnerable to such arguments, and there have always been people to make them.

Reform groups organized in many states, and a national organization was founded in 1845. Women made up a sizable portion of the movement. Michigan became the first state to ban executions within its borders (except for treason), after an extraordinary chain of events. The story begins in 1830, when a bartender in Detroit named Stephen Simmons went home drunk one night and beat his wife to death. Simmons was sentenced to die by hanging. The sheriff, however, resigned in protest, saying that Simmons had been too drunk to know what he was doing on the night of the murder. The new sheriff decided to make his mark with the execution, with brass bands playing and thousands attending the gala. When the prisoner reached the gallows, the sheriff asked if he had any last words and Simmons, with great dignity and in a rich baritone, sang out:

> *Show pity, Lord, O Lord, forgive*
> *Let a repenting rebel live.*
> *Are not Thy mercies full and free?*
> *May not a sinner trust in Thee?*

The crowd was deeply moved, many to tears, as the floor opened and Simmons dangled and died, and the witnesses filed away in silence. A debate over the fate of the death penalty in Michigan began. Finally, in 1847, after Michigan became a state, the first official act of the judiciary was to abolish the death penalty, a ban that remains.

Gallows and Gospel

A few years later Rhode Island and Wisconsin followed Michigan in abolishing the death penalty—in Wisconsin, after a hanging in which the victim had struggled at the end of the rope for more than five minutes. Increasingly, abolitionists put forward as an alternative the notion of strict life imprisonment (an echo increasingly heard today, as we have seen). This was morally preferable and gave the prisoner a longer time to repent, they argued. It had deterrent value as well—evildoers might fear life behind bars more than a quick hanging.

Yet there were several problems with these arguments (as there are today). If life imprisonment was more dreadful than execution, didn't that make it even more inhumane? If there was no chance for parole, didn't this make useless the notion of rehabilitation? And if the prisoners truly repented, and yet never emerged from behind bars, what use were they to God or society?

Because of these and other questions, most of the clergy continued to support capital punishment, sometimes thunderously, derailing abolitionist legislation in key states. John Greenleaf Whittier, a Quaker and a former Massachusetts legislator, denounced what he called this union of "gallows and gospel" in 1843, in his poem, "The Human Sacrifice." Walt Whitman felt much the same way, exclaiming in 1845 in his essay "A Dialogue," "O Bible! . . . what follies and monstrous barbarities are defended in thy name!"

The phrase "gallows and gospel" suggests the formidable duality of all religion: a dogmatic side that imposes its vengeful judgments and a compassionate side that stresses openness and love. Hence, those who invoke religion have been the most intense advocates *and* opponents of the death penalty. For many of the clergy, relying on the deterrence argument is beside the point, even offensive. For them, as with an increasing number of other Americans today, it is simply a question of justice, retribution, and the "expression of the moral sense," as one minister put it.

At the core, it is a struggle over the concept of "humanity." Justice and retribution can always claim this high ground. They are compelling, they articulate a moral universe, they can be life-affirming. Aligning themselves with the killer's victims, advocates of the death penalty can and do claim appropriate outrage at the taking of innocent life.

The leading death penalty advocate of the time was the Presbyterian minister George Cheever. Humanity, he said, meant the greatest good for the greatest number, not merely one particular prisoner. Capital punishment was far more humane than any of the alternatives. In fact, he predicted, the moral imperative was so strong that if the state abolished the gallows, citizens would probably take justice into their own hands as vigilantes. And, in a reverse of the argument heard in America today, Cheever pointed out that only three nations in the world had abolished the death penalty— so how wrong could it be?

For most Americans, these points were persuasive, and the abolition movement soon subsided. Much of the moral force was drawn into the fight to abolish slavery, and then the Civil War consumed all.

Lynchings: A "Peculiar Form of Chivalry"

Following the Civil War, the movement to abolish the death penalty would not soon catch fire again in many major states. Increasing crime, disorder, and instability bolstered capital punishment.

Especially in smaller states, public opinion would often rise and fall alarmingly. One especially gruesome murder could send an abolitionist state back into the comfort of capital punishment. Maine abolished hanging, then restored it, then abolished it again. After Colorado did away with capital punishment in 1897, groups of citizens carried out a few lynchings (as many had warned would happen), and the death penalty was restored four years later.

There has been an uneasy link between legal hangings and vigilantism in our history. According to the authors of *The Rope, The Chair, and the Needle: Capital Punishment in Texas,* lynchings "were thought by many on the western frontier to be a guardian of the otherwise precarious social order. . . . What mattered was dominance and control." Lynching also made things simple: evil was confronted directly and erased. People could feel closer to fundamental moral truth. But there was undoubtedly an element of doubt, of inner question on the part of many about this version of justice.

Abraham Lincoln once told a story about vigilantes who strung up the wrong fellow. Learning their mistake, they cut down the young man—too late—and carried the body to his mother. "Well," they told the grieving mother, "the joke's sure on *us*." At bottom, the meaning of the "joke" is potential error inseparable from barbarism.

Mainly in the South, but also in scattered states in the Midwest and West, more than 3,000 men and some women, overwhelmingly black, were lynched by white mobs between 1880 and 1920—even though lynching was a capital crime in many of the states. ("So much for deterrence," Jesse Jackson would comment years later.) By most accounts, Georgia, Mississippi, and Texas led the nation in lynchings. Often the victims' only crime was associating with white women—leading to the popular depiction of lynchings as a "peculiar form of chivalry."

Lynching was more raw, much less controlled, than state killing, but we can learn much from it about capital punishment. It tore the veil away from killing—it was nothing *but* killing, as opposed to the more structured executions by the state. And in targeting one race, lynch mobs hinted at the more covert singling out of convicted black criminals in years following. There was, after all, considerable truth in calling certain state-sponsored executions an official form of lynching. By the 1920s, however, the number of lynchings had declined, while the number of interventions by citizens to prevent these hangings had increased.

The Modern Era: Variations on Old Themes

Early in the twentieth century, abolition sentiment continued to rise and fall, in scattered settings. Several states (Kansas, Washington, Oregon, the Dakotas, Minnesota, Tennessee, Arizona) barred

executions, as progressive reform took hold, but by 1921 five of
these states had reversed themselves. Most of the executions took
place in southern states, or in heavily populated New York and California. The Catholic church continued to endorse capital punishment strongly, claiming that its bishops could not stand against the
wishes of the state. New, efficient, and purportedly more humane
methods of execution—the electric chair and the gas chamber—
slowly replaced the gallows as the killing devices of choice. Two-
thirds of those executed for murder in the North and West were
white; the reverse was true in the South. About one or two women,
and only a few teenagers, were executed per year.

In the fear and chaos of the Prohibition era and the Great Depression, executions increased, to roughly 170 per year. They
might have multiplied if not for the attorney Clarence Darrow and
other leaders of the newly formed American League to Abolish
Capital Punishment. Darrow pressed the argument of social deter-
minism: society made murderers what they were. He also argued
that the state "continues to kill its victims, not so much to defend
society against them . . . but to appease the mob's emotions of hatred and revenge." William Randolph Hearst, who was hardly soft
on crime, asserted, "Cruelty and viciousness are not abolished by
cruelty and viciousness—not even by legalized cruelty and viciousness. . . . We cannot cure murder by murder . . ."

Dozens of other countries, meanwhile, abolished the death
penalty (in some cases retaining it only for military crimes). The
new state of Israel retained the death penalty only for war crimes
and genocide. Between 1917 and 1957, however, not a single state
in America abolished the death penalty.

During the 1950s the mood of the nation apparently changed
again. The execution of the Rosenbergs, convicted as Soviet spies,
outraged many, even among those who believed they were guilty.
Caryl Chessman, imprisoned in California, drew national attention
as he won appeal after appeal (filing his own legal briefs) and wrote
several books, including a bestseller, *Cell 2455 Death Row*. His
pleas for a new trial inspired the first mainstream churches, such as

the Methodists, to join the so-called "peace" churches in taking a stand against capital punishment. (He was executed in 1960.) Albert Camus's essay "Reflections on the Guillotine" became a revered text for abolitionist activists. "Let us call [the death penalty] by the name which, for lack of any other nobility, will at least give the nobility of truth, and let us recognize it for what it is essentially: a revenge," he advised, adding that there would "be no lasting peace either in the heart of individuals or in social customs" until the death penalty was outlawed.

Hawaii and Alaska entered the union as abolitionist states; voters in Oregon abolished the death penalty; and Iowa joined Michigan, Rhode Island, and Wisconsin and about five others as an execution-free zone. In 1959, Susan Hayward won an Academy Award for her portrayal of a condemned murderess in *I Want to Live*, based on the true story of Barbara Graham. The film concluded with a graphic and disturbing depiction of the woman's prolonged execution in the gas chamber at San Quentin.

More nations abolished executions. In 1965, England suspended the practice, as an experiment, after a series of controversial executions; four years later it decided to make the ban permanent.

In America, a significant decline in the number of executions occurred, from about 120 during the 1940s to about 70 per year during the 1950s, and then to 21 in 1963, seven in 1965, and two in 1967—the last executions for a number of years. There were several reasons for this. New studies suggested that the deterrence theory was a sham; in fact, in some states, the murder rate appeared to *rise* after a wave of executions. Arthur Koestler called belief in deterrence "perhaps the saddest aspect in this whole heart- and neck-breaking business. For it shows that an officially sponsored lie has a thousand lives and takes a thousand lives."

Yet the claim of deterrence can never quite be overcome. Whatever the lack of evidence for it, it is constantly invoked. And the further claim can then be made that we need *more* executions in order for deterrence to take effect. The belief that deterrence *should* work is so strong that this feeling often takes precedence over evidence.

It has to do with a view of fear as salutory, so that the fear of retaliation (it is thought) creates a predictable cause-and-effect process. For better or worse, however, minds do not work that way. We are more complicated and can in fact be deeply attracted to that which we most fear.

Public opinion had slowly turned against capital punishment in the 1960s, so prosecutors were hesitant to seek it and juries reluctant to grant it. A new generation of anti–death penalty lawyers, led by the NAACP Legal Defense and Education Fund, adopted a strategy of contesting nearly every capital conviction, logjamming the death penalty machinery, hoping this might lead to a permanent shutdown. A kind of moratorium on state killings was established while numerous legal issues were decided in the courts. Few could deny that the death penalty had been exacted disproportionately on the poor and minorities. For the first time, in the late 1960s, surveys showed that a majority of Americans, influenced by all of the above trends—and a general period of economic well-being and social stability—opposed the death penalty.

Matters came to a head in 1972 when *Furman v. Georgia* reached the Supreme Court, and the justices essentially were asked to rule on the validity of the death penalty in light of the Eighth Amendment. The justices split into three factions. Thurgood Marshall and William Brennan felt that executions indeed amount to cruel and unusual punishment *per se*. Each cited "evolving moral standards" as one reason for this belief. Brennan, in addition, argued that capital punishment was degrading and humiliating and "does not comport with" the fundamental right to "human dignity."

Four other justices ruled that capital punishment was clearly permitted by the Constitution (although two of them indicated that they personally abhorred the death penalty). That left a swing group of three, who took no position on the validity of capital punishment but ruled that it had been applied unevenly, arbitrarily, especially in regard to defendants who were poor or black.

The 5–4 ruling, then, was a compromise, reflecting American opinion at the time. The *Furman* decision halted all pending cases but left the door open for the return of executions if the death penalty could be applied less capriciously. In several countries abroad, as we will see, unexpected decisions such as this, which merely put a temporary hold on executions, led instead to permanent bans. It could even happen this way in America some day, but it did not occur in the 1970s. Most states struggled to reform their death penalty laws, as public opinion shifted again in favor of executions, part of a general call for the courts to "get tougher" on criminals of all kinds.

And so, in its decision in *Gregg v. Georgia* in 1976, the Court ruled that executions could resume, as states took some discretion away from judges and juries in capital sentencing, and ordered that so-called "mitigating" factors must now be considered before sending someone to death row. This promised to reduce (if far from eliminate) some of the racial imbalances and other blatant forms of bias. Only Marshall and Brennan, the two abolitionists, held out. Two weeks after *Gregg*, the Canadian Parliament, moving in the opposite direction, outlawed the death penalty.

The following year Gary Gilmore became the first condemned American to die since 1967, after refusing to appeal to higher courts. In 1979, John Spenkelink became the first American prisoner since *Furman* to go involuntarily to his death, via the electric chair in Florida. Soon, nearly 700 prisoners resided on death rows across America—over 100 in Texas and Florida alone. By the early 1980s, backing for capital punishment had topped 70 percent in national polls, with majority support crossing all racial, gender, religious, and geographic lines.

Then, in 1982, in Texas, as the pace of executions picked up, Charles Brooks, Jr., became the first prisoner executed by a mixture of sodium thiopental, pavulon, and potassium chloride—the so-called lethal injection. This was America's latest attempt to put a more humane face on the killing of one of its citizens. But, like all of the earlier methods, it would not preclude botched executions, and the bad publicity and protests that inevitably follow, weakening the institution of capital punishment even as the pace of executions accelerates.

3

METHODS OF EXECUTION

Seeking a "Humane" End, from Noose to Needle

In a few years' time, with God's help, all this will appear
as unthinkable as drawing, quartering and pressing to
death appear to us today.

—*Arthur Koestler*

AS the electric chair totters on its last legs in America, it follows the
historical sequence of seeking, then discarding, ostensibly more humane ways of execution: from hangings and firing squads to electrocution and the gas chamber. Interestingly, each of these methods is still used somewhere at some time in the United States, as if
we, as a culture, are unwilling or unable to shed images and rituals
of our execution heritage.

The electric chair and the gas chamber are also peculiarly American: they are used for executions nowhere else in the world. Every
few years, one of three states (Delaware, New Hampshire, or Washington) hangs a prisoner. Three other states (Utah, Oklahoma, and
Idaho) still use firing squads. Lethal injections are mandated in a
majority of places, and a dozen states give prisoners a choice between injection and one other method. We have come this far: centuries ago only the well-to-do were ever given a choice.

Each method of execution has its own special lore. Each has an
aura and a relationship to legend.

The firing squad conveys a sense of military honor—being put to death by soldiers—which makes the condemned man something of a warrior himself. Hanging conveys a history of heroes and martyrs and rogues whose bravery or bad deeds led them to "the gallows." The electric chair is associated with sensational twentieth-century crimes and their Hollywood versions. ("He'll fry!") There's something fascinating about someone sitting down in a chair from which he never gets up.

Each method, as well, produces its own version of the botched execution, and each is grotesque in its own way. One of the most bizarre recent cases concerned a killer named Mitchell Rupe in the state of Washington, where condemned men were allowed to choose their poison—to die by hanging or lethal injection. Rupe picked hanging, then claimed he should be spared because this method amounted to "cruel and unusual punishment"; he weighed 409 pounds and would probably be decapitated in the process. As his attorney argued, "This case focuses in a very grisly and graphic way [on] what capital punishment is all about." A federal district court judge ruled that hanging the prisoner would indeed offend "basic human dignity" and "go against standards of decency"—ordering that he die by the needle, like it or not.

Lethal injections have yet to create much legend or lore, but the method seems to appeal to Americans in its promise of simply putting the condemned "to sleep" rather than violently breaking their necks or shooting or electrocuting them. Surprisingly, our history in this matter goes back more than 150 years. Shortly after anesthesia was introduced to America in 1846, some reformers advocated using chloroform to make prisoners lose consciousness before going to the gallows. One commentator observed that while the law mandated that the inmate hang by the neck until dead, no one said he had to be conscious when it happened.

A literary critic and lawyer of that era named G. W. Peck advocated the use of chloroform for the "social health" of America, arguing that what preserved society in a civilized state was "true refinement" and "healthful quietness." He supported capital punishment but wondered whether executions "must be made more painful than absolutely necessary." Shouldn't society, "now that science has found a means of alleviating extreme physical suffering . . . allow the benefit of it to the miserable wretches whom we simply wish to cast contemptuously out of existence?" It was "against good manners" and "unbecoming to civilized Christian people" to inflict pain, he wrote.

Chloroform never caught on, and thousands of the condemned would continue to go to the scaffold in varying shades of terror, but always quite conscious. Yet we still hear the same arguments about social health, offered by those who wish to abolish every method of execution, save one—the "civilized" form, lethal injection. "For all the fervor among death-penalty adherents," the writer Russell Baker recently observed, "they are curiously squeamish about how the thing is to be done." Americans remain in the grip of a paradox. Few of us, when the time comes, will die painlessly, yet most of those who support capital punishment nevertheless wish to execute the worst among us—convicted murderers— with as little suffering (and as little fuss) as possible. As Sherwin B. Nuland, author of the book *How We Die*, has observed, we seek for them "a quietus of which they have deprived others." Surely this reveals, in sharp relief, the conflicts beneath the advocacy of executions.

In fact, one might consider the history of executions in this country as one long, futile search for the ultimate oxymoron—the *humane killing*.

By Rope and Bullet:
An Attraction to "Things Gruesome"

Hanging was the method of choice in America for hundreds of years, a "compassionate" alternative to stoning, burning, or beheading. If all went well, when the trapdoor opened and the prisoner dropped, death came quickly. But often all did not go well. The drop might be too short, causing slow strangulation, or too long, ending in decapitation. As decades passed, this happened less often, as prisoners were carefully measured and weighed so the optimal length of rope could be determined.

Montana once operated four "galloping gallows" which traveled around the state, as needed. When Tennessee switched from hanging to electrocution, the state, in a sentimental mood, used wood from the old gallows to construct its first electric chair. Later, when it asked a specialist in executions, Fred Leuchter—the subject of the recent Errol Morris documentary *Mr. Death*—to build a new chair, officials sent him pieces of the original chair (made from the gallows) to incorporate in the new one. Leuchter said, approvingly, "They're keeping their tradition alive and well in Tennessee."

The execution of Westley Allan Dodd in Washington in 1993—the state's first hanging in thirty years—inspired more than 100 reporters to vie for one of the twelve seats available for witnesses. Afterward, a local Catholic pastor declared that a "morbid sense of attraction to things gruesome . . . brought this circus to our town." It was "a show not intended to do justice but to give us our turn to say, 'Hang the son-of-a-bitch!' It is our chance to see vicariously what our forebears actually saw: a man swinging from a tree by the neck . . . so that we might feel for ourselves the surge of satisfaction at having killed the beast. . . . The truth, of course, is that the beast is not really dead."

In Delaware, the rickety wooden scaffold, built in 1986 by Fred Leuchter, seems to come right out of the Old West, or a Hollywood version of it. A prisoner still must climb twenty steps to his doom. In January 1996, Delaware hanged Billy Bailey; this was only the third execution at the scaffold in the United States since 1965, when four went to the gallows in Kansas alone (including *In Cold Blood* killers Richard Hickock and Perry Smith). After Bailey climbed to the platform, a noose was placed around his neck and a hood pulled over his head. A trapdoor was sprung, and Bailey's body twisted in the wind as it dropped.

Running for Congress in Illinois in 1998, a leading Democrat said we should go back to hanging killers on the very spot the murder took place. Present-day executions, he explained, are too abstract to be effective as deterrents. After the hanging, the dead man should be left there "until his flesh rots," he added. "That's the way it was used in the West, and it worked." This nostalgia for frontier justice expresses a contemporary longing for a time and place where justice was simple, swift, and total. There remains a conflict between harking back to the vivid execution drama of those days (to "hang the son of a bitch") and bringing to the process forms of technical muting that would domesticate it.

Like hanging, death by firing squad can seem fast and relatively painless, although always bloody. Utah's retention of the firing squad, in fact, stems from belief of its founding Mormon settlers that one could atone for murder only by the shedding of actual blood; hanging was insufficient.

Sharpshooters aim at a target, usually over the inmate's heart, with a large pan positioned under the chair to collect the blood. A survey of thirty-nine executions by firing squad in Utah—most prominently, that of Gary Gilmore—found that the prisoners had taken from fifteen seconds to twenty-seven minutes to die. A British commission once declared that execution by firing squad "does not possess even the first requisite of an efficient method, the certainty of causing immediate death." What makes marksmen miss the mark is that the emotional element comes into play when men squeeze triggers that fire bullets into another man—a far more personal gesture than simply opening a trapdoor or flicking an electrical switch.

The "Easy" Chair

While the gallows and firing squads are still occasionally used today, they began to lose favor more than a century ago. In the 1880s the state of New York began a landmark study seeking "the most humane and practical method known to modern science" of carrying out a death sentence. A new possibility had emerged a few years after Thomas Edison invented the lightbulb. Electrocution was thought to be neater, more scientific, more compassionate. An invisible charge would surge through the victim and kill him quickly.

At the time, Edison was in fierce competition with George Westinghouse. Edison was establishing himself in the utility industry with his direct current (DC) service, while Westinghouse had pioneered alternating current (AC) technology. The latter was thought to be more flexible and economically viable. So Edison set out to prove that his rival's AC was more dangerous than his own DC, and how better to do that than to promote AC as an execution tool? In 1887, in West Orange, New Jersey, the inventor publicly electrocuted stray cats and dogs by luring them onto a metal plate wired to an AC generator. Westinghouse recognized what Edison was up to and declined to promote AC for executions, asserting that the task could be "done better with an axe." In any event, the term "electrocution" was coined to describe the new phenomenon of execution by electricity—a term which suggested drama and mystery as well as efficiency.

The following year the New York legislature established electrocution as the state's method of execution and asked the Medico-Legal Society to recommend how to implement it. The society funded researchers allied with Edison who electrocuted dozens of dogs, two calves, and a horse—using AC. Other researchers recommended that the condemned be electrocuted in a chair rather than in a tank of water or on a rubberized table, and the New York prison system decided to buy AC generators to power the chairs (to be placed in three prisons, including Sing Sing).

Crucially, the U.S. Supreme Court ruled that the Eighth Amendment did not bar electrocution. Cruel "implies . . . something inhuman and barbarous, something more than the mere extinguishment of life," the justices explained. They endorsed a state court determination that "it is within easy reach of electrical science at this day to so generate and apply to the person of the convict a current of electricity . . . to produce instantaneous, and therefore, painless death."

Soon, a man named William Kemmler, who had killed his lover, was slated to become the first to lose his life in the chair, at New York's Auburn Prison. And who helped fund his appeals? George Westinghouse, of course, while Edison testified for the state. The appeals were denied. Edwin Davis, the Auburn Prison electrician, designed an electric chair which closely resembles models used today, and tested it using large slabs of meat.

Finally, on August 6, 1890, Kemmler became the first person to make the trip to the electric chair. Unfortunately, it took multiple attempts to complete the job. Then, as now, electrocution provoked widely varying responses. According to an assistant to the executioner, "The man never suffered a bit of pain." Recognizing both the technical advance and a need to believe in its benefit for humankind, a promoter of the method asserted: "We live in a higher civilization from this day on." (One is reminded of Harry Truman's declaration on learning of the successful use of the first atomic bomb, "This is the greatest thing in history.") But the *New York Herald* reported that among the witnesses "strong men fainted and fell like logs on the floor," and other newspapers called the first test a fiasco.

Still, the electric chair gained ground, with Ohio, Massachusetts, and New Jersey being the first of more than twenty states to follow New York's example. In many southern states portable electric chairs were shuttled from county to county, as needed. Alabama switched to electrocution, and since then 169 people—136 blacks and 33 whites—have been executed in the state, making famous the brightly colored chair in Atmore known as "Yellow Mama." The word "Mama" suggests both a jaunty domestication and, underneath that, a Medea-like figure who, driven by revenge, kills her own children. Something about the electric chair has fascinated or haunted Americans, inspiring dozens of Hollywood movies, such as *Angels with Dirty Faces*. It has to do with being "zapped" in histrionic fashion. Also, there's something more directly human—more concrete and specific—about killing a man in a chair than inserting him in a gas chamber or injecting him with lethal medicine.

Witnesses to electrocution, however, almost always notice that it is a less than tidy procedure, physically and morally. In the standard procedure, the electrical system delivers three jolts without interruption: roughly 2,300 volts for eight seconds, then about one-third that level for twenty-two seconds, then 2,300 volts for another five seconds or so, intending to kill "by a combination of massive shock and gradual cooking" (as one observer has described it). Inmates, nevertheless, usually buck in the seat and strain mightily at restraining straps; vomit, defecate, or urinate, or all three; lapse into convulsions and facial contortions; and sometimes emit cries, the cords on their neck standing out like steel ropes. Burns mark their bodies around the electrodes—a halo effect on their skulls and a smaller mark on their legs—and the smell of burning flesh sometimes fills the room. "Only the greenhorns sit in the first row," a veteran witness once explained. "We sit behind. The smell is too bad."

Chamber of Horrors

When it became clear, by the 1920s, that electrocution could never be anything but messy, officials sought a less dramatic and more "humanitarian" form of execution. Gassing prisoners would put them out of their misery without (it was said) even a first surge of pain. They would simply nod off, as if sleeping—a kind of anesthesia. Initial plans called for construction of special holding cells; gas would be released without warning at night while the inmate was *already* asleep, sparing him and family members (and, incidentally, the witnesses) the agony of the final countdown.

When this proved unfeasible, the gas chamber was invented. A pig was executed in it to prove that it worked, and the first inmate was killed by cyanide in the chamber in 1924. Soon it was adopted for use in several states, most prominently California. The state's first gas chamber was installed at San Quentin in 1937, using prison labor. (One inmate helped install gauges and pipes and witnessed several tests. Within a year of his parole, he killed three people and ended up sitting in the execution chamber he had helped to assemble.) Many world-famous prisoners, such as Barbara Graham and Caryl Chessman, would later occupy the chamber.

It is a kind of pod, not much bigger than a large freezer, generally with small windows for observation, and often likened to a diving bell or something out of Jules Verne. The inmate is strapped in with a stethoscope taped to his chest so his heartbeat can be monitored. An official pulls a lever, releasing sodium cyanide capsules into a dish of sulfuric acid resting directly under the seat. The seat of the chair is made of mesh, meant to hasten absorption of the deadly gas. The cyanide is so toxic that prisoners wear no underwear, preventing any gas from being trapped in folds where it could prove dangerous to an undertaker.

The condemned are often advised to breathe deeply if they wish to get it over with quickly. Essentially, they are asked to facilitate their own demise, and many willingly follow this advice. Quickly they sink into unconsciousness, although death requires a few more minutes.

Considering how the Nazis had put cyanide gas to use, it was strange that after World War II there was not more association with Hitler's Germany. Instead, the use of the gas chamber thrived during the 1950s, the latest manifestation of ever-present pressure in America to become more up-to-date, more technologically advanced. But the gas chamber would prove only a little more reliable and efficient than the electric chair.

Botched Executions and the Reality of Death

The list of gruesomely botched executions, by every one of the allegedly more humane methods, is a long one. The cause may be equipment failure, poor preparation by the prison staff, or a prisoner struggling for life. A famous example occurred in 1865, when four conspirators in the assassination plot against Abraham Lincoln went to the gallows. One of them, Lewis Paine, twitched at the end of the rope for five minutes while onlookers gasped.

With any botched execution we encounter a mask of civility

being torn away. A smooth, routine, technicized or medicalized procedure suddenly gives way to a more accurate rendition of what is actually happening. Botched executions provide grotesque images that bring us much closer to the truth. We see blood or a foaming mouth or hair catching fire, and we are reminded that someone is being killed.

However botched, an execution is rarely stopped. The problem is usually seen as nothing more than a glitch, something that has to be "fixed." The execution is a matter of law that must be carried out. One of the century's most contested executions—that of Ethel Rosenberg (convicted as an atomic spy)—required a second and third cycle of electricity. Decades ago, such problems were more common, but they have by no means disappeared, as we will see. Perhaps this is God's way of saying that killing a person should be difficult to do.

The phenomenon of the botched execution has a particular grotesqueness in the case of the electric chair, with the victim emitting an odor of "something burning." There's a sense of a "burning alive," an electrical return to burning at the stake. One of the most hideous legal killings was the execution of 17-year-old Willie Francis in Louisiana in 1946. When the electricity was turned on, the prisoner bucked so hard that the chair came off the floor, and after two more surges he cried out, "Take it off, let me breathe." Guards removed the hood and unstrapped him. Francis was one of the few to live to describe the experience. "My mouth tasted like peanut butter," he explained. "I felt a burning in my head and my left leg. . . . I saw little blue and pink and green speckles." The U.S. Supreme Court ruled against his claim that a second trip to the chair would represent cruel and unusual punishment, arguing that the Eighth Amendment prohibited "infliction of unnecessary pain," not suffering created by "unforeseeable accidents." Francis was executed a year later.

In 1983, when Alabama strapped John Louis Evans into "Yellow Mama," sparks and flames erupted from the electrode attached to his left leg and smoke poured out from under his hood. An overpowering stench of burned flesh and clothing filled the witness room. Doctors examined Evans and declared that he was still alive. Evans was given another thirty-second jolt of electricity—but still his heart would not stop beating. After fourteen minutes and a third jolt, he was finally pronounced dead.

In 1985 a prisoner in Georgia named Alpha Stephens struggled for breath for eight minutes after being electrocuted. A second attempt produced a similar result, and a third surge was needed. Stephens was "just not a conductor of electricity," a prison official explained. The same year, William Vandiver required five charges and seventeen minutes to expire. Six years later, poor prep work by prison officials in Virginia caused steam pressure to build inside the skull of Albert Clozza, popping out his eyeballs and causing blood to flow down his chest—after four jolts of juice.

Still, most experts contend that the lightning bolt to the brain caused by the first surge of electricity shuts it off so completely that when the pain signals from the nerves arrive they are not felt—"the body screams into a dead receiver," as one writer put it. If this is true, multiple shocks are not especially brutal; they do nothing but make sure the heart quits. "If you overload an individual's body with current . . . you'll cook the meat on his body," Fred Leuchter explained. "If you grab the arm, the flesh will fall right off in your hands. That doesn't mean he felt anything. It simply means that it's cosmetically not the right thing to do." (Leuchter, for a time, was America's only execution entrepreneur, offering for sale lethal injection systems, gallows, electric chairs, and gas chambers. Orders dried up, however, when he served as an expert witness for a neo-Nazi who denied the Holocaust—after Leuchter went to Auschwitz and "proved" that cyanide gas had not been used there. Leuchter was psychologically consistent in his embrace of death and killing.)

The gas chamber gained grim notices in 1983, when Jimmy Lee Gray was executed in Mississippi. After Gray thrashed about wildly for eight minutes, his head smashing an iron pipe behind him, prison officials ushered witnesses out of the viewing room before he finally lost consciousness. The official response? The prison installed a headrest on the chair to forestall another such incident. Soon, however, the state legislature adopted a bill that would eventually replace gassing with lethal injection.

Nine years later, California planned to use the gas chamber for the first time in twenty-five years. Attorneys for Robert Alton Harris argued that it was cruel and unusual punishment, and U.S. District Court Judge Marilyn Patel temporarily barred the proceedings on grounds that the gas chamber was "inhumane and has no place in civilized society." Reportedly, this was the first time a court in the United States had declared any method of execution unconstitutional. Patel was overruled on appeal, and Harris was executed. Later, a federal appeals court ruled that the gas chamber could still be used because a new state law gave prisoners a choice between that method and lethal injection.

In North Carolina, meanwhile, legislators voted to shut down their chamber following the gruesome gassing of Ricky Lee Sanderson in January 1998. Sanderson choked violently and strained against his chair straps, causing three witnesses to flee the viewing room. The chief sponsor of the measure to switch exclusively to lethal injection said he was concerned not so much with torture as with workplace safety issues. Cyanide fumes lingering in the gas chamber after executions pose a hazard to prison workers, he argued, although he acknowledged that the gassings are "not pleasant to watch."

The legality of the electric chair has also come under attack. In April 1985, lawyers for a Louisiana prisoner named Jimmy Glass asked that the U.S. Supreme Court halt his pending execution on grounds that "electrocution causes the gratuitous infliction of unnecessary pain and suffering and does not comport with evolving standards of human dignity." The Court rejected this argument by a 7–2 vote, with Justice William Brennan writing an impassioned dissent.

Justice Brennan, as we have seen, had come to the conclusion that the death penalty, in *any* form, was prohibited by the Eighth

and Fourteenth Amendments. He observed that the Court had always emphasized that the Eighth Amendment forbids "inhuman
and barbarous" methods of execution that cause "torture or a lingering death" or "unnecessary cruelty" or "terror, pain, or dis-
grace." On the basis of "considerable empirical evidence and eyewitness testimony," electrocution violates every one of the
principles set forth, he added.

Some authorities agree. Donald D. Price, a neurophysicist who
studies how the brain processes pain, agrees that electrocution is "a
form of torture." He claims that autopsy photos, eyewitness accounts, and new brain research all suggest that prisoners do not die
instantly but remain conscious, at least in parts of the brain, after
the electricity is switched on, suffering a slow-motion death. Price's
research helped persuade the Indiana legislature to retire that
state's electric chair.

"Courts are not clear on when pain is truly gratuitous," observes
Deborah Denno, a law professor at Fordham University, adding
that the high court's vagueness had allowed states to set high pain
thresholds and tolerate botched executions by every method.
Nowhere has this proved more frightful than in Florida—the sun-
shine state—and the potential effects are far-reaching.

The Rise and Fall of "Old Sparky"

Florida's dance of death with the electric chair epitomizes America's romance with the machine. For decades prison officials and
the press have called the state's execution device "Old Sparky," the
kind of affectionate nickname often given to instruments of destruction, even atomic bombs (the devices dropped on Japan were
known as "Little Boy" and "Fat Man") to domesticate them and
blunt their terror. Florida refused to abandon the chair despite a series of widely publicized botched executions, because it had become part of state legend.

Florida officials seemed to want it both ways: painless, humane
death brought about by an efficient technical instrument—but also

a threat of extremely painful death brought about by an unreliable appliance held over from the past. Even in Florida, however, the electric chair finally overstayed its welcome.

This turn of events began on March 25, 1997, just another execution day on Florida's death row. Prison officials shaved the head of the prisoner, Pedro Medina, and applied an electroconductive gel to reduce the amount of burning to his scalp. Medina was then ushered to the three-legged electric chair, carved out of oak by inmates in 1923. More than 200 prisoners had made this trip before him, including the mass murderer Ted Bundy. Guards placed straps around Medina's chest, abdomen, arms, and legs and secured his head firmly to the back of the chair by a mouth and chin strap. They attached a large, wet sponge, soaked in saline solution, to his right leg and strapped on an electrode. Then they lowered a black leather face mask over his head. His last words were, "I am still innocent."

Medina, thirty-nine, a former mental patient, had come to the United States from Cuba in 1980 in the Mariel boat lift. Two years later he apparently stabbed to death an elementary schoolteacher who had befriended him. His lawyer had argued that he was innocent and, in any event, he was deranged; he had taken to drinking toilet water and eating his own feces. Pope John Paul II pleaded for mercy, and the victim's daughter opposed the execution on grounds that the state had not conclusively proved Medina's guilt.

Just before 7:05 A.M., the first jolt of electricity coursed through Medina's body. But something went terribly wrong. Within a few seconds a little smoke drifted from under the right side of the headpiece, followed by a four- to five-inch yellow-orange flame, which flared for a few seconds, then disappeared. More smoke rose from Medina's head, dense enough to fill the chamber. Appalled, some of the thirty-nine witnesses noted an unsettling odor, like something burning. After thirty-five seconds, the current was switched off, as planned, and Medina, visible through the smoke, appeared lifeless, but witnesses noticed his chest moving two or three times during the next few minutes, as if he was trying to breathe. At

7:10, five minutes after the juice was turned on, a doctor declared Medina dead. But the controversy over his electrocution had only begun.

A visibly shaken spokesman for the state's Department of Corrections, who had witnessed eleven previous executions, admitted that this was "something entirely out of the ordinary." One witness called it "a burning alive, literally." With executions becoming routine in America, the death penalty had faded from newspapers, but the botched job in Florida brought it back to the front page. The tabloids had a field day, with the *New York Post* headlining "Sparks Fly Over Execution." A Vatican newspaper charged that Medina was "burned like a torch" and pleaded that this "tragic event" might force America to reflect on abolishing the death penalty. A pastor of a New Jersey church who had tried to keep Medina off death row called the smoke the wrath of God and charged that Florida had "burned a man at the stake."

This was the second time in recent years a condemned man had caught fire in Florida, one of the few states that continue to rely solely on the electric chair for executions. One of the most gruesome executions in memory occurred in Old Sparky in 1990 when a sponge ignited and flames shot from the headpiece worn by Jesse Tafero. His body was charred in places, and blood poured from his face. In 1995 another man sitting in the chair let out a muffled scream as the juice was turned on.

Even after Medina, most Florida officials stood behind the use of electrocution. "People who wish to commit murder better not do it in the state of Florida, because we may have a problem with our electric chair," Attorney General Bob Butterworth announced. This warning painted an image of uncontrollable technology, the threat of death intensified by the unpredictability of the death machine. (It's somewhat akin to cold war nuclear strategists conveying a sense of their own "craziness" to scare the Soviets—what used to be known as the "madman theory.") The majority leader of the Florida legislature, Locke Burt, asserted that "a painless death is not punishment."

Editorials in many newspapers criticized those officials, however, for flouting human decency and perpetuating the fallacy that capital punishment—the crueler the better—deters crime. A columnist for the *Miami Herald* pictured Butterworth as a "chest-thumping super sheriff. . . . One imagined Butterworth hoisting his gun belt and punctuating his observations with tobacco spit." The institution of capital punishment seemed to be taking a toll "on the ethical and constitutional literacy of those who administer it in at least one state," the *Arizona Star* opined. "Instead of regretting the cruel mess that state had made of Medina's punishment, . . . Florida's leaders brandished the atrocity, gleeful."

At first, Governor Lawton Chiles suggested that the state indeed might have to consider other execution options. "We've had smoke before," he observed. "But the question is really, 'Is this something that is torturous or painful?' . . . Right now we do not have any indication that it is." After consulting with prison officials, Chiles announced that the presiding doctor believed Medina's death was "very quick" and "humane" and that he had felt no pain, while admitting that "putting people to death is not the most friendly thing that you can do."

A leading Republican legislator said that at worst all Florida needed was a new electric chair. "The whole thing could have been avoided," he pointed out, "had Mr. Medina not murdered a woman in 1982. That is the easiest way to stay out of the chair." An investigation found that a dry sponge had ignited, causing the unsightly execution, seemingly a simple problem to resolve. A circuit court judge in Florida ruled that executions could resume, since experts had testified that Medina suffered "no conscious pain. . . . The Florida electric chair—its apparatus, equipment, and electrical circuitry—is in excellent condition."

While one electric chair was shut down, another was about to be fired up. Managers of the new WonderWorks tourist attraction in Orlando announced that they planned to let visitors sit in a mock electric chair, which does not deliver a jolt but produces smoke if you sit in it too long. In Tallahassee, someone started selling repli-

cas of Old Sparky for $995, along with a T-shirt bearing the slo-
gan, "Only sissies do the injection." Reportedly, the chair comes
with leather straps and a copper skullcap, and when you throw a
switch the chair seat vibrates. John Pauley, the entrepreneur, who
admitted he has a "warped sense of humor," reported, "We're having a ball; this is all in good fun." Let's face it, he argued, "people
are fascinated with death," pointing out that they rubberneck at
highway car crashes and other accident sites.

Seven months after Medina's execution, the state supreme court
ruled 4–3 that the electric chair did not deliver cruel and unusual
punishment—but it recommended that the legislature find another
method of execution. The state's Corrections Commission began
studying alternatives, but its executive director complained that
there was "no science in execution," especially since the Hippocratic oath discourages doctors from designing execution technology.

This is a revealing plea for medical and scientific expertise in
methods of capital punishment. Officials want the method to be
based on physiological knowledge, so that the killing is smooth,
precise, quick, and humane. The Nazis, too, aspired to this in de-
veloping their early "euthanasia" project, the murder of people
considered in one way or another impaired, mostly mental patients.
Karl Brandt, then Hitler's chief doctor, had a certain amount of
idealism and apparently wished to employ the most painless
method of killing.

A reporter for the *St. Petersburg Times* observed that for
many legislators the possibility of losing the chair was "as heart-
wrenching a prospect" as losing campaign contributions from lob-
byists. Other lawmakers were more concerned about a delay in re-
suming executions, no matter which method was employed. "I
don't care if it's firing squad, public hanging, lethal injection, or
whatever, so long as the legislation we pass doesn't diminish the
carrying out of the death penalty," a Republican leader argued. Another lawmaker, Charlie Crist, who was running for the U.S. Sen-

ate, said that he didn't care "if we fry them or inject them." A Democrat reasoned, "Dead is dead."

Then, a little less than a year after Medina's execution, legislators in Florida voted to keep the electric chair in service and Governor Chiles signed the bill. Days later, four executions, including that of Judy Buenoano, the so-called "Black Widow," proceeded as planned. Seven legislators who had voted to bring Old Sparky back on line attended one of the executions, explaining that they wanted to make sure it was working properly. Afterward, the Senate majority leader, Burt, pronounced the procedure "antiseptic," like "a grim ballet. . . . When they pulled the switch it was over." Another senator, Fred Dudley, who was running for state attorney general, said he was "very surprised and pleased" at how smoothly the execution went, while admitting, "It's never pleasant to watch somebody die." Judy Buenoano, he reported, "died much more humanely than those she murdered."

It looked as if Old Sparky was back for a long run—or rather, its offspring, what some called "Son of Sparky." More than forty executions in twenty years had caused a lot of wear and tear on the original, so the state produced a new version of the old favorite, a process ingenuously referred to by prison officials as "routine maintenance." But then, two years after Pedro Medina burst into flames, a 350-pound inmate named Tiny Davis sat in the new chair and bled all over himself while being electrocuted, and suddenly the chair appeared headed for the junk heap of history once again.

Pictures at an Execution

As condemned men go, Alvin "Tiny" Davis was perhaps among the worst. A former child molestor, he had survived on death row for seventeen years after bludgeoning a pregnant woman to death, then shooting and killing her two young daughters. He had never expressed remorse. One would have expected his execution on July 20, 1999 to cause barely a ripple in Florida. Instead, it would lead to a temporary halt to all executions by electrocution in every state, and the introduction of lethal injection in Florida.

Everything went normally at first that day, if you consider normal strapping a grossly obese, nearly comatose man into a chair he will never rise from alive. And, indeed, he died more or less on schedule. The problem was that he screamed in pain when the first jolt hit him, and then a large blot of blood appeared on his shirt. After two more jolts, his chest still heaved a bit before he succumbed. Journalists sent the graphic details all over the country, creating a storm of editorial protest.

According to Governor Jeb Bush, all that blood was merely caused by a little nosebleed, made more dramatic by the unfortunate fact that the prisoner was wearing a white shirt. An autopsy, he said, proved that Davis had never felt a thing. Others disputed this, citing the screaming and heaving, and noting that blood had never appeared in any of the many executions since 1979. Then there was State Senator Ginny Brown-Waite of Brooksville—a witness who thought the bloodstain on Davis's shirt resembled a cross and interpreted it as a sign from God. What this meant, she announced, was either that Davis had made his peace with God—or that God was giving his blessing to Florida's execution policy.

Clearly, with supporters invoking miracles and visions, the electric chair was in trouble in Florida. The speaker of the Florida House lamented that it was all the fault of that "soulless monster," Tiny Davis.

In any case, it appeared that Davis, the three-time killer, had now saved one life, at least for a while. Embarrassed by his bloody end, the state postponed the execution of another killer, Thomas Provenzano, scheduled for the following day, while they studied what went wrong (continuing to claim that the chair "functioned properly"). Attorneys for Provenzano appealed to the state supreme court, calling executions in the chair cruel and unusual punishment. They took advantage of a novelty: because of what had happened to Pedro Medina, the state, apparently for the first time, had asked a photographer to snap pictures of an execution.

The photos, entered as evidence in the hearing, appeared to show Tiny Davis grimacing or howling behind his leather face straps, his face turning purple, as blood flowed and covered much of his chest.

The court, however, in a narrow 4–3 decision, ruled that expiring in the chair was not cruel and unusual punishment, despite what some physical evidence or eyewitness testimony might imply. But this was far from the end of the matter. In his dissent, Justice Leander J. Shaw wrote, "Execution by electrocution, with its attendant smoke and flames and blood and screams, is a spectacle whose time has passed," and then he did an extraordinary thing: he requested that the photos from the death chamber be posted on the Court's website so that citizens could judge for themselves.

Over the next several days, the site received more than a million "hits." And no wonder. The photos held grim fascination, as few Americans have ever been exposed to visual images of an actual inmate—not a Hollywood actor—in the process of being executed. A new state poll revealed that 58 percent of all Floridians now supported a state law to switch from the electric chair to lethal injection. As a practical politician, Governor Bush proposed a special legislative session to consider it. He was under tremendous pressure, as the U.S. Supreme Court, responding to an appeal from yet another condemned Florida prisoner, had just agreed to reconsider the constitutionality of the electric chair for the first time in years, on "cruel and unusual" grounds.

The death penalty scholar Deborah Denno remarked that while the Court had always applied fairly "generous" standards in this matter, it "has never seen pictures of an inmate sitting on a chair with blood on his face." Governor Bush did not savor defending Florida's recent experiences with the chair before the high court, and if the state law was changed to allow for the option of lethal injection, that might end the appeal. Many Florida lawmakers, who had steadfastly defended the chair, had now seen enough (or else bowed to shifting public opinion). "For some reason, we just can't seem to pull the switch and get people to die instantly," complained Walter Campbell, a state senator from Coral Springs. Finally, both chambers of the legislature overwhelmingly passed a bill giving prisoners the option of choosing execution by injection. And within a few weeks in early 2000, two had done so, and had died by the needle.

Politicians can develop a passion for the death penalty, or at least for its existence as law. There is a need for an ideology of purification through capital punishment—along with some reluctance to carry it out. So we find in Florida some of the most intense expressions in favor of the death penalty along with a relatively limited number of actual executions. It may be more important for Florida's leaders to sustain the ideology than to carry through the killing. Sometimes, however, truths arise from such debate, as with the simple expression, "Dead is dead."

Humanity may indeed have been served by Florida's allegiance to the electric chair. If the instrument of execution is itself controversial in terms of the pain and suffering it causes, and considered by some to be barbarous, everyone concerned (politicians, prosecutors, judges, juries) has greater difficulty carrying out capital punishment. One can contrast this with the state of Texas, where lethal injections have eased the performing of a record number of executions.

The Needle and the Damage Done

The preference for lethal injection can be explained by its apparent ease, cleanliness, and relative lack of drama. Lethal injection is a quantum jump in medicalization, and in the overall numbing surrounding capital punishment. It is clinical in ways that are familiar to anyone who has ever visited a hospital: there are IV lines, gurneys, a doctor, technicians, prescription drugs. Sedation is the word. "They put you out," a victims' rights advocate in Tennessee explains, "but in this case you never wake up." A Baptist chaplain in Texas who has witnessed almost forty executions calls it "as humane as any form of death you can find. Basically, they go to sleep."

The sleep metaphor suggests that the execution is merciful, peaceful, for the prisoner's own good, as well as society's—like having compassion for a favorite old dog who has turned rabid. When he was governor of California, Ronald Reagan likened lethal injections to putting an injured horse out of its misery—"The horse goes to sleep—that's it."

As the death penalty moratorium of the 1970s ended, many states began to pick up the needle. The British had rejected lethal injection in the 1950s, feeling that it was an undignified way to die and preferring hanging instead. In the United States, however, growing discomfort with the aesthetics of gassing and electrocution promoted a slow changeover. In 1982, Texas prisoner Charles Brooks, as we have observed, became the first person executed by the so-called lethal injection. The dream of an anesthetized execution, proposed by G. W. Peck in 1847, was finally realized, if in a different form.

After witnessing an execution by needle in Missouri, the writer Christopher Hitchens observed that this method "is supposed to be more tranquil and predictable and benign than the various forms of burning, shooting, strangling and gassing that in the past have squeezed themselves through the 'cruel and unusual' rubric. It looks and feels—to the outsider at least—more like a banal medical procedure but this medicalized 'putting down' is designed to leach the drama and agony out of the business; to transform it into a form of therapy for society."

Whether death by needle is easier for the executed is an open question, but surely it is easier for the executioners. By wrapping punishment in a therapeutic cloak, the process feels less morally offensive to those who are required to participate, and it is therefore more bearable. There is a deeper issue as well. "The use of a well-known medical tool, general anesthesia, for execution blurs the distinctions between healing and killing, between illness and guilt," observes Dr. Jerome D. Gorman, a general practitioner in Richmond, Virginia, who has spoken out strongly on this issue. "Those distinctions between illness and guilt, between therapy and punishment, are important to a just society. Once before in the twentieth century, physicians [in Nazi Germany] allowed themselves to play a role in blurring these distinctions, with disastrous consequences." (Nazi medicalization of killing meant either carrying out the murders within medical structures and institutions, or involving doctors directly in killing situations—so much so that at Auschwitz, doctors were in charge of the killing process from beginning to end).

One can also speak of the guillotine, gas chamber, and electric chair as medicalized killing, since doctors helped create and administer them, but lethal injection comes closer to direct medical killing. The entire process is a medical procedure, though it does not take place in a medical institution. Rather, the hospital equipment is brought into the prison, so that a room within the prison becomes a kind of small medical facility. This creates an "as-if" situation, a kind of illusion that a dire but necessary medical procedure is being implemented as a "cure" for a severe ailment. Mass killing often has a medicalized aura, but in capital punishment the focus can be more precise and the aura more readily established.

Inevitably, as lethal injection takes hold in our society, there is a sense that the electric chair and the gas chamber are old-fashioned and crude. Any new technology, if perceived as more humane and therefore more acceptable, helps sustain the policy of capital punishment. The new execution method, the needle, consists *only* of elements ordinarily associated with medical treatment, and therefore doesn't just blur but obliterates the distinction between healing and killing.

People often use the phrase "too easy" concerning lethal injections. Some think the condemned man has it too easy—while others feel that the method makes it too easy to execute someone. Everything, in fact, becomes "too easy."

From the first point of view, the relative tranquillity is regrettable. Supreme Court Justice Antonin Scalia once called "enviable a quiet death by lethal injection" compared with that of a brutal rape or murder. The California-based Children's Protection and

Advocacy Coalition charged that lethal injections sanitized executions, a misguided form of euthanasia. "Learn to burn," one member of the group advised the public, adding that "rapists don't burn by themselves, they need your help."

The federal judge Alex Kozinski, a well-known death penalty proponent, comes at this from the second angle, agreeing with abolitionists that it is "creepy that we pervert the instruments of healing . . . by putting them to such an antithetical use." It bothers him that "we mask the most violent act that society can inflict on one of its members with such an antiseptic veneer. Isn't death by firing squad, with mutilations and bloodshed, more honest?"

In this now familiar procedure, the prisoner is strapped to a gurney and needles are inserted in his arms. At a signal, three chemicals begin to flow in succession: an anesthetic, a drug to paralyze the respiratory muscles, and a third drug to halt the heart. During the early years of lethal injection, prisons designed their own procedures in a somewhat experimental, haphazard fashion, often leading to glitches.

Then, in 1989, Missouri tried out the new lethal-injection system designed by none other than Fred Leuchter in the execution of George Mercer. It became the subject of a widely viewed documentary that some found "eerily reminiscent of Nazi nightmares," as James Megivern put it in his theological survey of the death penalty. Still, even with improved delivery systems, mistakes occur. One prisoner remained conscious, struggling, for about ten minutes, due to a clogged catheter. In another case an I.V. popped out of an inmate's arm, spewing deadly solutions toward the witness box. After jabbing a prisoner's arm for several minutes trying to find a vein, officials in Louisiana finally had to insert the needle in his neck. In Texas, a condemned man had such a violent physical reaction to the drugs—gasping and choking—that one of the witnesses fainted, knocking over another witness. In several cases officials have had such a hard time finding a vein that an inmate lay strapped on his cot for more than forty minutes, awaiting death.

Joseph Cannon, who was condemned to die in Texas when he was 17, repeatedly said he was sorry for what he had done, and closed his eyes peacefully as the chemicals flowed. Then he opened his eyes, turned to a window where witnesses were standing and said, "It's come undone." The drapes were pulled, and a prison chaplain informed the witnesses as they were led outside, "His blood vein blew. He is doing fine. They are just going to restart it." Fifteen minutes later the witnesses were brought back in, and the execution proceeded. Cannon, no longer "doing fine," was pronounced dead thirty-four minutes after the first injection was aborted.

Florida, which had just stepped away from the electric chair due to botched executions, couldn't even get the lethal injections right. Its third execution by this method in June 2000 went horribly wrong when it took more than half an hour to insert the IV in prisoner Bennie Demps. According to a prison spokesman, "It was necessary to do a surgical procedure to find a suitable vein" in one arm after flubbing a hook-up in the other arm and in his leg. "They butchered me back there," the prisoner told stunned witnesses before his passing. "I was in a lot of pain," he said, adding that it amounted to a "low-tech lynching."

In other cases, a small error in dosage may leave prisoners conscious but paralyzed—seemingly dead but perhaps still slowly dying. Of course, the only person who knows that for sure is not in any position to testify to it. Several lethal injections as recently as 1999 took far longer than the normal five to seven minutes to produce a certifiable corpse. An official in Texas complains that attorneys seeking to stop all executions sometimes demand proof that it is "totally and completely painless. I don't know how you go about satisfying that. You can never call them [the executed] back and say, 'Did this cause you pain?' "

Choices: "There Ain't No Humane Way"

Yet among those most affected—the condemned—lethal injection apparently seems like the best of several bad options. In states where prisoners are given a choice, they almost invariably select the needle. Those who dissent are likely to claim that they are doing so as a form of protest.

One convicted killer said he wanted his passing to be "ugly," in the gas chamber, where he figured it would look more like murder. An inmate in Maryland chose the gas chamber for the same reason, though he later changed his mind and switched to injection to spare his family needless pain. Paul Hill, convicted of gunning down a doctor and his bodyguard outside an abortion clinic in Pensacola, Florida, has asserted that he hopes the "gruesome" electric chair remains in operation because it "might bring more sympathy and attention" to his efforts to avoid execution. The daughter of Judy Buenoano said she prayed that her mother would go up in flames in the chair so it would hasten the end of capital punishment. "If my mother catches on fire," she added, "the world is going to know."

Some prisoners are more philosophical about it than political. In the autumn of 1998, Kenneth Stewart, Jr., shunned lethal injection to become the first killer to die in Virginia's electric chair since 1994. "There ain't no humane way to put a human being to death," he explained, "if you stop and think about it."

Those killers who opt for an "ugly" death to make it look like murder remind us of comments made years ago by American soldiers discussing how they preferred to die in Vietnam. One of them said that he "wanted to die clean, not with mud on my boots, all filthy" (this has some parallels to lethal injection). Another described how he feared and dreamed of being shot and then "lying along the side of the road, dying in the mud." A third spoke of an incident he had heard of in which a helicopter pilot carrying a portable toilet crashed and he was "buried under the whole shithouse and all the shit"—which would be the appropriate way *he* wished to die in Vietnam. Most condemned criminals want the easiest death, but like these soldiers a few may wish their means of dying to embody their protest or express their sense of filth or absurdity.

John Albert Taylor, who claimed to be innocent of raping and murdering an 11-year-old girl, chose the firing squad in Utah in 1996, saying that he did not want to "flop around like a dying fish" on a gurney, but also insisting that he wanted to make the process as expensive and embarrassing for the state as possible. Indeed, by 1996, executions were becoming so routine in America that it required an unusual method—such as hanging or shooting—to generate much attention.

Taylor's execution went off as planned, but he succeeded in his goal of embarrassing the state, aided by prison officials who naively showed reporters a hole in the death chair made by a bullet that had passed through Taylor's heart. A local ACLU director said that it made Utah "seem backward." Even some Mormon leaders got behind a legislative drive to abolish death by firing squad in the state.

In the wake of the Pedro Medina fiasco in Florida, and subsequent debates and legal appeals, several states embraced lethal injection as an alternative to gassing or electrocution. Kentucky made the switch after a poll found that 63 percent of its citizens favored lethal injection over the electric chair. State officials in Georgia and Nebraska, two of the four remaining electrocution-only states, proposed studying the same change rather than risking the entire right to execute in the short term. But an anti–death penalty legislator in Nebraska announced that he opposed the move, arguing that all executions are "inherently barbarous and inhumane" and "there is no humane way to commit an inhumane act."

What options remain? A member of the commission probing alternatives to the electric chair in Florida wondered if there was a science fiction or Star Trek solution—"At what point do we have a vaporizer?" He was presumably joking, but this reflects a yearning for a still more advanced, humane, and efficient killing mechanism: a fantasy of a method so perfect that it *completely* removes the killing from killing. Then there's Dr. Jack Kervorkian's idea of execution by surgery: anesthetizing murderers, then harvesting their organs for reuse. Legislators in Arizona recently proposed a bill allowing at least the harvesting part of it, a procedure reportedly used in China following executions.

There is a real question about what any particular society deems to be "unnecessary cruelty." It is always relative, depending on available technology and on the climate in relation to capital punishment. Shooting, hanging, and the electric chair seem more violent than the gas chamber or lethal injection, but the true violence is the killing. In that sense all methods are equally violent.

One recalls Franz Kafka's short story of 1914, *In the Penal Colony*, in which he described an ingenious killing machine called "The Harrow." Equipped with sharp needles, it slowly etched a condemned man's crime into his back over a twelve-hour period until he died of his wounds. Over time, however, the machine inevitably broke down and began to cruelly carve up its victims. "This was plain murder," Kafka wrote.

America appears to be constantly looking for ever more efficient ways to kill people as a form of respect for their humanity. Precisely that "improvement" not only makes killing easier but serves to justify retaining the death penalty in general. Will executions continue to evolve in more palatable and "modern" ways, ever more distant from the executioner? Or will we give up the quest for the perfect method, recognizing that the strongest testimony to how little we have evolved since frontier days is the fact that we still do it at all?

PART II

EXECUTIONERS

4

WARDENS AND GUARDS, CHAPLAINS AND DOCTORS

I am the limbs and the wheel—
the victim and the executioner!
—*Charles Baudelaire*

THE direct responsibility for performing an actual execution is delegated mainly to wardens and prison guards. Despite constant improvements in efficiency, many among them experience painful symptoms that reflect their deep ambivalence about what they do. Other professionals—chaplains and physicians—play a more ambiguous role in the execution process, but a very important one nonetheless. Their unease can be compounded by conflict about this use of their ordinarily healing professions. In members of all these groups, the discomfort, at times extending to excruciating guilt, has to do with a perception of the essential wrongness of killing a fellow human being, no matter what the cause.

One rarely finds in America the sense of pleasure and "fun" Albert Camus described in some French executioners half a century ago, to the point of being "batty about the guillotine" and spending "days on end at home sitting on a chair, ready with hat and coat on, waiting for a summons from the Ministry." Norman Mailer points out that prison administrators everywhere in America now share the goal of attempting to carry out executions "without looking sadistic or ridiculous."

Many officials and staff appear sincerely troubled and divided about their duties on death row. They avoid using boastful language and will often say that they are just doing their job, with "professionalism," aiming for a high degree of "dignity" in the killing process. To a degree this may be a moral—and public relations—requirement of the work. Occasionally, officials will voice callous views or, even more rarely, refuse to take part in the procedure, but generally they explain that they derive no pleasure from planning to put someone to death and are intent only on making the process tolerable for everyone involved, including the inmate. These varying attitudes provide considerable insight into the psychology of those involved in hands-on killing.

Correctional Officials: "Unfortunately, That's My Job"

When Peter Matos, a former prison guard and warden, became deputy commissioner of corrections of the state of Connecticut, one of his new duties was to plan, and be prepared to carry out, executions; and he put a lot of thought and work into it. Connecticut last executed a prisoner in 1960, but changes in state law have made death sentences more common. So, starting from scratch, Matos set up the execution machinery and assembled and trained the teams that will carry out the law.

"I'm a pretty happy-go-lucky guy," Matos told a reporter, "so people are surprised that I'm even involved. They say, 'Jesus, Pete, you're doing *this?* " *This* is something extreme, unmentionable, or at least not quite in the realm of ordinary, acceptable behavior. It is a euphemism for killing.

His task attracted unusual interest, frequent black humor, and some criticism. People often sent him gifts. A skeptical friend presented him with a guillotine for Christmas. Matos interpreted the message as, "You're into the death penalty? Here's a guillotine for you, pal." A supportive colleague in the Department of Corrections gave him a tiny replica of the state's old electric chair, enclosed in a glass dome. One day Matos arrived at his desk to find that someone had opened the dome and placed in the hot seat a tiny doll with flaming orange hair and a twisted grin.

In any event, to Matos the death penalty is no laughing matter. He claims that he has an open mind about capital punishment, and he sparked a brief controversy when he told a *Hartford Courant* reporter that there was *no* humane way of killing someone—rare language for someone in his position. Still, he asserted that he would carry out the law if required. He had come up through the ranks of the criminal justice system over a long career, not imagining that he would ever be in charge of orchestrating executions: reading research reports, remodeling the death chamber, planning crowd control for the inevitable protests, running execution drills. He also must anticipate the psychological fallout among his staff. "A lot of people always say, 'Oh, I have no problem, I can handle it.' Well, I don't really know if people can handle it until after it happens," Matos observed. "Even if they're not in the room, they [may be] in the building and they know that someone's being executed down the hall. We probably have to work with some depression and psychological effects on staff after the fact."

But what about the effects on those actually participating in the execution? Matos favors lethal injection because the medicalized procedures make it easier for executioners to carry it out. He spoke with emotion, however, in describing the mock executions he and his staff have witnessed in other states on training missions. In some states, staff volunteers practice executions for weeks. Officers playing condemned men faint or thrash about, and the warden times how long every step takes, including his own reading of the death warrant. "I was really surprised at how much information the prisoner got, and how much he knows [about] what's going to happen," Matos explained. "Weeks prior they start to counsel the person and work with him. The day of the execution they actually tell him, from A to Z, this is what's going to happen. This is what's expected of you"—besides dying, that is.

Matos refers to trained staffers as "execution teams," but hates to call them that because it makes them sound like torture squads

in South America. Back in the mid-1990s, when he began his new
duties, a newspaper reported that he was looking to hire someone
to undergo training for the team. When he got home that night his
wife said that one of her friends at work had commented, "Jesus,
your husband is looking for an executioner." His wife complained
to him that he hadn't told her about it. He replied, "I'm not running a guillotine or anything, honey. I'm only setting up the
process." Nevertheless, he affirmed, "she had a hard time with
that."

She wasn't the only one. Besides receiving unsolicited and sometimes unnerving gifts, and hearing a lot of gallows humor, he's also
received many letters. "People have gotten morbid since they know
I was handling this," he said. Some letters declare that what he's
doing is "great," while other people "think I'm Saddam Hussein's
little brother."

Matos expressed disapproval of the large number of people who
stepped forward to volunteer for execution duty claiming they had
no qualms about it whatsoever. "I don't really think they understand, and I think those are definitely the people I would *not* have
as part of the team," Matos observed. "I want somebody who's
going to be concerned about what they're going to do. I don't
want it to have [such] a negative reaction that it's going to destroy
their personal lives, but I want to make sure they understand the
consequences of what we're doing."

Like many who plan and manage executions, Peter Matos conveys
a compelling struggle to balance feeling and nonfeeling. He insists
that people working with him realize that "someone's being executed down the hall," but he favors lethal injection because it gives
the person doing it "some peace of mind." The mock executions
and the careful scripting of every detail of the event contribute to
the professional numbing Matos and others seek to achieve. His
goal is to make efficient use of the best available technology, to "do
it right."

This type of numbing is necessary for all who work with death, the threat of death, or with suffering and pain. A surgeon, for instance, cannot afford to experience the emotions of the patient's family; he must maintain sufficient detachment to enable him to make best use of his technical abilities—while at the same time retaining sufficient humanity to enter into a concerned dialogue with family members. Matos knows that "callous" people are incapable of such an equilibrium because they are insufficiently concerned about what they're going to do. Their problem is that, unlike the surgeon, they are not seeking to *preserve* life.

His bitterness toward those who are too enthusiastic about participating in killing mirrors his own conflicted feelings, which spilled out in the interview in which he—rather too frankly—averred that there really was no humane way to carry out an execution. In any case, he emphasizes that, humane or not, the execution can at least be carried out with dignity. "We want to make sure that we don't botch things up," he explained.

Matos appears honestly torn, at least until that first execution, which may or may not set him on a clearer path. "People say, 'Well, are you for the executions or against?' Well, I don't know, I'm, I'm—this is my job. People say, 'Well, if I had a job like that, I'd leave it.' Well, yeah, well—this is the profession I have chosen. If we have to carry out an execution, I would hope that it's something that's being carried out by the letter of the law. Yeah, I may feel uncomfortable with it. But I'm obviously going to carry it out. . . . Unfortunately, that's my job."

One senses that Matos is a decent man, but he is psychologically enabled to do what he does through a pattern of "doubling." Matos forms what could be called an "execution self," which does the dirty work. He tries to instill into that work whatever professionalism is possible, but he and others know that it is dirty work nonetheless. The execution self is morally at odds with his everyday self, since he would not ordinarily have anything to do with killing another person. The execution self performs what is expected of it within the killing institution and in that sense behaves "normally."

Matos tries to avoid the ethical questions surrounding executions by insisting that this is "the profession I have chosen," but when he says "Unfortunately, that's my job," he is articulating his ambivalence and discomfort. Yet he could conceivably become slightly more comfortable with every execution, slightly better adapted to killing. This would be reminiscent of the phenomenon of the "decent Nazi," the professional who is well trained, thoughtful, likable, even charming socially, who sees himself as combating callous people and cruel tendencies within his domain, but because of his intelligence and ability ends up doing much of the crucial work of the project.

Of course, Matos is no Nazi, and no American prison is a full-time killing institution like Auschwitz and other death camps. But executions render our prisons at least occasional or part-time killing institutions. And well-meaning men like Matos enable our killing institutions to achieve maximum function.

Wardens: Varieties of Conflict

Peter Matos has spoken with more frankness and emotion than most in his position, but many wardens voice some of the same views.

Warden Wayne Patterson of Colorado insists on sharing the responsibility with citizens in general: "As far as I was concerned, every person that voted for it in Colorado at that referendum [favoring executions] had his hand on the lever, same as I did." His attitude parallels that of many Vietnam veterans who insisted that all of American society share responsibility for the killing they did in that war. The implication in both cases is that there is something wrong, something dirty, about the killing, and that all who supported the overall project must bear their share of responsibility and guilt.

"As prison officials, we just adopt the policy of going about our business in an extremely professional and sober manner with the policy handed to us by those in the legislature," a director of public information for the Texas Department of Criminal Justice said recently. Such professionalism diminishes what we might call "executioner stress." One assistant superintendent in Missouri, Don Roper, goes so far as to say that there's "much more stress" when the process is interrupted by a stay of execution.

But Roper made clear that, having experienced the condemned prisoner as a human being, one must fend off feelings of guilt—often by invoking the authority of the state and the prisoner's original misdeed: "People say, 'Well, you're right there in the execution chamber with them. I mean, you're the last person to see them draw breath. You're the last person that gives him a cigarette and lets him smoke. Does it bother you?' And I say no. And it doesn't bother me. As a professional in the Department of Corrections, I know my duty. These people killed somebody. I didn't. All I'm doing is a job that the state says I should do."

Toward the end, the defenses become both more difficult to sustain and more urgent. "Certainly, that last thirty minutes, when you're in preparation of actually taking a human life—you have to look into your own self and say, I'm an instrument of the state, I have a job to do, and I chose to do it," Roper explained. The inner pressure to avoid discomfort and self-condemnation undoubtedly contributes to his insistence that "it would not bother me whatsoever to push the button."

Another warden, Charlie Jones, candidly admits that the process of carrying out an execution is "a hell of a time, stressful and scary." He handles his anxiety by invoking the authority of law over the original transgression ("I don't carry the load for what the inmate did") and by committing himself to carrying out the execution "in the most humane way possible." Others, like Bill Armontrout, warden at the Missouri Penitentiary, invoke a claim of legal fairness. Armontrout insists that he has "made peace with myself on this thing by knowing that the fellow that's being executed has had every chance of appeal. When you know that the case has been scrutinized this closely, then it makes you feel much easier." This distancing mechanism is built upon illusion, however, because of many capital cases are not at all closely scrutinized and do not even include competent legal defense.

Armontrout actually went to Mississippi once to help a friend, Donald Cabana, with his first execution, or as he put it, "do a complimentary one for him." The newcomer is socialized to killing by one who has already undergone that socialization.

Because he's never had to "manhandle" prisoners to get them onto the gurney, Armontrout believes, undoubtedly falsely, that none of them felt any "animosity" toward him or his staff. Still, killing an inmate a warden has been watching over for years—as a ward of the state, so to speak—can be traumatic, even if he feels the prisoner deserves it. Armontrout considered one prisoner he executed, Tiny Mercer, to be a "friend" and admits that it was "hard doing him." Yet he seemed a bit perplexed afterward about why Mercer's widow greeted him with, "Hi, Bill. God loves you, but why did you kill Tiny?"

Wardens frequently enlist the condemned man as, in effect, part of the execution team, insisting to him that "We've got to get through this together." They mean to express sympathy, to show that it's painful for them, too; and the "teamwork" may, in fact, benefit the prisoner by making his death a bit easier. Yet the claimed mutuality is also a bit spurious, since in the end only one of the parties will "get through this."

One official went further in articulating a principle of transcendence. When the legendary executioner Albert Pierrepoint testified before a British commission in 1950, he spoke proudly of his work. Questioned on whether people often asked him about his official duties, Pierrepoint replied: "Yes, but I refuse to speak about it. It is something I think should be secret. It is sacred to me, really."

Pierrepoint's statement suggests what may be an inevitable sacralization of the execution process. People concerned with death and killing are likely to connect their work with religious meaning of some kind. Death itself—even more so, the taking of life—evokes in us a need for an immortality system of the kind provided by religion. There are also reverberations of the "sacred executioner" who presides over human sacrifice, described by the Judaic scholar Hyam Maccoby as "the figure of a person (either a God or a human being) who slays another person, and as a result is treated as both sacred and accursed." Pierrepoint's overt sacralization of his execution function enabled him to continue it for several decades. But since, in his memoirs, he would declare himself against capital punishment, we may assume that some part of him came to be sensitive to the "accursed" side of the executioner.

Guards and Staff—"Our Executioner Is a Team"

> *No one wants to touch a smoking gun*
> *But since they got injection*
> *They don't mind as much I guess*
> *They just put 'em down at Ellis Unit One*
> —Steve Earle, *"Ellis Unit One"*

Unlike wardens and correctional officials, prison guards and staff who take part in executions often express a blasé, at times even self-satisfied, attitude about this aspect of their work. They are the foot soldiers of execution. Blending as they do into execution teams, they can feel themselves less responsible than wardens for the project and its outcome, but at the same time even closer to the direct experience of killing.

One coping mechanism can be a form of crass detachment. A Florida guard in charge of the generator that fed the electric chair, denied having any moral qualms about his work: "If you've got a problem with your job, then you've got to get another job." He added, "I pretty much support the death penalty. Anyway, I get paid for it." A member of another execution team declared that he could "take or leave executions. It's a job I've been asked to do. If they would stop the death penalty, it wouldn't bother me. If we had ten executions tomorrow, it wouldn't bother me. I would condition my mind to get me through it."

Individuals are encouraged to melt into the elaborate team structure—escort teams, strapdown teams, injection teams, and others, all with multiple backups. Typically, the inmate is moved to a special cell near the death chamber and guards are posted outside to prevent a suicide, while other officers prepare the electric chair, gas chamber, or lethal injection circuitry. Thus begins what one writer has called the "deathwatch," moving the prisoner through "a series of critical and cumulatively demoralizing junctures": the boxing up of his possessions, his last meal, a final visit with loved ones and his spiritual adviser, a change of clothes, a picture taken, the reading of the death warrant, and then the "last walk."

Individual responsibility also dissolves, as each member of the team is given only a limited task. A participant in Missouri executions put it this way: "We all work together. It's a collective thing. Everyone is properly trained. They know what they're supposed to do, and take care of business." A warden in Missouri refers to this as being "task-oriented." Each member of an execution team can concentrate on a limited, specific task, rather than the overall process—or the end result. "Our executioner is a team," declares the director of the Texas Department of Criminal Justice. "I haven't heard of a single problem. Some retire or move on, and we have had people say they've had enough, but there are always others. The sterility helps. Everyone volunteers their services and everyone is guaranteed anonymity."

The result, as one outspoken critic of the death penalty observes, is that "thicker and heavier layers of denial and obfuscation have already begun to encrust this new, pristine, hygienic, pain-free system." The dissolving of responsibility is further enhanced by an aura of militarization and "battle preparedness." A staffer in Missouri compares it to his experience in Vietnam, where he recognized the chain of command and "knew . . . what job I had to do. And . . . that people were going to be killed."

Whatever the dissolving of responsibility, there is evidence, as we will see, that members of an execution team share a sense of collective taint. They alone are chosen to handle the killing and its preparations, as well as the corpse. In this they resemble groups in the past designated as outcasts who were assigned death-related professions in Japan, India, and elsewhere, so that the rest of the population could be distanced from such tasks, and from death itself. Of course these hardworking Americans are not cast out by their communities. Yet their relationship not only to death but to killing creates in them some sense of being psychologically or morally defiled.

Spiritual Advisers—"God Stands by All His Children"

Members of the clergy have a particularly excruciating role in the process. A pending execution raises all the ultimate moral and spiritual questions for which they, as spiritual advisers, are supposed to have answers—questions about mortality and immortality, about living, dying, and taking life. Yet like others, they are very divided in their views on the death penalty, and therefore, in their approach to condemned prisoners.

The numbing we've seen in others who take part can infect even spiritual advisers. Asked to describe his reaction to executions, a prison chaplain at Potosi in Missouri replied: "Exhausting. You're running on adrenaline. You're stressed out. And when it's all said and done . . . it's anticlimactic . . . There's nothing there. You keep thinking there's going to be some emotion. You're searching for something. *How do I feel?* It's just a blank."

Death penalty supporters can, like Ron Mosby, a visiting minister at a Tennessee prison, insist that the Bible "certainly endorses capital punishment" and that "a severe God" sanctions states like Tennessee to execute convicts. Mosby chides clerical colleagues who deny this "severe side" of God, and declares: "I'll pray with you, baptize you, hold your hand until they put the needle in your arm." Another chaplain went further. When a strapped-down prisoner making his final statement asked, "What is capital punishment for?" and lifted his head and strained at his ties, pleading with the chaplain, "Don't let them do this, I'm not done yet," the man of God eased him back down on the gurney so that the chemicals could flow, and he was soon dead. While such physical participation is unusual, chaplains in this category offer active spiritual participation that helps energize the overall execution process.

Many spiritual advisers struggle with an in-between position. A Baptist minister in Tennessee, for instance, referring to the condemned prisoner, insists: "You make a choice, you have to pay consequences." But he describes his support of the death penalty as "reluctant." Similarly, a rabbi in the same city points to what he considers the general "ambivalence" about the death penalty in Jewish tradition as a way of justifying his own.

Sister Helen Prejean established a highly visible model of a very different kind: the spiritual adviser as an anti–death penalty activist. She is not alone. Jerry Welborn, a prison chaplain in Tennessee, had himself laid out and shackled on a gurney, had a colleague pray over him and ask for last words, and then even had intravenous needles inserted into his arms. While this was considered a "routine trial run" for a state execution, with Welborn playing the part of the condemned criminal, he made it into a personal and broadly moral demonstration. He described it as a "trying and stressful . . . experience [that] will make me more available, more empathetic to the inmates," while also pointing out: "The only thing that didn't happen was I didn't die." His general philosophy, "God stands by all his children and so do I," is echoed by other clergy who point to Jesus' teaching as "all about love and mercy," and the insistence in the Gospels that "your sins are forgiven."

Yet when, spiritual advisers lend support to the condemned man—even when they are uncertain about or clearly opposed to the death penalty—they become part of the execution project.

Staff Interplay: Gentle Collusion

During the prisoner's final hours, the atmosphere around him softens. Staffers tend to become kind and generous, prompting some inmates to ask aloud why they never received this level of concern and respect before, going back to their often miserable childhoods. The reasons for the staffers' relative warmth are no doubt varied and complicated. Some certainly feel sympathy for a person about to lose his life, or feel painful regret for volunteering to take part in this process. But others know that this is a kind of ritual, not unlike those of centuries past, where all participants, including the condemned prisoner, follow a script or act out certain roles to guarantee that things go smoothly—and also to help all involved to distance themselves from what is about to happen. Some refer to these final hours as switching over to the "execution mode."

In that mode, as a shrewd observer notes, "The officials' goal, and in the end perhaps the prisoner's as well, is a smooth, orderly, and ostensibly voluntary execution, one that looks humane and dignified and is not sullied in any way by obvious violence." In exchange for the inmate's not raising a fuss, the executioners "will do the job cleanly and without a hitch." The prisoner—who is by this time, psychologically speaking, already dead—tends to cooperate. Thus everyone shares in an illusion of nonviolent decency, as opposed to the reality of the impending killing.

This is why prison officials in Texas could claim, if with some exaggeration, that over a period of seventy-five years not a single condemned man had to be forcibly taken into the execution chamber. But their record of cooperative numbing was shattered in November 1999, when Desmond Jennings, a convicted killer, declared that he would literally fight for his life all the way to the gurney. Officials at Huntsville prison had to use pepper spray to subdue him in his regular prison cell, and later turned to a special five-guard "extraction team"—wearing body armor and plastic face guards—to get him out of his cell near the execution chamber.

Throughout the process, members of the execution team struggle against their own discomfort and potential guilt. Guards often reacquaint themselves with details of the murder or murders committed by the prisoner. As one put it, "You try to find out all the dirty things that he done. So you say, 'Well, okay, it's okay. It's all right, all right to put him to death.' " They need to evoke those "dirty things" of the past in order to overcome their perception of the quite ordinary, sometimes even appealing, man they have come to know on death row. That is, they must kill not the human being they know but the murderer of the past.

Yet some officers are deeply distressed, like the member of the strapdown team at Angola prison who told Sister Helen Prejean that he couldn't square with his conscience "putting them to death like that," and then asked for a transfer. A former prison warden observed "the terrible pain of guards who would turn their face from you, not in shame, but because they didn't want you to see the emotions and the pain and the burden on them."

Afterward, according to Don Roper, the assistant superintendant at Missouri's Potosi facility, staffers feel "very relieved . . . very calm, cool, and collected." He told writer Stephen Trombley, "People have met the challenge, if you will, and have taken the stress in stride and moved right along. Very professionally." Once an execution is over, "people just basically go home," but he added that in his own case he and his wife "sit down, talk and discuss" before he goes to sleep. Moreover, it turns out that before returning to their homes, many of his staffers first go out drinking. Participants may indeed feel relieved that their demanding task has been carried out, but this does not mean that they get off scot-free, emotionally speaking. Alcohol can end up playing an important role in sustaining postexecution numbing.

The Executioner

> *The executioner's face is always well hidden.*
> —*Bob Dylan*

In former days, when hangings were common, there was no doubt about the identity of the on-site executioner. Each of the modern methods deliberately leaves it in doubt, for witnesses and participants alike. More than one member of an execution team commonly throws a switch or pushes a button or opens an injection line, not sure whether he or a colleague has administered the fatal blow.

Typically, in states using a lethal injection machine, one staff member mixes and loads the chemicals, another "arms" the machine, and at least two others actually push the buttons that send the chemicals into the inmate's veins. Steps are taken so that no one can be absolutely certain that he or she was *the* executioner. The control module, in a room adjacent to the execution chamber, has two separate sets of controls, marked station 1 and station 2. To arm them, one turns a key at the bottom. As the final step, two staff members press buttons that release the deadly medicine, but a built-in computer decides which of the buttons actually triggers the release, then *automatically releases from its memory* which button that was. One official in Missouri put it this way: "The machine decides which of the button pressers actually performs the execution." Another official remarked, "You have that external doubt whereby it probably gives someone a protective mechanism to say, 'I don't know that I did it.' " With the record erased, one can never know.

While considerable technological distancing could be achieved with gas chambers, with lethal injections the entire process can be computerized and robotized. The machine not only provides much of the numbing but can be seen as the actual executioner. Or, perhaps more accurately, human executioner and machine become indistinguishable in carrying out the killing.

One wonders what Camus would think of this. When he portrayed executioners harshly in "Reflections on the Guillotine," there was no such machine, and responsibility was neither technologically nor collectively dissolved. He insisted that the only sure effect of an execution was "to depreciate or to destroy all humanity and reason in those who take part in it directly," adding that "these are exceptional creatures who find a vocation in such dishonor." At least the second part of the observation would seem to be no longer true. Very ordinary people can be socialized into teams of amenable executioners, especially when they are psychologically protected by the distancing technology—the overall robotizing— of the lethal injection.

Whether or not they use lethal injection, most states shield the identity of those who push the buttons or pull the levers. In Florida, the man who activated the electric chair (until recently) was already wearing a hood over his head at 5 A.M., when a state car picked him up. The hood stayed on until he was dropped off at his home after performing the act and getting paid. A reporter once asked to interview the mysterious hooded figure, who seems to have emerged from a preceding century, but an official of the Department of Corrections replied, "You won't be seeing him. Not on *this* side of life." The hooded figure could be viewed as death personified, the grim reaper, in some form of morality play. But the morality of the morality play is attenuated and unclear.

After making the switch to lethal injections early in 2000, officials in Florida hastened to assure the public that they would still rely on a private citizen, not a prison employee, to act as chief executioner, pay him also in cash—and do away with the hood. "We've never had any problems whatsoever with the executioner," explains a spokesman for the Department of Corrections. "We've never had anyone say they couldn't do it at the last minute. They do their job and they get out." Florida is still working with a list of twenty volunteers who answered an ad for the job in 1979.

The hangman in Washington is visible only as a silhouette behind a screen. In other states, the personnel working the lethal injection controls are hidden from witnesses. The man who injects the chemicals in Texas stands behind a one-way mirror and witnesses peer in to "see their own reflections, which has some poetic justice," a writer for *Esquire* reported.

Recently, officials in Tennessee preparing for the state's first execution since 1960 identified a problem: They planned to pay $700 but didn't want to identify the executioner by writing his name on the check. "How do you pay this person who doesn't want to be identified?" the state comptroller said, indicating that he wanted to avoid cash payments. A state legislator explained. "We don't want hardworking Tennesseans to be scrutinized and criticized and embarrassed."

One member of a firing squad is always given a blank. This is "for the conscience of the executioners, so no one knows for sure who fired the live round," a spokesman for the corrections department in Utah has explained. Still, a former Utah warden who took part in planning the execution of Gary Gilmore has described the particular challenges of death by gunfire, noting the need to "give the firing squad members a chance to get over any emotional barrier to pulling the trigger." Even so, the human element sometimes cannot be denied. Half a century ago a condemned prisoner named Elisio Mares was so well-liked that when the firing squad was ordered to shoot, all five aimed away from the target, his heart, hitting the other side of his chest and causing him to bleed slowly to death. Efficiency in killing diminishes pain, while human emotions that interfere with efficiency can increase the prisoner's suffering.

Bad Dreams

Killing does take its toll. Donald Hocutt has been described as "the last of the old-style southern executioners." It was Hocutt who supervised the botched execution of Jimmy Lee Gray, when the prisoner banged his head on a pipe in the gas chamber for several minutes. Unlike many states, Mississippi did little to shield Hocutt's identity, which was all right with him, at least at the time.

His retirement in 1995, however, was caused not just by various physical ailments but also by psychological suffering diagnosed as depression. Hocutt now speaks painfully of executions, comparing them to "being in a car wreck that's going on forever." He speaks dismissively of those who claim they'd love to "throw the switch." They might be able to do it once, he claims, but you'd "have to be a pretty sick individual to do it twice." Nevertheless, he himself is proud of his work and would even be willing to "pull the switch" again if the money was right—say, ten times his original fee of $500.

But Hocutt is troubled by his dreams. He's had a series of nightmares in which he repeatedly kills a condemned prisoner in the gas chamber, while two others await their turn. At other times he'll be watching TV and will suddenly drift into a recurring dream, where he goes through his house opening doors and closets, looking for a man, Leo Edwards, whom he killed in 1989. Sometimes these dreams are followed by daydreams in which "I can't believe what I'm seeing . . . prisoners singing . . . in the fields. Shovels over their backs. Lined up in the field in rows, y'know, military rows, like we line 'em up, and me having to shoot 'em all, and they just keep on singing."

Hocutt seems to be haunted by guilt, as personified by the recurring dream of a specific prisoner he killed; and by the futility and meaninglessness of the executions, as reflected by the persistent singing of the rows of prisoners he is supposed to shoot. The latter scene is also reminiscent of slaves on a plantation seemingly at the mercy of a murderous master who, nonetheless, is awed by their mythic, impervious, even immortal demeanor.

The Field of Battle

Men will kill under compulsion—men will do almost anything if they know it is expected of them and they are under strong social pressure to comply—but the vast majority of men are not born killers.

—*Gwynne Dyer,* War

Those engaged in executions often draw analogies with a battlefield, but killing a strapped-down man, even a convicted murderer, in a prison chamber is, of course, quite different from shooting at an enemy in war. In both cases, though, one must be willing to kill another human being, or at least collaborate in that killing.

A former lieutenant colonel in the army, Dave Grossman, who has taught psychology at West Point, recently wrote an important book, *On Killing: The Psychological Cost of Learning to Kill in War and Society.* Grossman's book grew out of his shock at uncovering a little-known statistic: studies show that roughly four out of five soldiers in World War II *failed to fire their weapons directly at the enemy* on the battlefield. This made Grossman reflect on "the simple and demonstrable fact that there is within most men an intense resistance to killing their fellow man."

But Grossman went on to observe that the number of battlefield "aimers"—those who shot at the enemy—had jumped to 95 percent in Vietnam. This was not because men had become more bloodthirsty: only 2 percent of all soldiers were identified as "eager" coldblooded killers. Rather, it was because of the vastly improved psychological manipulation in training methods. His book, then, became a meditation on how Americans overcome strong resistance to killing, with several explicit references to executions.

Numerous researchers have found that soldiers will quite readily target the enemy (or even noncombatants) from a distance but are far more reluctant up close. As Grossman explains:

> When one looks an opponent in the eye, and knows that he is young or old, scared or angry, it is not possible to deny that the individual about to be killed is much like oneself. . . . At this range the interpersonal nature of the killing has shifted. Instead of shooting at a uniform and killing a generalized enemy, now the killer must shoot at a person and kill a specific individual. Most simply cannot or will not do it.

Not only are those taking part in prison executions in close proximity to the condemned man at the time of death, but they may have come to know him quite well over a number of years; and unlike soldiers, they are not imperiled by the man they are about to kill. A warden who supervised executions in Washington and North Carolina says that corrections officers told him the main difference between killing in the military and in the prison is that "this is not like defending yourself. This offender you've known, you've helped solve their problems, you've brought their food to them for ten years. And then you reach a point where their life is going to end and you may be a participant."

The improved psychological training methods of recent decades for making soldiers into killers are: desensitization (including the chant, "kill, kill, kill"), conditioning (the soldier learns to shoot reflexively and instantly), and cultivation of denial (instilling a feeling that the enemy is a mere target, not a human being). Again, we can consider the process as a form of doubling, the formation of what is effectively a second self, a "killing self," which contrasts strongly with prior relatively nonviolent civilian self.

Grossman points out that few soldiers have ever thrust a bayonet into an opponent's chest or abdomen. Bayonets are mainly used when the enemy is fleeing and can be stabbed in the back. That is because close proximity can be negated "when the face cannot be seen." This "enabling process" explains why individuals being executed by hanging, shooting, electrocution, or gas are always blindfolded or hooded. "The eyes are the window of the soul," he notes, "and if one does not have to look into the eyes when killing, it is much easier to deny the humanity of the victim."

The various enabling mechanisms Grossman describes apply to those who carry out executions: the desensitizing and conditioning effects of the repeated rehearsals; various forms of emotional and technological distancing; a high level of anonymity and the defusing of responsibility; and moral distancing from the prisoner, who is seen as in some way as nonhuman.

These enabling mechanisms help explain why there is no shortage of volunteers for executions, even in the case of lethal injections, where the prisoner is never hooded or blindfolded. Indeed, there have been only rare occasions, reports Grossman, when "those who are commanded to execute human beings have the remarkable moral fiber necessary to stare directly into the face of the obedience-demanding authority and refuse to kill." A soldier at My Lai (interviewed by one of us) not only refused to kill but pointed his gun at the ground to make clear to everyone that he was not participating in his group's mass execution of Vietnamese. He was highly exceptional, and afterward he seemed to suffer emotionally at least as much as the men who had done the killing. He was taking a great chance in pointing his gun at the ground because he was violating the immediate ethos of the group and in that sense being disloyal to his "team."

To do something like that would be even more difficult for a member of a tightly organized, technologically efficient death row execution team—but it is not impossible that a day will come when this happens. As Grossman explains, "In combat, each man *is* really a member of a huge firing squad." Correspondingly, each member of an execution team is engaged in a form of combat, however one-sided, and must overcome his resistance to killing.

Doctors: "A Host of Troublesome Questions"

It should not be forgotten that the medical profession resolved upon the guillotine out of humanitarian considerations. Here, in embryo, lies the logic of today's "art of death": the electric chair, the fatal injection.

—*Daniel Arasse,*
The Guillotine and the Terror

Doctors have been deeply involved in executions for centuries, and have had a hand in helping design many of the methods. Most notoriously, of course, there was the guillotine: designed by one doctor and fatefully promoted by another (who lent it his name). As Daniel Arasse observed in his study, the rationale for the guillotine "constituted a spectacular perversion of medical sciences," for, after all, "it was the medical profession that proposed, invented and, in the last analysis, exonerated a machine for decapitating people."

The claimed reasons, of course, were humanitarian, seeking to reduce the pain for the prisoner to what Foucault has called "zero-degree torture." But the guillotine was, in addition—or above all—intended to be humane toward the executioner, who would be freed from lengthy and intimate contact with the victim. An impersonal machine would do the dirty work; all the executioner had to do was set in motion one mechanical stroke "with clocklike precision," as Foucault observed. Still, Dr. Guillotin came to regret, if not the invention of the machine, at least his unshakable alliance with it. The doctor also must have come to doubt the machine's humanity, as he provided his friends with poison tablets, giving them a chance to take their own lives if they were ever sentenced to lose their heads to his machine. No wonder that a eulogist at Dr. Guillotin's funeral could declare: "How true it is that it is difficult to benefit mankind without some unpleasantness resulting for oneself."

As we have seen, medical personnel were also crucially involved in the invention of the electric chair. It was a dentist named Alfred P. Southwick who alerted officials to the fast and apparently painless death of a Buffalo man who touched an electric generator in 1881, and it was doctors who subsequently practiced electrocution techniques on animals and helped adapt the first electric chair.

Dr. Southwick, who became known as the "father of electrocution," attended the first execution in the electric chair, which attracted tremendous interest from the medical community; of twenty witnesses, fourteen were doctors. The actual executioners were electricians, but the men directing the event were two physicians whose specialty was mental illness. Before proceeding, the warden asked the doctors how long to turn on the juice (they guessed wrong and poor William Kemmler needed a second, lengthy jolt). Still, Dr. Southwick pronounced himself satisfied with the method, since the law had been "successfully carried out," and called it "the grandest success of the age." But medical ambivalence toward the killing machine was expressed in the response of one of the two presiding physicians, who said he felt disgusted and called the invention of the electric chair "in no way a step in civilization."

Then the gas chamber was invented by D. A. Turner, a major in the U.S. Army Medical Corps, largely inspired by the experience of gas warfare during World War I. Finally, many consider the "father of lethal injection" to be Dr. Stanley Deutsch. In 1977, Dr. Deutsch, chairman of the anesthesiology department at Oklahoma University's medical school, responded to a request from a legislator for an alternative to repairing the state's balky electric chair.

In addition, doctors have routinely participated in executions in

America by pronouncing the prisoner dead and setting the time of death. This meant that in the many cases where an initial electric shock, puff of gas, or snap of the noose did not result in death, the doctor had to call for another, fatal, attempt. Even in ordinary cases where the execution goes smoothly, this function connects the doctor with the execution team.

Consider the experience of a prominent American professor of psychiatry who traced his opposition to capital punishment to his seemingly benign role in a hanging in Iowa in 1952. On that day, in the course of a single hour, he learned, among other things, that "the heart stops reluctantly. As I listened (for an interminable thirteen minutes) to the dying heart of Edward J. Beckwith, there was time for me to ask myself a host of troublesome questions about what we had done that morning." Notice his use of the pronoun "we" to convey his own involvement in the killing.

Although there has always been some degree of conflict and soul-searching about physicians participating in executions, it has only been in recent years, with the rather sudden adoption of lethal injections, that the controversy has really flared. For that new method inevitably comes to involve either doctors themselves or medical surrogates, directly or tangentially.

These medical connections were very much at issue with the first lethal injection, of Charles Brooks in Texas in 1982. Officials claimed that no doctor was directly involved in the killing, but critics insisted that physicians had ordered the deadly drugs, trained the executioners and technicians who inserted the needle, and examined the prisoner's veins to determine how and where to insert it. William J. Curran, the Harvard law professor and dean of American legal medicine, urged the Texas Medical Association to revoke the medical license of any doctor directly or indirectly involved. "Not only is this unethical, it is illegal," he said. "There is no medical license that authorizes a physician to use medicines to kill."

Three physicians later wrote an article in a Virginia medical magazine calling lethal injection "a perversion of medicine"; they warned against "wrapping punishment in a therapeutic cloak" and using drugs tested and approved for humanitarian reasons in a killing process—a kind of "unauthorized experimentation on human beings." A medical ethicist at Georgetown University observed, "By using medical knowledge and personnel to kill people, we do more than undermine the emerging standards and procedures for good, ethical decision-making about the sick and dying. We also set off toward a terrifying land where the white gowns of physicians are covered by the black hoods of executioners."

He is referring to an alliance between the death penalty and the dark side of medicine—an alliance the Nazis made. For example, the Nazis had a slogan, "The syringe belongs in the hand of the physician," when the syringe in question was actually a gas cock to release the carbon monoxide that killed victims of "euthanasia." The idea of putting the condemned "to sleep" recalls the Nazi doctor who told one of us that killing children in the "euthanasia" project was easier than killing adults because they were simply given increasing doses of barbiturates so that "there was no killing, strictly speaking . . . People felt this is not murder, it is a putting-to-sleep."

Whether or not doctors are directly involved in the killing, they have something to do with any lethal injection. It is, after all, a medical procedure, like many others, except for its purpose of killing. So when William Curran makes the simple but telling point that any doctor involved *in any way* is not only being unethical but breaking the law (because a physician is never licensed to kill), he is saying something crucial to the moral function of physicians in a democracy. In totalitarian states a claimed higher purpose can supersede rules of medical ethics. If an individual physician follows official decrees, it does not matter if he appears to act unethically. Some German physicians made this clear by telling one of us that the oath of loyalty to Adolph Hitler superseded the Hippocratic oath. In a democracy it does matter, even if a machine takes over most of the function of a doctor.

*   *   *

At Missouri's Potosi Correctional Center the execution chamber is located in the heart of its hospital block. Stephen Trombley described the room as little different from any other in that wing, holding a plain gurney with an IV drip stand and a gray hospital blanket, which had been used in executions, folded lengthwise. "I looked at the coarse fabric [of the blanket] and noticed that it was stained," Trombley reported. "I looked away."

In the moments before their death, the inmates lie flat on the gurney, one IV drip in their arm, covered from toes to chin with a white sheet. They appear almost indistinguishable from any patient "prepped" for surgery. A Missouri prison official made another analogy, comparing a generally docile and tranquilized inmate to a "terminally ill person" who has "accepted his fate." All this terminology reflects the malignant medicalization of the whole process.

Of course, taking part in the actual killing is a breach of the Hippocratic oath, which counsels doctors, "Above all, do no harm." The American Medical Association's ethics policy declares that a physician "as a member of a profession dedicated to preserving life when there is hope of doing so, should not be a participant in a legally authorized execution." Indeed, in 1991, when the state of Illinois passed a law requiring the active involvement of two physicians in every lethal injection—the state promised to conceal their identity and pay them in cash—national doctors' groups fought it. A year later the law was changed so that the physicians only had to pronounce death.

Most medical societies seem to tolerate that limited but still significant role. When Kentucky recently changed its execution method from the electric chair to lethal injection, the state's medical association declared that it was unethical for a physician to participate "except to certify cause of death." In many states, doctors officially do little more than stand in a room adjacent to the execution chamber, studying a heart monitor for approximately four minutes, the time it normally takes for the line to go flat. But by doing just this, by examining a screen or the actual prisoner to determine whether he is dead, the doctor either authorizes or confirms this very effective killing measure.

When an execution is botched, the doctor can find himself at the center of a grotesque scene, as described by Warden White (recalling the killing of Jimmy Gray Evans): "I knew he was dead on the first surge but the doctors hadn't officially pronounced him dead. The doctors were too excited. Their skills are in saving lives, and here they were assisting in the taking of a life."

In some states, doctors have been quietly contracted to take a direct part in executions, in most cases by helping to insert an IV line while prison staffers connect the lines leading to the lethal chemicals. When it is hard to locate a vein (usually because of prolonged drug use), a doctor may take part in the "cut down"—digging out a fresh vein. In most cases, however, a nurse, perhaps specializing in anesthesiology, is called upon.

Fit to Die?

Doctors also participate in the execution protocol by examining death row inmates to help restore their health after a suicide attempt, or to guarantee that they are healthy enough to take their last walk. A physician once referred to this as the irony of working "long and hard to keep a man alive for the hangman"—thereby preventing him from "cheating" society of its revenge. (Or as Camus put it: "The animal that is going to be killed must be in the best condition.") This parallels an assigned role of doctors in many totalitarian states—examining a political prisoner to determine if he is well enough to be tortured.

Perhaps the most sensational and disturbing example of this syndrome occurred in early December 1999. David Long, on the eve of his execution in Texas for killing three women, was found in his cell unconscious from an overdose of anti-psychotic drugs. He was rushed to a hospital in Galveston and placed on life support. Would the state of Texas remove an inmate from intensive care so that he could be executed more or less on schedule? The answer was yes.

To make sure that Long arrived at the death chamber in Huntsville still breathing, the state chartered a plane and staffed it with medical personnel to monitor his condition during the twenty-five-minute flight.

A state spokesman explained that the Department of Criminal Justice had determined that transporting the prisoner from Galveston to Huntsville was "not life-threatening." Quite the contrary—David Long was executed the following day. The *Washington Post*, while observing that the episode appeared "comical-sounding" on the surface, chose the occasion to denounce the "veneer of civilization we have placed over an act that is inherently barbaric."

Psychiatrists frequently play a role in certifying that a prisoner is mentally competent to be executed, a requirement ordered by the U.S. Supreme Court in 1986. In Texas, Dr. James Grigson, who flaunted a gold cigarette holder and made his rounds in a white Cadillac, became known as Dr. Death because he had testified that 124 convicted killers were mentally balanced, and juries had then sentenced 115 of them to death. Psychiatrists are also asked to visit death row and not merely certify competence but *restore* it, through prescribing medication—so the prisoner can be executed sane. The AMA prohibits this policy, calling it "ethically unacceptable," and doctors often refuse to medicate prisoners for the purpose of paving the way for their demise.

Doctors, indeed, fit awkwardly into the execution regimen. Fred Leuchter once referred to doctors as a real "problem" because "they're afraid of the issue. They don't really want to get involved. They freeze up. Doctors save lives. Even when they have to participate [in executions], even when they have to supervise, they're not operating at full capacity, because they have to think backward. They have to think about destroying a life rather than saving it. It's like the difference between an engineer and a repairman." Leuchter felt bitter about doctors' standing by while wardens or other non-medical personnel mixed chemicals in the wrong amounts or amateurs botched injections.

Christopher Hitchens, who attended a lethal injection in Missouri and vowed never to do it again, now refers to death by needle as "medical butchery." Stephen Trombley interviewed the doctor Missouri employed in this process, who claimed he did nothing more than examine the inmate before the execution, administer one or more sedative shots to calm him, pronounce him dead, and sign the death certificate. Still, the doctor was "worried" about the AMA's attacks on physicians taking part in *any* way. "I don't want any flak from them," he told Trombley. "I got enough trouble of my own."

But the issue isn't merely how directly or indirectly physicians participate in lethal injections, but rather that the overall medical profession lends its methods and (in one way or another) personnel to a killing process. According to Dr. Jerome D. Gorman, it is "a hideous perversion and subversion of anesthesiology," so that "the whole process leading to that final moment feels less aversive to those who are required to participate and is therefore more bearable." But that is also "precisely why physicians should oppose it," he says. To maintain the distinction between healing and killing "physicians, even physicians who support the death penalty, are ethically constrained not to play an active role in capital punishment. Lethal injection, because it blurs these distinctions, is as much a perversion of medicine as is using doctors to perform executions." He continues:

> The integrity of society is much better protected with traditional means of execution, such as the electric chair, the gas chamber, or the firing squad. They leave no doubt that the act is one of punishment, not of healing, and that the subject is a convict, not a patient.

The story of Rickey Ray Rector, the mentally impaired death row inmate in Arkansas who became famous when Governor Bill Clinton flew home from the campaign trail in 1992 to oversee his execution, illustrates the essential problem. Taken from his cell for his death walk, the prisoner asked guards to save the piece of pecan pie left on his tray for when he returned. A few minutes later, on the hospital gurney in the death chamber, he helped the executioners find a vein for the IV because, as Christopher Hitchens observed, "he thought they were doctors come at last to cure him." But Rector was only responding to the medical aura experienced by everyone involved in the injection method. That is, he was responding to the "as-if" medical situation that predominates.

Executioners Who Say No

What the hell was I doing here? How had my career come to this?
—*Donald Cabana, former warden*

On January 1, 1924, Captain R. F. Coleman, warden of Huntsville prison in Texas, submitted a letter of resignation. The state had decided to abandon its tradition of scattered legalized hangings and execute all the condemned men in the Huntsville prison's new electric chair—and the first electrocution was scheduled in two weeks. "A warden can't be a warden and a killer, too," Coleman told reporters. "The penitentiary is a place to reform a man, not to kill him." As a warden, Coleman considered himself to be a caretaker, something on the order of a father, so that participating in an execution would be the ultimate form of parental abuse.

Unlike Coleman, some of the wardens who spoke out against capital punishment continued to oversee executions. The two most famous examples were Lewis E. Lawes, warden at Sing Sing; and Clinton Duffy, warden at San Quentin. Both joined anti–death penalty leagues and shared platforms with Clarence Darrow and other opponents of executions.

During his years at Sing Sing, from 1920 to 1941, Lawes became the most famous warden in America, writing several books, hosting a weekly radio program, and providing story ideas to Hollywood. Several of these were made into films starring the likes of James Cagney, Spencer Tracy, and Humphrey Bogart, including *20,000*

Years in Sing Sing. Despite his criticism of the death penalty, Lawes directed the execution of more than 200 men and women in the electric chair. He explained that while it was his legal duty "to be present physically in the death chamber," he always turned away when the juice was turned on; this allowed him to claim that he had "never seen an execution."

Turning away was in itself a powerful indictment of the execution process. By never "seeing" an execution, Lawes could imagine, in at least part of his mind, that he had given no such order, that no execution was taking place.

Lawes said that he opposed capital punishment not on moral grounds but because it served no purpose. He rejected the widely accepted notion of deterrence and complained bitterly about the selective and arbitrary application of the death penalty, as well as "the halo with which it surrounds every convicted murderer." But planning and enforcing the death penalty weighed considerably on his conscience. "When you have steeled yourself, as I have; when you try, as I try, to let routine rule while doing everything within the law to make the end as merciful as possible, it's heartbreaking to run against the raw of human suffering." Yet Lawes continued to take part in the death process, doing his duty as warden, as he explained, and apparently never seriously considered quitting.

It is quite possible that Lawes saw himself as "working from within" to change the system, but such involvement in killing is reminiscent of Eduard Wirths, the chief Nazi doctor at Auschwitz, who was horrified by everything he witnessed upon arriving at the camp and sought to make things better for the inmates, yet ended up rendering more smooth and efficient the overall Auschwitz arrangements for medicalized killing (which, of course, far exceeded anything in an American prison). Indeed, the attempt to work from within becomes darkly absurd when the institution in question includes a project of systematic killing. But a sense of one's humane professionalism can prevail on an everyday basis—as it did for Lawes and Duffy and Wirths as well—and can enable one to block out psychologically the connection between professionalism and killing.

There is no modern-day equivalent of Lewis Lawes. For one reason, there are no famous wardens today; and almost no wardens have taken a public stand against capital punishment. Some correctional officials, however, have spoken out in one way or another against the death penalty in recent years.

William Leeke, former head of corrections for the state of South Carolina, came to understand this near the end of his long career. He had wanted to retire without having to electrocute anyone, and he almost made it. But in the mid-1980's he finally had to oversee two executions. For the first one he recruited a clinical psychologist to attend, in case any of the guards or officials broke down—but it was the psychologist himself who nearly passed out.

"After it's all over, you feel like you want to go wallow in mud," Leeke said following his retirement. "Because although you didn't do it personally, and even though you don't want to be perceived as a total liberal or soft on crime, you feel like you sort of degraded yourself, and you feel so sorry for the people who had to actually carry out the execution. There is nothing in the law that says that you have to like killing somebody. . . . You can see the visible effects on the people that are doing it, especially the warden who has the responsibility in the death house, the trauma that comes." He used to favor lethal injection, but came to question it, finding it "so easy to put people to sleep. It becomes just too easy to make that decision to kill. My concern overall is that we can become so insensitive that we can just start killing and not think about it."

Another former warden was even more direct and outspoken. James W. L. Park, who began his career as a clinical psychologist, served the California Department of Corrections for over thirty years in a variety of tasks, including being assistant warden at San Quentin. Participating in the execution of a man in the gas chamber in 1967, Park realized how "task-oriented" he was, concerned not about taking a man's life but about the various duties he had to perform.

"It is just one of my feelings," he observes, "that it is bad for society to hire people to kill other people, because it becomes a task-oriented thing. I can believe, without really knowing, that most of the guards in the concentration camps were good family men. They simply had a *task* to do, they did it, and somehow it wasn't 'people'—it was 'units.' " Park mentions the gassing of mental defectives, Gypsies and Jews in Germany, noting that in America today "we have a lot of people in this society who are nuisances, who are inconvenient, and I would be afraid that a society that became too comfortable with killing people would extend that charter, so to speak, to dispose of other groups."

To combat this, Park always tried to use the word "kill" to describe what the state was doing, finding "execution" and "capital punishment" too sanitized—or something only other people do. (Similarly, the Nazis employed the euphemism "special treatment" for individual and mass murder.) Park believed that all citizens in California were doing the killing "and yet they don't take it personally, and I think that rather few of the people that agitate for the death penalty would be willing to actually do the killing." By rejecting all euphemisms for "kill" and "killing," he was trying to bring the truth in all its horror back into death penalty discourse. He was saying that one could be in favor of *capital punishment* or even *execution* but be profoundly reluctant to *kill*.

Still another former California warden, Lawrence Wilson, who supervised the gas chamber, reflected many years later on a sense of professional pride among his colleagues that caused them to be skeptical about or opposed to the death penalty. At annual meetings of the Wardens' Association of America, he claimed, only rarely does anyone speak out in favor of capital punishment. According to Wilson, most wardens feel that murderers, however evil, should be kept behind walls, contributing in some small measure to keeping the prison going. He was implying that there's something useful to be contributed, if only to prison life, by any man or woman allowed to live.

For Donald Cabana, a longtime supporter of the death penalty, what he calls "the moment of truth" arrived in 1987, when he had to execute Connie Ray Evans in the gas chamber at Parchman prison in Mississippi. Cabana was a Vietnam veteran who understood himself to be "hardened" to death and to "the sight of mangled bodies." But he had been shaken by several recent encounters with death. He had been "stunned" by the brutal suicide of a 20-year-old man who had slashed his wrists, leaving blood splattered throughout the cell. His assistant warden and closest friend had died painfully of a rapidly spreading cancer. And he himself had supervised the execution of a prisoner, which left him with overall "feelings of revulsion." Afterward he "felt dirty" and tried unsuccessfully to "scrub away such feelings in a shower," he recalled in his book, *Death at Midnight: The Confession of an Executioner.*

Connie Evans had insisted upon talking to Cabana about that initial execution, pressing on him the question of what he would have done if he had been shown clear evidence that the man was innocent (as he'd claimed). When Cabana tried to explain that such matters were outside his responsibility and he was only doing his job, Evans challenged him, saying, "*You* didn't convict him, the jury did. You didn't sentence him to die—the judge or the jury or some-damn-body else did. And when you kill him, it ain't really you that's doin' that, either. It's the state, the folks out there that's doin' it." Cabana could think of nothing to say; his psychological defenses had clearly been threatened.

With Connie Evans, Cabana faced "the difficult task of sending a young man whom I had grown to know and like to his death." He unsuccessfully requested the governor of his state, Bill Allain, to grant the prisoner a reprieve, explaining that Evans was not "the same man who came in here six years ago" and further insisting that "it was just a matter of luck, and lawyers" as to who got executed.

Now he found preparations for the gassing "ghoulish." The whole process seemed "insane" and had cast him into "a personal hell." But at the zero hour he called forth his professionalism and emphatically gave the order, "Do it!"—culminating in "a violent, repulsive death." Cabana worried what his wife and children would think of him, but most of all he wondered if God would forgive him. When he met his wife afterward, he said, "No more. I don't want to do this anymore."

Upon returning to work, he found a pall cast over everything, and he contemplated leaving corrections work. Soon he quit to take a college teaching job and began writing and speaking out against capital punishment, believing that his background and experience gives him special authority. Today, he condemns the "emotionalism" and "histrionics" that have led Americans to seek this "quick fix" to crime and violence when they should be fighting poverty, child abuse, and drugs.

Although Cabana, like any warden, had acquired a measure of selective professional numbing, he was sufficiently compassionate to open himself to painful death encounters. In relation to the two executions, he was both a perpetrator and a deeply troubled survivor. He could find meaning and a survivor mission by converting residual guilt into a sense of responsibility and knowledgeable opposition to all capital punishment.

Cabana believes that the executioner "dies with his prisoner"— whether it's "the general who gave Socrates the hemlock or that deputy warden in Nebraska who executed [the mass murderer] Charlie Starkweather." To die psychologically and morally is to be destroyed as a functional and ethical human being. "It didn't matter that Starkweather was one of the most hated men of the decade," Cabana observes, sadly. "They say the warden never got over it." It may be that no executioner ever really gets over it, and that Cabana is different mainly in realizing this, and acting on it.

5

PROSECUTORS AND GOVERNORS

Prosecutors

PROSECUTORS play a central, if little understood, role in the death penalty process. Their significance can hardly be overstated, for the machinery cannot grind forward at all without the original decision by a district attorney to seek a death sentence. Essentially, every other aspect of the process, in the years that follow, serves as a kind of check on, or endorsement of, that initial decision.

Some prosecutors claim they have never questioned capital punishment, and that they continue to have no qualms while aggressively seeking death sentences. Others, who originally opposed executions, have a kind of conversion experience once in office and selectively pursue capital cases, if with lingering ambivalence. A few refuse to press for capital convictions in any cases.

Whatever the opinion of local prosecutors, their decisions on choosing which (and how many) cases to prosecute as capital crimes take place in the political arena. In almost all jurisdictions and states, prosecutors are elected, not appointed. Sometimes they have made certain promises in running for office, or their office has recently lost a high-profile murder case and desperately needs a capital conviction to restore public confidence. Or a particular case has received sensational media attention because of the prominence, affluence, or tender age of the victim.

Not every crime, therefore, and certainly not every prosecutor, is created equal. Even within the same state each prosecutor operates in a different political context—and with a different demographic pool. In a high-crime county a district attorney is unlikely to seek a high percentage of capital cases, because of limited resources. The pressures are far different in a county that rarely witnesses a murder. There the decision the prosecutor makes in *each* case undergoes tremendous scrutiny, and a defendant is far more likely to face the ultimate penalty—if the county can afford it. Many of them can't.

All this contributes to the unfair, arbitrary, and capricious nature of capital punishment. Of the thousands of murders committed in America each year, only a few hundred end up as capital cases. Kill a convenience store clerk in one town and face the electric chair; commit the same crime five miles down the road across the county line and maybe get twenty years to life.

The Zealots: "A War on the Domestic Front"

Throughout their careers, as we will see, some prosecutors express moral reservations about their jobs or express doubts about the fairness or efficacy of the death penalty. Other prosecutors admit few misgivings, and indeed assert that they take pride in what they do, but even they may be suppressing inner doubts they must keep hidden.

Brandon Hornsby, an affable, handsome young attorney, was for several years a prosecutor in Georgia who specialized in setting murderers on the path to the electric chair. Hornsby, as assistant district attorney in Clayton County, asked reporters not to call him "Dr. Death," but he appeared to revel in the attention. Until he arrived in 1996, no prosecutor in the county had secured a death sentence in ten years; in the space of about three years, Hornsby had won four. He claimed that this made a statement to outsiders: if they come to Clayton they had better leave any violent tendencies behind. Unlike most prosecutors, he witnessed executions himself; before one of them he phoned a reporter and suggested he attend with him, adding, "It'll make a good road trip."

Hornsby worked hard to send killers to the chair, sometimes putting in 100-hour weeks, perhaps because he didn't see it as a job: it was a calling, a crusade, a mission. "Except for the Gulf War," he explained, "my generation has not had an opportunity to serve in a war. The way I see my service is very similar. It's a war on the domestic front." Hornsby thus cast himself as a dedicated warrior, but a "lifesaver," as he put it.

His aggressiveness angered some observers. A superior court judge in Clayton who has criticized Hornsby's courtroom tactics predicts that "one of these days Brandon is going to look back and ask himself, 'Why did I have all these people killed?'" But Hornsby's boss, Bob Keller, the Clayton district attorney, observed that he merely argued for the death penalty with the same flair and moral force normally displayed by defense attorneys. Why, Keller wondered, are defense attorneys praised for their passion while prosecutors who seek the death penalty are often described as "zealots"?

There is an answer to that: passion here is associated with compassion, with seeking to maintain human life, while zealotry becomes associated with killing or taking life. That distinction enables us to recognize, on at least some psychological level, that taking a life is an extreme act.

A mediocre student and self-described "party animal" in college, Hornsby found his calling when his father, a prominent local lawyer, died and a newspaper called him "an avenging archangel." Like his father, he believes he places a high value on human life (in punishing those who extinguish life). After witnessing his first execution from a front-row seat, he said he felt no guilt or remorse or compassion for the killer. "That," he said, "wasn't an emotion I got in touch with," suggesting an unusual degree of psychic numbing. Brandon Hornsby seems to be on a survivor mission—carrying out the work cut short by his father's death. By making it a crusade and calling it a "war," he invested it with an absolute dimension of heroic meaning.

Early in 1999, Hornsby left the prosecutor's office to go into private practice, without expressing any second thoughts about his work. Others found some problems with it. Two of his four death penalty victories have now been overturned (either the death sentence itself or the conviction) by the state Supreme Court. In both cases the judges found that Hornsby had made improper comments to the jury—in one case, arguing that the Bible instructed that the state "must" take the lives of those who kill others.

Another example of the power a committed prosecutor may exert can be seen most starkly in the career of John B. Holmes, Jr., a district attorney in Harris County, Texas. Since capital punishment was reinstituted in Texas in 1976 one county, Harris, has been responsible for one-third of the state's cases leading to executions (including that of Karla Faye Tucker). For nearly this entire time Holmes has served as the county prosecutor, with strong support from the voters.

Holmes has sent more men to their death than any other D.A. in America. A survey in 1999 found that Dallas County had thirty-seven inmates on death row, while Harris had exactly 100 more, even though its crime rate is lower.

Familiar throughout the state because of his handlebar mustache and blunt talk, Holmes directs his 200 prosecutors to seek the death penalty aggressively. Critics, even some who favor capital punishment, claim that Holmes pushes his office so hard for executions that it becomes "abusive"—especially since Harris County has no public defender agency, meaning that defense attorneys are hard to find and must work cheap. Holmes claims he is not "bloodthirsty"; he's "just a lawyer. I follow the law. . . . We're good at it because we never let up on the pressure."

Yet how tough is Holmes, really? He never attends an execution, though he claims that "there are some I would be tickled to death to do myself." And, like so many others caught up in the killing process, he is all too willing to pass along responsibility. "Everyone who got death in Harris County," he said, "has gotten it from a jury."

Brandon Hornsby and John B. Holmes, like most prosecutors, insist that they are not engaged in a popularity contest, and are not attempting to influence potential voters. Prosecutors are sensitive about such charges, which are aired frequently. When the district attorney in Monroe County, New York, seemed intent on seeking the death penalty against a man who appeared mentally retarded and was suffering from AIDS, *New York Times* columnist Bob Herbert commented that prosecutors in general "tend to salivate over the benefits, political and otherwise, of sending someone to the great beyond. . . . Death penalty cases excite them. . . . A successful capital prosecution can make a prosecutor feel powerful, popular and righteous all at the same time."

Herbert captures something of what we might call the omnipotent righteousness that some prosecutors (such as Hornsby and Holmes) can actually experience. But Herbert had painted with a broad brush, and the reaction was predictable. The Monroe County D.A. wrote an angry letter to the newspaper asserting that prosecutors in his office "are not looking for notches on a belt. We are seeking some semblance of justice in a court system overwhelmed with cases."

Still, whatever their beliefs and actions, the emotional toll on prosecutors, one suspects, can be high. An assistant district attorney in Texas, Joetta Keene, speaks of "crying at night because you're involved," and feels relief when prosecuting a truly monstrous killer, as this reaffirms her belief in this "necessary evil." Susan Bolyn, as assistant state attorney general, who represents Georgia in capital appeals, once said, "Since the first day I came here I've heard, 'All you are is a Nazi taking orders.' " An attorney who has defended several death row prisoners in the South tells us that even in that region he saw a lot of "deep moral ambivalence" among prosecutors and always privately took that into account in seeking plea bargains that saved inmates' lives.

Norman Mailer claims that even the attorney who prosecuted Gary Gilmore did not want him to be executed and always assumed that his death sentence would be commuted to life imprisonment.

"He was not unique among prosecutors," Mailer explains. "Capital punishment is to the rest of all law as surrealism is to realism. It destroys the logic of the profession." He continues:

> Until one gets to capital punishment, law is a game. A most interesting, valuable, and serious game. To the degree that a case is brilliantly argued for both sides, justice, if not done, is at least approached. . . . Capital punishment, however, says: The penalty no longer fits the crime. You are being moved from the court to the tomb. The prosecuting attorney is transmuted into an avenging angel.

The Uncertain Prosecutor: From Moral Skeptic to "Instrument of Retribution"

A familiar figure in popular fiction and Hollywood movies set on death row is the attorney (or warden or judge) who once favored capital punishment but comes to oppose the practice when exposed to a particular prisoner or immersed in a specific case. It even happens that way, at times, in real life. Sometimes, however, attorneys experience a kind of reverse conversion, when outrage at cruel murderers turns them around in the opposite direction, from skeptics to advocates of executions.

When Ron Sievert applied for the position of assistant district attorney in Grayson County, Texas, a member of the search committee asked if he favored the death penalty. It was an important question, for that county ranked third in the state in capital cases. He risked losing the job when he replied that the death penalty could be defended only if it served as a deterrent, and he didn't think that had been established. Sievert, who comes from what he calls a "Catholic, respect-for-life, blue-collar" background, always felt the state had to have "an awfully good reason to kill someone," and he came out of law school (under the tutelage of generally liberal professors) feeling even more strongly that capital punishment was "stupid, useless."

He got the assistant D.A. job anyway, and a year later, Sievert was handed his first murder case (though not a capital offense). For the first time in his career he had to study closely autopsy reports and photographs of murder victims. They revealed, coldly, the damage done and the death agonies of a human brutally slaughtered. Sievert had often felt compassion for defendants from poor backgrounds, but this time he felt deep anger rising within him, anger that would only deepen as he took on other murder cases over the following year. Sievert came to see the perpetrators as "animals"—or "domestic terrorists"—who seemed to feel no remorse or display any feelings about snuffing out a life. "In my own mind," he reflects, "it was now enough that I could deter this one defendant from criminal acts regardless of whether his death would deter others." At the same time, the old-fashioned concept of public retribution was beginning to make more sense.

The following year he plunged into his first capital case and, as he recalls, "I was suddenly engaged in devoting all of my energy to accomplishing a goal which a short time before I had publicly and seriously questioned." Before long, four men he prosecuted received the death sentence. This experience saddened him, he explains, because of the atrocities perpetrated on the victims "and by the fact that human beings exist who could do these things—and with the thought that they too may now need to be executed for the good of society."

At the same time, Sievert acted to limit the number of capital cases in his office. The public and the media often assailed the district attorney's office, demanding capital charges that Sievert felt could not be sustained at trial. Sievert tried to impose what he considered a "rational order to the process," targeting certain defendants for capital trials and others to be indicted on simple murder charges.

Being selective about seeking the death penalty was necessary, as

Sievert recognized that jurors in capital cases "hold us to the highest possible burden of proof before they feel justified in assessing the death penalty." Another factor was far more subjective. Did this crime "cry out" for the death penalty? Was Sievert certain in his heart that the defendant deserved to die for what he had done? "There was no set rule for that determination," he admits, "and it depends greatly on the individual beliefs of the prosecutor." For Sievert, the murder had to be premeditated and the perpetrator's history had to indicate that he was a truly dangerous and evil individual.

What Sievert calls the ultimate highlight of a prosecutor's career comes in convincing a jury "to make the supreme decision, the decision to take someone's life." Among what he describes as his typical lines of argument addressing the jury:

- The *atomic bomb* argument: "No one likes the death penalty, but it will have absolutely no deterrent value if the bad guys believe we are afraid to use it."
- The *stay focused* argument: "It is not up to you to forgive this defendant, only Mr. and Mrs. Jones, the people he killed, could do that."
- The *they* argument: "You hear about this type of crime and wonder why *they* don't do something about it. The police and prosecutors have done their jobs. Did you ever wonder who *they* are? The *they* who can do something about this crime right now is *you*."

More effective than anything, he feels, was the moral force he brought to the argument, fueled by anger. "I had come from being doubtful about the death penalty," he recalls, "to the point that as I personally approached the defendant in some of these cases, reciting what horrible acts he had done, . . . I was filled with such outrage that I sometimes felt that if I had a weapon I might have executed him right then and there." He felt like "the avenging voice of the community," representing "a just society." At the high point of a final argument "you felt this emanate from your very being as if you were somehow spiritually connected with the county's 600,000 people and you were energetically, persuasively, thunderously speaking their words. You were an instrument. I cannot overstate this feeling. It is a very powerful moment. The jury could not help but get the message."

When his first capital case concluded with a death sentence, Sievert went back to his office and, with colleagues and friends, got "very intoxicated." It was partly a celebration for achieving what they had set out to do, but he also felt "moved, awed, permanently affected." He tried to explain it to his wife that night: "We have just spent thirty days of our life working unbelievably hard to kill a man, don't you understand? Someday it's going to happen, because of what we did." She didn't understand, Sievert believes, "nor will anybody who has never prosecuted a capital case."

Sievert's role in sending violent criminals to death row brought general support from his friends and family, although a few relatives from back home in New York called with some questions after the mother of a killer he had convicted called him "Mad Dog Sievert" on national television. By his fourth case, Sievert felt much less troubled by the trials and the penalties. This worried him, indicating that it was time to move on. He applied for the position of assistant U.S. attorney, and he now serves as chief of the Austin Division. Sievert handles corruption and drug cases instead of murder cases, although he was appointed special state prosecutor in one successful death penalty case.

One day at his new job he received a call from someone in the D.A.'s office informing him that one killer he had prosecuted long ago, named Elliot Johnson, was scheduled for a lethal injection the following evening. Sievert was stunned. He had not thought about the case, or about Johnson's possible execution, for years. He shut his door and asked his secretary to hold all his calls as he pondered what he had done. At first, Sievert felt he did not want to see Johnson die, but then he forced himself to "relive" the evidence. He recalled Johnson's long record of assaults and robberies, the savagery of his attacks on a jeweler and his assistant, and the families they had left behind. Sievert felt sorrow for killer and killed alike, but decided that he had no objection to the execution.

Today, Sievert continues to harbor ambivalence about capital punishment. He still feels it should be justified primarily on grounds of deterrence, and that this is *still* unproven. The farther removed he becomes from death penalty cases, the more he begins to look at the question "academically" and reconsider his feelings. But every time he examines a murder file, he knows that he would "go for it" again, and feels that even a small deterrent effect makes it worthwhile. For Sievert the solution is not to do away with the death penalty but to sharpen its deterrent edge by tightening the appeals process and making sure that when someone commits a capital offense "within a few years he will be executed for his act."

Adapting to Death: The Execution Self

No doubt Ron Sievert felt genuinely appalled, even sickened, by his exposure to the violent acts of killers he was called on to prosecute. But there is another way of looking at his overall feelings about capital punishment. In seeking the job of assistant D.A. in Grayson County, he was gravitating toward a death penalty environment. It is possible that he was unconsciously drawn to the death penalty, and that this tendency had been long suppressed because of a combination of Catholic influences and his response to liberal professors.

To be sure, people can be greatly influenced by what they discover in their professional work, especially in the case of a prosecutor, but it is also true that we tend to seek out environments in which our deepest inclinations can find expression, even when we are largely ignorant of them. Sievert's "conversion" enabled him to sweep aside troubling doubts about the death penalty, at least for a while, and to experience transcendent feelings of righteousness.

There is another related point about his feelings as an assistant district attorney: people tend to become what they do. When you are a prosecuting attorney in a death penalty environment you are likely to become execution-oriented. It has to do with overcoming the "cognitive dissonance" between your own inclinations against the death penalty and the professional expectation of prosecuting capital cases. You seek a sense of inner integrity, which requires that you come to believe in what you're doing.

In cases like Sievert's there may be a certain amount of doubling, that division between an "execution self" and a prior self opposing, or at least uncomfortable with, participation in killing.

While Sievert was not himself related to any murder victims, in becoming a prosecutor he took on what can be called a survivor mission of retributive justice. To carry out such a mission, one immerses oneself in the grotesque deaths encountered by victims and family members and retains that imagery as a basis for moral and professional action. But paradoxically, maintaining that sense of mission requires more and more death penalty cases, and ever-increasing executions. Each new case can supply the kind of imagery—an image of ultimate horror—that further propels the survivor mission. Should such cases diminish or disappear entirely, the earlier self, the self opposed to the death penalty, can reemerge and make its claim, as may be happening with Sievert now.

Sievert's adaptation to capital punishment was helped by his sense of exerting restraint in choosing death penalty cases. By acting to limit these cases, he resisted more aggressive and "bloodthirsty" forces in the system that he is part of. Sievert could see himself as "moderate" and "reasonable," as could others. All this has to with the psychology of "working from within," and the contribution to killing that one may make in the name of moderation.

By his fourth death penalty case, Sievert felt less affected by the notion of state killing, suggesting the effectiveness of his professional numbing (which itself worried him and influenced his job change). But later the shock he experienced when told that someone he had prosecuted was actually to be executed suggests that the numbing was fragile and that he was susceptible to feelings of remorse and responsibility. He had to call forth the grotesque image of the original murder to get through the night.

Sievert knows one district attorney in Texas who reluctantly pursued a death penalty case, then bowed out of it and asked a subordinate to argue it in court. He was a veteran D.A., and Sievert believes that as prosecutors—and potential jurors—get older they often become "more forgiving." Why that is true is not clear. It suggests a kind of fatigue over maintaining the motivation for execution, and also, possibly, a "retirement syndrome"—upon retirement or anticipation of it one allows suppressed doubts to surface and take hold. This is especially true when the project one has been involved with concerns killing.

Reluctant Prosecutors: Living with Deadly Contradictions

There's a third type of prosecutor: one who publicly, or privately, opposes the death penalty but, having sworn to uphold the law and the wishes of the people, nevertheless continues to work on capital cases.

One of them, though it's not widely known, is Attorney General Janet Reno, who has authorized seeking executions in more than 125 federal cases around the country (while declining to seek death after reviewing more than 300 others). Many U.S. attorneys who work under her feel the same way. Karen Rochin, for example, says it is morally wrong to take a life, yet leaves her personal beliefs outside the courtroom when she seeks death sentences in federal cases in Florida. Vermont's top federal prosecutor, Charles Tetzlaff, shares that sentiment, explaining that he took an oath to enforce and carry out the law "and I'm prepared to do that."

The possibility of executing an innocent man or woman "frightens me," Attorney General Reno has said in demanding that her prosecutors "do everything we can to prevent it from happening." This led to criticism from some prosecutors, who believe that qualms about capital punishment inevitably affect judgment and cripple the vigorous pursuit of executions. John Holmes, the D.A. in Houston who has won so many capital trials, denounces prosecutors who oppose the death penalty yet maintain that this doesn't affect their actions. "If you're president of the United States," he asserts, "you shouldn't put anybody in the position of having to enforce the death penalty who doesn't believe in it."

Ron Sievert feels much the same way. "You take an oath as a prosecutor to bring out the truth and convict," he observes. "If you don't believe in your heart in executions you shouldn't be up there before a jury trying to convince *them* to do it."

This conflict between personal values and professional duties has come to a head in New York, even before the state has witnessed its first modern execution. As it happens, three popular, high-profile district attorneys in New York City—Robert Morgenthau in Manhattan, Robert Johnson in the Bronx, and Charles Hynes in Brooklyn—passionately oppose the death penalty. Each claims that he remains willing to uphold the law and seek executions, but (as we complete this book) only one of them, Hynes, has done so.

"As D.A. I've had the responsibility to apply the law," Charles Hynes told political audiences in 1998. "As a leader and as someone running for governor, my responsibility is to tell you the law is a sham." The law, of course, is the 1995 statute that reintroduced the death penalty to New York. Hynes, the longtime Brooklyn district attorney and before that a well-known lawyer, was the only candidate for governor in 1998, in either party, who took a public stand against capital punishment. He has opposed it for decades because it is morally "questionable," because it does not serve as a deterrent, and because it gives killers an easy way out compared with life without parole. "You're playing God," he says. He promised that as governor he would try to repeal what he considers an obscene law, and if he failed, he might commute all death sentences.

Yet it was Hynes who brought the first case resulting in a death sentence under the new law, and it was Hynes who during the first two years under that law sought executions in five cases, far more than any other prosecutor in the state. He called these decisions among the most difficult he has ever made, but "I will be in a better position to continue my opposition to the death penalty by prosecuting a death penalty case," he explained. A local magazine called him a "reluctant hangman," noting that his position was "neither consistent nor logical."

Conflicts between duty and inner conviction in this case become especially wrenching because the end result may be a killing. Prosecutors who want to sustain their careers can be reduced to intellectual incoherence, as in the case of Hynes. By pressing to have someone killed, one purportedly can better *oppose* the process. There is something wrong with an arrangement that brings compassionate and intelligent public officials to this deadly contradiction.

Still, it earned Hynes the admiration of some advocates of the death penalty who called him the one prosecutor willing to make the threat of execution real—and criticism from opponents of the death penalty who believed he was just trying to jump-start his political career. Still others believe he seeks the death penalty to throw this issue in the face of the public, making them confront the execution machinery in the state before it actually lurches into operation. Perhaps there's an element of truth in each of these views.

In any case, Governor Pataki, who promoted and signed the death penalty law, applauded Hynes for being able to "put aside his personal opposition and . . . doing what is right for the people and required by law." The governor had quite a different reaction, however, when Robert Johnson, the Bronx district attorney, stuck to *his* principles.

Refusing to Seek Death

Governor Pataki had signed the death penalty statute into law in 1995, using a gold fountain pen that once belonged to a police officer slain in the Bronx. The same day, Bronx District Attorney Robert Johnson suggested that he would continue to settle for life without parole for those convicted of first-degree murder. The death penalty, he explained, was extremely costly to implement, did not serve as a deterrent, and might lead to executing an innocent man, and in any case juries were reluctant to vote for it. The 48-year-old D.A., the first African-American to hold that post anywhere in New York state, had started his career as a Legal Aid attorney, and this helped shape his stance on the death penalty, as did his religious beliefs. He remains "haunted," he says, by a case early in his career when he successfully prosecuted a man for murder—a man whose brother subsequently confessed to the crime.

Johnson's announcement didn't cause much of a stir at the time, as prosecutions were still far off, and a few months later voters in his borough returned him to office with overwhelming support. But a year later, he made front-page news and provoked a political and legal showdown with Governor Pataki.

It began when a police officer was murdered in the Bronx. After claiming that he'd never said he would never *consider* the death penalty, Johnson announced that indeed he would not seek it in this instance. "I don't feel any pressure," Johnson explained. "I answer to my own conscience. . . . Clergy and community people are telling me to hang in there," he said.

Pataki intervened, taking what he admitted was an extraordinary leap of executive power by removing Johnson from the case and replacing him with the state attorney general. It was an unprecedented action; governors had replaced prosecutors previously only when they were clearly corrupt or incompetent. Johnson responded by taking Pataki to court, pointing out that the Supreme Court had declared that the death penalty should never be considered mandatory, no matter how evil the crime. "The governor seeks to use the power of his office to impose on prosecutors throughout the state his beliefs as to the appropriateness of the death penalty," Johnson argued.

The dispute became moot when the alleged cop killer committed suicide in his prison cell. But the incident raised a tangle of fascinating questions. Can an elected prosecutor, sworn to uphold the laws of the state, refuse to fully enforce *one* of them? Can he follow his conscience, or must he bend to the will of the legislature? Which political figure represents the will of the public—a governor elected by the entire state or a district attorney elected by the people who live in the county where the murder occurred? In any case, can any state afford to have two, or perhaps dozens of, different standards for prosecuting murder cases? "We cannot have the death penalty in New York state except in the Bronx," Pataki observed. "I will not allow certain areas of the state to become death penalty–free zones."

A state judge later rejected Johnson's suit, ruling that Pataki had legitimate concerns in deciding that the D.A. would not faithfully execute the law; the governor had a constitutional obligation to "take care that the laws are faithfully executed." Yet, months passed and Johnson, unbowed, continued to eschew capital cases.

Robert Johnson's personal belief system (powerfully affected by his experience of having prosecuted the wrong man for murder) comes up squarely against the actions required in his professional life. In a sense, Johnson was expressing a form of professional lawbreaking in connection with what he considers an unjust law, and civil disobedience is never easy, particularly when it occurs at the center of one's professional life.

This is true, as well, with the most famous and powerful prosecutor in the state, Manhattan D.A. Robert Morgenthau, another longtime foe of the death penalty. More politically entrenched and skillful than Johnson, Morgenthau has managed to avoid capital cases without incurring the wrath of Pataki. Unlike Johnson, he has never said "never" in public, and he claims that he closely considers every case on its merits. Yet the result—no capital cases—is the same. Morgenthau, as a critical *New York Post* editorial pointed out, walks a thin line between Hynes and Johnson: "He's never explicitly ruled out the possibility of a capital prosecution in Manhattan—but he's never initiated one, either. . . . The time has come for Morgenthau to make clear whether he intends ever to enforce this law."

Morgenthau has served as district attorney since the mid-1970s.

The last time he ran for office, he received 90 percent of the vote and it was no secret where he stood on this issue. Capital punishment, he declared in an article in *The New York Times*, is "a mirage that distracts society from more fruitful, less facile answers. It exacts a terrible price in dollars, lives and human decency. Rather than tamping down the flames of violence, it fuels them while draining millions of dollars from more promising efforts to restore safety to our lives."

Like many other prosecutors (who may not admit it publicly), Morgenthau feels that the amount of money and attention needed to seek the death penalty could be much better spent elsewhere. He points out that Philadelphia and Manhattan, with nearly identical populations, had virtually the same number of homicides in 1990. Then the Philadelphia D.A., Lynne Abraham, gained national renown by promising to seek the death penalty in every possible case, while Morgenthau declined to seek a single one. Six years later, Philadelphia's murder rate stood at twice Manhattan's.

The Geography of Executions

While they exert tremendous influence in their own boroughs, Robert Morgenthau and Robert Johnson can do little to halt the death penalty throughout the state or nation. Or can they? Their ability to promote a double standard for capital crimes (and survive in office) may threaten the very future of the death penalty.

During the first years after capital punishment returned to New York, prosecutors upstate were nine times more likely to seek capital verdicts than their counterparts downstate, according to a 1999 study. Although the New York metropolitan area is more highly populated than upstate counties, and experiences many more murders, prosecutors there (a group that includes Morgenthau and Johnson) produced only thirteen capital cases, compared with twenty-three in the rest of the state.

Practically every state with a death penalty has a story like that to tell:

- The city of Baltimore averaged 320 murders a year during the 1990s but had only one inmate on death row. Suburban Baltimore County, which averaged less than thirty murders a year, had four.

- Under the direction of aggressive prosecutors, Hamilton County in Ohio has more inmates on death row, about fifty, than any other county in the state—even Cuyahoga, which has over half a million more residents. In fact, if you slay someone in Hamilton, you're seven times more likely to face the death chamber than in the state as a whole.

- Tiny Baldwin County, Georgia, population 42,000, had five people on death row in 1999, one more than Fulton County, which includes the city of Atlanta, and has 772,000 people. Baldwin averages about two murders a year, Fulton about 200.

One of the most amazing stories in this regard concerns Raymond Patterson, who shot and killed a man during the 1980s in the parking lot of a motel in South Carolina. As it happens, the line dividing Richland County and Lexington County runs right through the parking lot. This was a matter of some importance, as Lexington was known as a "hang-hard" county, while Richland was not. Unfortunately for Patterson, an investigation determined that he would stand trial in Lexington. He presently resides on death row, where he is appealing his case on grounds of the arbitrariness of the death penalty.

This, in fact, is a growing trend. Attorneys with New York state's Capital Defenders Office are currently appealing capital charges against a resident of upstate Rochester, a man named Jose Santiago, arguing that different policies by local prosecutors produce "stark geographical disparities in the death penalty's use." They argue, further, that New York's death penalty law violates both the state and federal constitutions because it is applied differently throughout the state, and geography is an arbitrary factor that "impermissibly affects the use of the death penalty."

David Baldus, a law professor at the University of Iowa who has studied this question for years, believes that the Santiago case, or one like it, could affect the "whole system" of capital punishment. "It would open the system to tremendous vulnerability," he observes. Just raising the "geography" issue can prove valuable, as it shows that, contrary to conventional wisdom, enthusiasm for executions is far from uniform, and in fact, varies absurdly from region to region—practically, from town to town. And if the U.S. Supreme Court ever makes a landmark decision in this area, it won't much matter if a prosecutor is a zealot or an objector. Capital punishment would be outlawed everywhere.

Governors

LIKE many prosecutors, state governors often have great difficulty balancing mercy, justice, and public opinion. They never initiate a capital case, but they have the option of halting most such cases, short of the death chamber, by granting clemency.

Precedents for clemency go back to the most famous capital case of all. Jesus was brought before Pilate, governor of Judea, after being found guilty by elders and priests of the capital offense of blasphemy. Pilate asked the crowd whether he should commute the sentence—a crude form of polling—and they screamed back *no*. He washed his hands of the matter and Jesus was led to his death, on the cross.

The idea of clemency is grounded in the foundations of the American republic, according to Richard Blecker, professor at New York Law School. The reason we appoint Supreme Court justices for life and give U.S. Senators six-year terms is that we believe that some public officials need to feel less pressured by momentary public passion. Society is furious at the murderer "and yet we don't want to put it beyond our ability to change the situation," Blecker observes. "So now it's ten years later, emotions have settled, the passion has settled. The question is whether we are going to act on the passions of the earlier moment and forever blind ourselves against rationality later."

Today, clemency procedures vary widely from state to state, with governors and parole boards sharing responsibility in some of them, and with procedures ranging from rigorous to casual. According to defense lawyers, officials usually embrace the sentiment expressed by the Nebraska Supreme Court when it rejected an inmate's appeal, explaining that the "exercise of executive clemency is a free gift from the supreme authority to be bestowed according to its own discretion."

Until recent decades, clemency was quite common—offered in perhaps 15 to 30 percent of all capital cases. Even in conservative Florida, governors granted clemency in nearly one-quarter of all death sentences between 1924 and 1966. It's possible that a few decades ago there were more governors philosophically or morally inclined to show mercy, but clemency was mainly used as a check on the many faults of the legal system in capital cases, such as arbitrary indictments, poor defense work, and racial discrimination. That was before the Supreme Court in the 1970s ordered the states to reform their death penalty laws and procedures to make them less capricious. Now there are fewer cases (though still plenty enough) that seem *clearly* unfair; if anything, the public feels that inmates now have too much protection and that appeals drag on far too long.

And so, in today's atmosphere, the quality of mercy has become strained to the breaking point. In the final quarter of the century less than forty men and women of the thousands on death row were granted clemency. In about one-fourth of those few cases clemency resulted from doubts about their guilt; in about the same number it was granted because of mental illness. Only one act of clemency, it appears, occurred in 1998—in Texas, when it was proved that a man on death row had been in Florida when the killing took place. "The whole idea of clemency no longer exists in California," charges San Francisco defense attorney Robert R. Bryan. "They give lip service to it, but it's a joke."

Clemency has become so unpopular that it often occurs only when a governor is about to leave office—and then it is often challenged by his successor. This happened in Ohio when Richard Celeste commuted eight cases on his last day in office, and the new governor asked the state attorney general to investigate the legality of the action. That clemency is likely to occur only when a governor is ending his term in office suggests the "retirement syndrome." The outgoing governor can now afford to permit suppressed feelings of compassion to emerge and become central to his decision.

Political considerations may have much to do with the lack of mercy. "There is a perception, whether or not it is based on reality, that a governor who exercises executive clemency in a capital case commits political suicide," observes Neal Walker, an attorney in New Orleans who has defended scores of death row inmates. Governors running for reelection in his state, he reports, routinely boast about the number of executions they have presided over.

The trend toward turning a deaf ear played out most dramatically in Texas in the Karla Faye Tucker case. By state law Governor George W. Bush could grant clemency only if his pardon board recommended it. The board could have done so on numerous grounds: Tucker had expressed remorse for her actions, was apparently sincere in her newfound devotion to God, and had cooperated with prosecutors by testifying against her former boyfriend. Faxes and phone calls flooded Bush's office appealing for mercy; the governor had appointed the members of the board and surely they would have followed his wishes. But he refused to intervene and ask the board to request clemency, and they voted 16–0 to deny it—with polls showing that the public favored their position.

Bush, who was about to launch his race for president, then had the option of granting a thirty-day reprieve, but he refused, after seeking "guidance through prayer," he explained. "I have concluded that judgments about the heart and soul of an individual on death row are best left to a higher authority." Bush's claim becomes another invocation of God as a means of withdrawing from human responsibility. His statement, however, could also be taken to mean that invoking the death penalty *should* be left to a "higher authority"—that is, human beings have no right to take each other's lives.

Later, during his presidential run, Governor Bush appeared on *Larry King Live* and told the talk show host that his televised interview with Karla Faye Tucker the previous year had "affected me more than I wanted to admit." The prelude to her execution, he added, "remain the longest twenty minutes of my tenure as governor." In an autobiography he later claimed that it felt like "a huge piece of concrete . . . crushing me." This suggests that he experienced a certain amount of doubt but had not permitted himself to act on it.

In succeeding months, he refused to intervene as his state sent dozens of other prisoners to their doom. By the spring of 2000, in more than five years as governor, Bush had presided over the executions of 130 men and one woman, by far the highest total in the nation during this period. Bush responded to criticism by saying that he felt that in all his years as governor he was confident "we have not executed an innocent person."

When Charles Baird, a judge on the Texas Court of Criminal Appeals until 1998, went to Washington recently to announce the formation of a committee to prevent wrongful executions, he was asked about this assertion by Governor Bush. He replied that he did not "share his view," as problems with the death penalty in other states (including bad lawyers, overzealous prosecutors, and elected judges eager to appear tough on crime) were also rife in Texas. To believe Bush, one would have to "take the position that this very fallible system has worked flawlessly," Baird explained.

Governor Bush himself seemed to show he had doubts of his own when, in June 2000, he delayed an execution for the first time in five years, citing concerns that adequate tests on DNA evidence in the case (involving Ricky McGinn) had not been performed. Skeptics, however, wondered if the governor—with sentiment rising against executions outside Texas—simply sought to soften his harsh pro–death penalty image among voters.

Attitude and Altitude

Governors are part of a kind of killing hierarchy, sharing the top level with Supreme Court justices. They make crucial decisions about (and set the tone for) the death penalty—nationally and in individual states—but are removed from the execution machinery.

Below them are the district attorneys and their legal staffs who designate capital cases and try them. While they do no direct killing, they become quite familiar with the men and women they prosecute, but can resist painful feelings about them by focusing on the extremity of their crimes. Below them, in turn, are the wardens and staff who conduct the actual executions and experience all the emotions related to hands-on killing. They too have protective mechanisms, but they are unable to avoid the pain of their direct involvement in the killing process.

One can make a loose but instructive comparison to the relative altitudes of aircraft carrying out bombing and strafing missions during the Vietnam War. Pilots flying high-altitude bombers saw nothing at all of the people they were killing on the ground. These pilots required an act of moral imagination to experience anything of what they were doing. Pilots flying medium-level bombers saw little figures that would provide a modicum of reality, but those flying helicopter gunships at low altitudes saw everything on the ground and experienced all the emotions of ordinary grunts. Like the death penalty hierarchy, these levels represent degrees of numbing in carrying out a killing project.

Yet governors testify that considering mercy for those on death row puts them through considerable torment. "I think that's the toughest thing we do," Governor Tom Ridge of Pennsylvania, a death penalty supporter, recently said.

When governors consider clemency, what is crucial for defense attorneys is to make sure the *specific person* about to be put to death is made real. This ensures that the governor is brought down from his "high altitude" to a "medium altitude" where he can identify the person he colludes in killing—or even to a "low altitude" where he can absorb a fuller dimension of that person. The more the governor permits himself to closely consider the human being to be executed, the more he opens himself up to conflict, guilt, and responsibility.

But as a recent case involving Governor Parris Glendening of Maryland illustrates, one can experience such conflict but overcome it sufficiently to permit the execution to go ahead.

It was the spring of 1997, and Governor Glendening felt that his lifelong support for capital punishment was being put to the test. A killer named Flint Gregory Hunt was slated for execution—the first during Glendening's three years in office. More than that, it would be the first time in thirty-six years that the state would put to death a prisoner who did not go willingly to the death chamber. Weighing clemency, the governor called it "probably the single most difficult type of responsibility that goes with the office. No matter how comfortable you are philosophically with the broad issues of the death penalty, when you are dealing with a specific person, it is very difficult. There is nothing as focused and immediate as deciding whether a person is going to die or not."

Glendening had been reviewing the Hunt case for about a year as it wound through its final appeals. Hunt had gunned down a Baltimore police officer in 1985, shooting him in the back, so there was much clamor from the media, officials, and the public for an execution. The governor read files of material prepared by his staff and a seventy-four-page petition filed by the condemned man's lawyers, and watched a fifty-minute video featuring Hunt and his family; but he refused to meet with the Reverend Jesse Jackson to discuss the case. Hunt's attorney asked that he be sentenced to life without parole and found three jurors in his original trial who testified, on the video sent to the governor, that they would have chosen that option over the death sentence if given the chance.

Letters poured into the governor's office, about evenly divided. But Glendening insisted that "this was not about political pressure or public perception or anything else. This was about making the right decision in the context of the responsibilities of this office." And that meant denying clemency; he supported the state's death penalty law "and if there was a case that fit" it, this was the one.

The week of the execution Glendening canceled most of his public appearances, including meetings with Vice President Gore and President Clinton. The night of the execution he remained at home and was surprised at how slowly time seemed to pass as the countdown continued. He wondered how he would feel afterward.

Near midnight a staff member called to say that guards were about to escort Hunt to the death chamber, leaving the door open for the governor to reconsider. He did not.

The morning after the execution, Glendening woke up feeling that "a weight had been lifted from my shoulders." He said he had no doubt, "not the slightest second guess," that he'd made the right decision. When he said a "weight had been lifted," it meant that the human being whose fate so troubled him no longer existed, so the conflict, and the burden, had largely disappeared. Psychologically, he could not afford to consider the possibility that he made a mistake. Yet it would be very surprising if he didn't, now and then, think or dream about the man whose appeal he refused—and struggle to fend off feelings of self-condemnation.

Illusory Safety Valves

Clemency may be rare, but as we have seen, a few surprising examples in 1999 suggest that, more and more, governors may be weighing the acceptability of life without parole, particularly when reminded to do so by the pope, local bishops, or other religious leaders.

But there is a flip side to this that actually encourages *more* executions. The possibility of clemency (even if rarely exercised) probably increases the number of death sentences, as jurors and the public at large may feel confident that a governor will surely intervene to prevent a tragic miscarriage of justice. Daniel Kobil, a professor of constitutional law, compares this to a bait-and-switch scheme. "Justice systems tend to operate on the assumption that clemency is available," he said, "and so we can have capital punishment because of this safety valve."

The possibility of clemency creates an illusion of compassion, and is only one of the perceived safety valves that make capital punishment possible—others (often illusory as well) being the promise of a fair trial, adequate defense attorneys, and a painstaking appeals process.

This extends as well to what could be called the preclemency phase. Governors in some states actively take part in deciding if and when to issue a death warrant for the many eligible candidates on death row. When this happens, they hold life-or-death power almost as surely as when the time comes to consider clemency. Through the media, the public learns that everything has been carefully weighed—laying the groundwork for accepting the fairness of the governor's decision, and the "justice" of a planned execution.

Executing, with Guilt, in California

Probably no governor personally opposed to the death penalty allowed more inmates to be executed than Edmund G. "Pat" Brown of California. During his eight years as governor he let thirty-six prisoners "go to their deaths," as he put it late in his life. Eventually, however, he became an eloquent spokesman against the death penalty, pointing the way to a transition that, perhaps, many governors may follow.

Early in his career he had pressed for the death penalty as a district attorney and then as state attorney general, and he criticized "softheaded judges" who granted unwarranted stays of execution. At one point back then, Brown decided to attend an execution at San Quentin, but he was talked out of it by two homicide detectives, who told him that if he did he would never be able to advocate a death sentence again. But should decision-makers really be kept far above the consequences of their decision? How many governors or senators or presidents have witnessed an actual execution? It is like keeping a general away from the actual battlefield where he might view killings resulting from his decisions.

Late in his final term as attorney general, however, Brown's belief in capital punishment was shaken when Governor Goodwin Knight ordered a last-minute stay for a condemned man—and the message reached San Quentin two minutes after the cyanide pellets had dropped into the sulphuric acid in the gas chamber. This incident defined the profound fallibility of human beings in relation to how and when they make decisions to carry out or interrupt executions. In the public uproar that followed, Brown called for a five-year moratorium on the death penalty in California, to give the state a chance to reform the system, but it was not approved.

When Brown became governor in 1959, he considered the death penalty an evil—but a necessary one. It might work as a deterrent, and it certainly served as "an emotional purge for society." In any case it was one of the laws of the state he had sworn to uphold. Within six months of taking office, however, his beliefs were undermined again when the case of a man wrongly convicted of murder came to his attention, resulting in his granting a pardon. Over the next seven years he decided the fate of fifty-nine condemned men, sending the majority to their death but commuting the sentences of twenty-three. This far outstripped acts of mercy shown by his predecessors, including Governor Earl Warren, who made only six commutations while allowing eighty-two prisoners to die.

Reading the files on the murderers, Brown was often filled with rage but, he explained, "anger is a luxury that a governor can't afford" as the last stop on the road to the gas chamber. Some of the men Governor Brown spared eventually emerged from prison and went on to live peaceful, productive lives, but one of them killed a woman. Years later, Brown confessed that he wasn't sure he would have spared anyone if he'd known that even one of them would take another life.

Brown's tendency toward clemency, however, became a political liability, and Ronald Reagan used it against him with much success, defeating him for reelection in 1966. Still, his opposition to capital punishment remained firm, and his son Jerry Brown, also a two-term governor, inherited this stance.

More than two decades after leaving office, Pat Brown paid a visit to death row at San Quentin for the first time. He felt he was paying a debt to the thirty-six men he had sent to their deaths. By then there were 224 men on the row, and that number would continue to grow (to more than 500) in subsequent years. Brown decided to write a book, called *Public Justice, Private Mercy*, an attempt to find out whether his opposition to capital punishment had "made any difference"—therefore, perhaps, redeeming the lives of those executed. Sadly, Brown had to admit in the book that while his public stance may have contributed to the slowdown of the execution machinery during the 1960s and 1970s, the practice, in California and elsewhere, was gearing up again.

Indeed, in California in 1998, all the candidates in the campaigns for governor and U.S. senator took pains to paint themselves as fierce advocates of capital punishment. Senator Barbara Boxer, a staunch liberal, declared that she had voted 100 times in Congress to impose the death penalty, balking only at executing juveniles. Her fellow Democrat Gray Davis, in the governor's race, cited repressive Singapore as a model for effective capital punishment. ("You can't punish people enough as far as I'm concerned," he added.) They both won their races. The support of the death penalty by Democrats, perhaps feeling tainted by "soft" liberalism, suggests the macho component of advocacy. It is a combination of political macho (being tough on crime) and personal macho (I'm the toughest on the block).

Pat Brown once asked an interviewer to imagine someone sitting alone in an office with the knowledge that "thumbs up they live, thumbs down they die." And then imagine that lonely official thinking about an actual person on death row and realizing that if the decision is "thumbs down," he really does die. "Nobody should be forced to do that," Brown said. "What did the good Lord give me that I should have the right to determine whether even the most abject, horrible character lives or dies?" Brown closed his memoir on a melancholy note, an 83-year-old public servant still bedeviled by his reluctant involvement with death:

> The longer I live, the larger loom those fifty-nine decisions about justice and mercy that I had to make as governor. They didn't make me feel godlike then: far from it; I felt just the opposite. It was an awesome, ultimate power over the lives of others that no person or government should have, or crave. And looking back

over their names and files now, despite the horrible crimes and the catalog of human weaknesses they comprise, I realize that each decision took something out of me that nothing—not family or work or hope for the future—has ever been able to replace.

Pat Brown's final confession suggests the mental cost of letting into one's psyche the actual image, and knowledge, of killing a particular human being. At the end of his life he was haunted by the people he had not saved, the people he had "killed."

Cuomo's Declaration of Life

The man who succeeded Pat Brown as the nation's most applauded and reviled anti–death penalty governor was Mario Cuomo of New York. Unlike Brown, Cuomo had always opposed capital punishment, and he came to office in a state that had recently outlawed executions. Cuomo didn't have to consider signing death warrants or clemency petitions. All he had to do was keep vetoing legislation that sought to reinstate the death penalty in the state, hope the legislature would never manage to overturn a veto (it didn't), and keep getting reelected (he did, twice, but then lost to George Pataki in 1994).

For years, Cuomo was a lightning rod on the issue, orating eloquently against the death penalty, swaying some voters to his side and convincing many others that he did not deserve to be removed from office for taking a principled stand they happened to disagree with. It is unclear how large this issue loomed in his loss to Pataki, but by 1994, Cuomo felt so vulnerable on it that he extended an olive branch to advocates of the death penalty, hinting that he might carry out the law if the legislature did manage to overturn his veto.

In 1998, running for and winning reelection, George Pataki revisited the issue, introducing legislation to strengthen and expand the state's new death penalty law. The intensity of Pataki's advocacy of the death penalty could be at least partly a reaction to Cuomo's opposition. Everything in public life becomes a combination of inner conviction and political efficacy; but in the case of the death penalty these have a particularly uneasy—and unsavory—interaction.

Since leaving office, Mario Cuomo continues to denounce the death penalty at every opportunity. Cuomo's reasons for opposing capital punishment are little different from Pat Brown's but, characteristically, he states them more profoundly, declaring that the death penalty "lowers us all," represents "a surrender to the worst that is in us," and "uses a power, the official power to kill by execution, which has never elevated a society, never brought back a life, never inspired anything but hate." Indeed, all it accomplishes is showing "the barbarians . . . that we are capable of official barbarism."

More significantly, Cuomo describes capital punishment as not merely an important issue but a central one with "transcendent significance: one that describes in fundamental ways what we are as a people, one that projects to ourselves, and to the whole world, our most fundamental values—one, even, that helps configure our souls." He has spent considerable time with victims of crime, including the widows of slain police officers, and says he understands their cries for retribution. He recognizes that he might very well feel exactly the same way, but he asserts that "society should stand for something better than what we are in our worst moments."

Cuomo, now a private lawyer, has put his political beliefs into personal practice, signing the Declaration of Life, a document distributed mainly by religious activists. The Declaration of Life—in effect, an insistence that society not "kill my killer"—connects opposition to the death penalty with events beyond the grave. Cuomo, like thousands of other signers, declares that if he should be murdered he does not want the killer put to death "under any circumstances, no matter how heinous [the] crime or how much I have suffered." He calls it a supreme example of victims' rights, which he supports. "In capital cases," he says, "a relative or a prosecutor sometimes says the death penalty would do justice to the deceased. Well, in my case, they're not going to be able to make that argument because I don't consider it justice."

6

JURORS AND JUDGES

Jurors

The jury system probably demands more of people than
they can be expected to deliver, especially under stress.

—*Wendy Kaminer*

CAPITAL trials are special in our system, for juries generally decide
the sentences. In most other cases, judges impose the penalty, as
they commonly have a background in criminal justice and wide
knowledge about sentencing options and precedents. This type of
experience is practically useless in a capital case, however. The
judge is no more of an expert in moral choices than any juror; and
juries, at least in theory, better reflect the values and conscience of
their community.

Still, jurors have an incredibly difficult task, not only making
moral choices, but measuring aggravating and mitigating circumstances that point to life or death, and deciding which outweighs
the other. They leave behind the world of eyewitness testimony and
physical evidence—fingerprints, bloodstains, murder weapons. As
one juror explained: "Did he do the crime is much different than
trying to figure out why he did it, will he do it again, what kind of

person he is. Those questions are much more difficult. So we relied more on gut feelings." Rules of logic do not seem to go very far here. Jurors must ponder the ultimate value of the convicted murderer as a human being, and whether, in this instance, society is justified in killing him.

In recent years the U.S. Supreme Court has appeared ambivalent about how strongly to guide jurors' discretion in capital cases. Yet it has articulated a concept of what the life-or-death decision *should* be based on: a "reasoned moral response" and an "individualized assessment" of the character and record of the defendant and the circumstances of his offense. Significantly, the Court now makes little reference to deterring other killers and has characterized "incapacitation" of the inmate (preventing him from killing again) as a secondary consideration, never "sufficient justification for the death penalty."

But there can never be an adequate set of instructions for jurors in capital cases. The Supreme Court's principle of a "reasoned moral response" is never quite attainable. So heavy is the burden that many jurors depend on a moment of epiphany to justify imposing the death penalty; hence the reliance on "gut feelings"— what we usually call intuition. This can draw on a juror's most complex perceptions and emotions, but it hardly constitutes reasoned reflection, and it may be difficult to articulate. No wonder jurors now appear more willing to consider alternatives to executions, satisfied that the correct moral response need not require more killing.

Selecting the "Death-Qualified"

Jury selection is much more rigorous in capital trials than in other proceedings. Commonly, it takes weeks. Potential jurors are usually asked to fill out a lengthy questionnaire—forty-seven pages long in a recent case in New York, more a final exam than a court proceeding. A questionnaire used in Sedgwick County, Kansas, for a murder trial in 1998 asked: "Do you have any moral, religious, or personal beliefs that would prevent you from sitting in judgment of another person?" "What do you consider the main purpose of the death penalty?" "Do you believe the death penalty is a necessary punishment in our society?" A prosecutor in Macon, Georgia, recently dropped a capital case against a man who had fatally stabbed his wife, his daughter, and two others, after questionnaires revealed that the prospective jurors overwhelmingly favored life without parole.

In a state poll in New York, 60 percent of the respondents claimed that as jurors they would be able to vote for death; one-third said they could not. Many people who say they cannot vote for death are surprised to learn that this view effectively bars them from serving on capital juries. The U.S. Supreme Court ruled in 1985 that jurors whose beliefs "substantially impair" their ability to vote for death should be excused. This appears to weigh juries in favor of death from the outset, and certainly affects the dynamics of any such group.

That doesn't mean, however, that juries are routinely packed with avid proponents of executions. For one thing, anyone who would *automatically* return a death sentence is supposed to be barred, just like those who would automatically insist on life. Most often the panels are a mix of strong backers and people described as "neutral"—willing to bring in a death verdict, but not by rote. Law merely requires that they be capable of considering both aggravating and mitigating conditions in weighing the sentence. Yet no jury can include opponents of executions, and therefore a capital jury cannot represent a true cross section of a community. To be a player in the game, you must not oppose the death penalty on principle—this is an "extreme" position that disqualifies you. The game can be played solely by those willing to consider the death penalty; the only question is whether or not it should apply in the particular case at hand.

The legal claim is that the exclusion of those inclined against executions is necessary; otherwise, every jury would probably be hung in the sentencing phase. An appeals court in Tennessee recently denied a class action lawsuit brought by two citizens who were denied a chance to serve as jurors in a capital case because their religious convictions led them to oppose executions. A deputy district attorney who opposed the lawsuit argued that religious belief was "just like any other bias. It could be someone's religious belief that everyone who commits a murder should be executed. It works both ways."

Before the trial, each potential juror may face interviews with attorneys that can stretch for more than an hour. One prosecutor explains that many jurors arrive without having given a lot of thought to the death penalty. "Some people were probably thinking about their attitudes and opinions for the first time as they filled out the questionnaire," he adds, "so it's important to use this process to dig a little deeper." Jurors may not give much conscious thought to the death penalty, but it nonetheless connects with primal feelings in them. Indeed, the issue for most people combines minimal reflection with powerful emotion. That emotion is related to anger and vengeance, but it also has to do with feelings about death, killing, punishment, and the sanctity of life.

During the selection process for a recent trial in New York one potential juror said he'd want to hear about the defendant's character and background before deciding on a death sentence. When the judge asked why, the man replied: "It's a big decision. I'm the one going to sleep at night knowing that if someone is convicted that I put him there, and I'd want to be sure that, yes, he deserves this." A prosecutor may decide that such a juror is suitably open-minded—or may attempt to strike him, fearing that he may be swayed too much by mitigating factors.

The jury that sat in judgment of Terry Nichols, a conspirator in the Oklahoma City bombing (and eventually decided not to recommend a death sentence) included a woman who admitted that she felt uncomfortable being asked to make a decision on life or death "that isn't ours to make," and a man who said he wished there were some "formula" that could decide who lived and who died. Both made the jury because they said they were, nevertheless, open-minded concerning capital punishment in this instance. Others were dismissed after revealing that they firmly believed in an eye for an eye and would certainly call for death if Nichols was convicted.

Whatever their views on the death penalty, jurors may doubt their capacity, as ordinary mortals, to make such ultimate decisions. They often invoke a larger system, and usually a higher power. We are, after all, ingrained with the idea that only God can decide matters of life and death, that these decisions are not "ours to make." *Hubris*, man playing God, has the psychological effect of transgressing, of violating one's human limits and seizing a divine entitlement. That's why jurors tend to invoke God and the Bible.

Defense attorneys, knowing they're going to end up only with jurors who believe in the death penalty, need to find shades of difference between them. David Wymore, a public defender in Colorado who has handled many capital cases, explains that in the *voir dire* he concentrates on potential jurors whom he considers "pro-life," but not to the extent that prosecutors will strike them. He tries to determine whether they will carefully consider mitigating factors, and he assures jurors, in advance, that bringing back a verdict for a life sentence is a perfectly proper choice. He asks potential jurors these questions: "Are you aware that you should not allow yourself to be browbeaten by other jurors into voting for death? Will you act with the knowledge that you have the right to have your decision, even if unpopular, respected by everyone in your community?" Indeed, the pressure of the group, of *groupthink*, can be inexorable, and standing up against it probably requires a prior capacity to find autonomy in such instances.

The Weight of the Word "Death"

How do jurors feel about their responsibility in deciding the fate of a defendant, and how does that color their decision? What factors most influence jurors as they determine whether a convicted killer may live or die? Consider what occurred in a recent landmark trial in New York City.

At the start of deliberations in the penalty phase, the jury of five men and seven women found themselves evenly split. Five favored a death sentence for Darrel K. Harris, five supported life in prison, and two remained undecided. It was early June 1998. The jury had already convicted Harris of brutally murdering three people in a Brooklyn social club in the first capital trial since the death penalty returned to New York.

The jurors had surprised no one when they returned their guilty verdict, but sentencing was another matter. Prosecutors were pessimistic, doubting that the jury would vote for death. To serve on the panel, jurors (as in every capital trial) had to declare that they were not fundamentally opposed to capital punishment, but Brooklyn jurors were perceived as generally liberal in outlook. Most of the jurors were black, like the defendant, and African-Americans often are suspicious of police and prosecutors.

Also, Harris's attorney, in the penalty phase, had articulated a number of "mitigating" factors suggesting that he should be spared. As a corrections officer in Brooklyn, he had once saved another guard's life during a prison riot, and had received a medal of honor from the mayor of New York. A psychologist asserted that Harris felt an "enormous amount of remorse." He apparently had severe psychological problems and had been addicted to cocaine and alcohol. And his mother appeared on the stand to ask for mercy, describing a devoted son who had pretty much stayed away from serious trouble until one fateful, murderous night. Harris's brother, an ordained minister, asked the jury to "dig deep in your hearts and search out the truth and know that one day shouldn't count for someone's life."

As they began deliberating at the State Supreme Court building in Brooklyn, the jurors knew that a unanimous verdict was necessary for death. Juries in these cases often end up split 11–1. "We felt the weight of just the word 'death,' " one juror later recounted.

Jurors carefully weighed aggravating factors versus mitigating ones, as instructed. What began to sway many jurors was the brutality of the crime. Harris had shot two men in cold blood in the course of a robbery but had run out of bullets with a female witness left alive. She begged for her life, crying that she had five children to support—but he stabbed her to death anyway.

One juror later explained that most of the panel found these murders "just too cruel for words." Another resented the fact that Harris had not testified or said anything on his own behalf in the penalty phase. After three days of arguing, crying, finger-pointing, and shouting, only two jurors held out for a life sentence. They declared that Harris might find spiritual redemption, even rebirth, in prison. The arguing continued. Some jurors started complaining of headaches.

Then one of the holdouts, an immigrant from the West Indies, changed her vote to death after consulting the Bible and praying to God. She said she identified with the mother who had begged Harris for her life—this juror had a 14-year-old boy herself—and she admitted that she had originally sympathized with Harris partly for "selfish," racial reasons. Now she came to feel that she could not do "anything else" but call for Harris's execution.

This made it eleven to one. That evening, the final holdout, a registered nurse, called for a moment of meditation to ease the tension. In the silence she felt something stirring within her—God granting her "peacefulness," she later explained. The following morning she opened her Bible and found a passage in the Book of Galatians. "It said something about how the wicked must be destroyed," she said. "Everything I read pointed to wickedness, destruction, reaping, and repenting. I took it as a strong sign of what my decision should be." The twentieth ballot finally produced a unanimous verdict. As the forewoman delivered that verdict in court, one juror sobbed uncontrollably and nearly collapsed.

The psychosomatic symptoms of Harris's jurors, notably their numerous headaches, suggest the anxiety that can occur in death penalty cases. Such headaches can also be an expression of hostility (resentment at being put in such a position) or entrapment (reluctance to kill a person, along with a sense that one must do just that).

That is what the juror meant in saying, "We felt the weight of just the word 'death.' " Invoking God, the Bible, and religious visions is a frequent and intense phenomenon in death penalty cases because it tends to be related to ultimate issues of life and death. Indeed, religious feelings tend to be evoked wherever there is death and loss. Resorting to prayer or making associations to God helps relieve jurors of the psychological burden of their task—and, even more, of the responsibility for their decision. God is doing it; God is deciding that this criminal should be put to death.

Judging the Life Story: Man or Demon?

Once a trial begins, the issue of how much jurors learn about the person they might condemn to death becomes critical. That knowledge can be divided into the story of the crime and the larger story of the defendant's life. The more emphasis given to the story of the crime, the more likely a death judgment. Hence, the prosecutors represent the crime itself as, essentially, the entire life story. But if a broader biographical narrative emerges, the condemned murderer may emerge as deeply flawed, but human. The murder itself can then be seen in the context of lifelong personal struggles. It is harder for jurors to condemn to death a man whose whole life has been spread out before them.

The penalty phase of Timothy McVeigh's trial brought into sharp legal and emotional conflict what types of testimony should be allowed as jurors weigh a death sentence. The American legal system has long held that sentencing should be determined not only by the defendant's background and motive but also by the pain he inflicted on his victim or victims. Nevertheless, standards covering what can be said about this, and by whom, varied. A decade ago, the Supreme Court ruled that introducing evidence about the pain and suffering of the victims was indeed constitutional; fairness to the killer did not require "turning the victim into a 'faceless stranger.' "

The judge in the McVeigh case, Richard Matsch, took the middle ground when he ruled that he would not allow testimony that "could inflame or incite the passions of the jury with respect to vengeance." He emphasized that a "penalty-phase hearing cannot be turned into some kind of lynching."

The judge's concern in this specific case expresses a more general feeling that such a danger *always* exists in capital trials. Permitting victims' families to testify forces jurors to focus on a survivor's excruciating experience of the murder itself, rather than focusing on the next unsavory step: a possible execution. While that focus seems reasonable, it can so intensify feelings of vengeance as to exclude any other response. Judge Matsch ruled, therefore, that a 9-year-old boy could not talk about the loss of his mother. Survivors would not be allowed to show wedding photographs or home videos of their loved ones. This, the judge ruled, might distract jurors from a calm and "deliberate moral judgment as to whether the defendant [McVeigh] should be put to death."

This ruling struck many observers as fair—in this case—since even the barest testimony about the killing of 168 innocent people, including many children, was certain to outrage and inflame the jurors. Others felt that it went too far. Laurence Tribe, the prominent Harvard Law School professor, argued that the judge had "sanitized" the testimony, seeking to "anesthesize the hearings." Victims should be allowed wide latitude, he declared, for "they add something unique to the proceedings. Their suffering is not a distraction to be minimized, but a reality that a jury must confront in assessing the gravity of the offense." He went further, linking the judge to those who "regard victims as barely relevant to the criminal justice system, people whose involvement is to be tolerated but not welcomed."

Still, the prosecutors were allowed to put on the stand more than a dozen grief-stricken people who testified to the horror and results of the bombing. The defense then brought forward friends and rel-

atives of McVeigh. "He is not a demon," his attorney Stephen
Jones told the jury, "though surely his act was demonic." Another
defense lawyer suggested that the jurors, and other Americans,
would not "feel a clear conscience" if McVeigh was killed, "and
that is why we ask that you sentence him to life in prison without
the possibility of parole. . . . Choosing life over death does not
mean that you in any sense excuse these crimes. It means only that
you have found some reason to exercise a small measure of compassion. It is crucial that you appreciate this distinction."

A prosecutor countered by asking the jurors to "look into the
eyes of a coward and tell him you will have courage. Tell him you
will speak with one unified voice as the moral conscience of the
community, and tell him he is no patriot. He is a traitor and he deserves to die. . . . It's time for justice."

One potential obstacle for advocates of the death penalty is the
human status of the murderer. After one of us interviewed a few
Nazi doctors, a survivor of Auschwitz asked him, "Were they men
or were they beasts?" When told that in fact they were men, and
that this was the problem, the survivor observed sadly that it was
"demonic" that they were not demons. Probably we'd all prefer
that those who murder would reveal themselves as other than
human. If that were so, we could feel completely removed from
them and readily apply to them the most extreme penalty.

By calling McVeigh a "traitor," the prosecutor was partly suggesting that he was less than human or at least an unusually evil
human being. By asking the jurors to look into his eyes and to
speak as the "moral conscience of the community," the prosecutor
was rallying them for the difficult task of directly confronting another human being with their decision ordering his death. The
crime was so extreme that the jurors in this case were able to do
what the prosecutor suggested. When called on in court to affirm
the verdict, they each looked straight into the mass murderer's eyes
and said, "Death."

Even in this case, however, there was pained reflection. One juror
later spoke of a highly emotional atmosphere in the jury room giv-

ing way to methodical attention to McVeigh's fate. "We said, this is a young man's life. We have got to give it every thought, every prayer," she reported. "Everything we could think of, we went over. You know what a terrible thing he did. But when you have never had to do it [consider a death verdict], it weighs a little heavy."

"I Felt Like a Murderer"

> Capital punishment inspires pure dread in judges and juries. Your dream life can be changed forever by bringing in such a verdict.
>
> —*Norman Mailer*

The moral conflicts reported by jurors in press accounts that follow capital verdicts are confirmed by research. We observe, quite strikingly, the same pattern that unfolds in public opinion polls: most of the jurors who vote for capital punishment at a trial nevertheless feel that the death penalty is too arbitrary (some people are executed, others not, for the same crime), and that defendants with good lawyers almost never get the death sentence. In one study, more than one-third of jurors who had endorsed executions at trial admitted they had "moral doubts about death as punishment."

Although many jurors are willing to impose the ultimate penalty—this enabled them to get on the panel in the first place—they often find they can't do it in deliberations; or they voted for death but then had second thoughts. "This was very difficult for all of us," explained a member of a jury in Randall County, Texas, which recently sentenced a woman to death for killing an elderly man (by stabbing him fifty-eight times). "When I walked back into the jury room after delivering the verdict, I felt like a murderer." There are many such jurors, who, without being opposed to the death penalty, are deeply uneasy and incapable of endorsing it without a sense of guilt. And no wonder, as Norman Mailer relates:

> It is one thing to read about a wanton slaying and tell your family they ought to kill the scummy son of a bitch who committed

the act: it is another to sit on a jury and stare at your potential victim. He does not look that different now from anyone else. Yet you are going to order this stranger—and how strange he is—to death. . . . Think then of the boiling pits in any judge or juror who has to condemn another to death.

In 1997, a jury in Orange County, California, quickly found David Von Haden guilty of killing his daughter and son after the breakup of his marriage, but then the panel deadlocked when a lone juror held out against the death penalty. Another juror later complained, "We weren't able to give them [the children] justice." In a similar case in Louisiana the following year a lone holdout apparently felt that the killer deserved death, but, as the forewoman revealed, "death could not come out of her mouth. She just found that out about herself." A jury in California deadlocked at 11–1 for death in a case involving a man who had doused a woman with gasoline and ignited it. The holdout juror said he wouldn't have been swayed "if there had been a million people on the other side." The murderer, he said, was "not acting like a normal person" when he committed the crime. "If he got life in prison, I felt that would be enough. The rest is savagery. I think people were overpowered by emotion and the way [the victim] was killed."

Kevin Doyle, the chief capital defender in New York state, believes that many jurors perceive crazy people as "scary but not absolutely evil. They're fearful enough to put them in prison for the rest of their lives, but they're not harsh enough to kill them." Executing a "crazy" person may conjure up images of medieval cruelty.

Many jurors apparently open deliberations feeling overwhelmed by the responsibility—or asking why it has fallen to them. "The first thing we did," a juror in Indiana related, "was everybody just collapsed literally in each others' arms and cried, knowing that we had to do that. . . . Somebody just said, what right do we have to decide if somebody should live or die? And then we had a large discussion about that, about whether we as people had that right." Some take refuge in jokes or alcohol; some seek strength through prayer, like two of the jurors in the Harris case in New York. It is as if everyone concerned is in an unfamiliar, highly threatening realm, one that is outside his or her perceived moral competence.

Jurors have told interviewers: "I could vote for the death penalty, in the case of a very vicious crime. This was not . . . a sadistic crime." "There were too many people involved, and it wasn't a Ted Bundy type thing." "Because of the severity of the death penalty, there was some concern about what if the evidence was wrong." "I never felt that he was in control of his faculties when he committed the crime." "The boy had a rough life."

William Bowers, a leading researcher in this area, found few shared beliefs among jurors who voted against death, but the leading belief they did share was that defendants who can afford good lawyers almost never get executed. "Perhaps this belief," he writes, "leads them to observe that the defendant in their case is not getting an adequate defense, or perhaps such an observation leads them to believe that the imposition of the death penalty is economically or socially biased."

A common feeling that no doubt influences most jurors was expressed by a juror in North Carolina who confessed that "it's hard when you sit there and it's time for you to say—should this person get life or get the death penalty? It's harder than you're thinking it's going to be when you go in there. In other words, when they're talking to you about being on the jury . . . you feel that, yes, I would, if enough evidence was there, I could do it [impose death]. But when that moment comes to do it, there's a little reservation in there because you start thinking, well, if you kill this person, what good is that doing?"

Often, a juror may overcome these reservations, only to feel them resurface a few months or years later. Attorneys for death row inmates sometimes approach jurors with fresh information, pointing to the prisoner's possible innocence, or to the fact that he may not have received a fair trial, or to something in his background that cries out for mercy. Jurors may then make statements in which they essentially recant their death verdict.

In a recent case in Virginia, for example, two jurors signed notarized affidavits asserting that they would not have sentenced the killer to death if they had known he was brain-damaged (and had an IQ of 75). It was to no avail, as is often the case, and the inmate was executed. In February 1999, a juror who had helped sentence a man to death for a murder committed in 1984 appeared at a clemency hearing for the alleged killer and said he was ashamed that he had voted for an execution. "I knew if I had held out and really did what I should have," he said, "I would have been some sort of pariah in the community."

It is unclear, from studies, how many jurors remain troubled by a death verdict in the months and years that follow. William S. Geimer, a professor who interviewed jurors in Florida, reports that most were not "emotionally torn up," and he attributes this to "insulation." Many claimed that at the trial they were told it wasn't really their responsibility and anyway "we did the best we could." But some were "just wrecks," or "ripped to pieces," he revealed. One woman he interviewed broke down and cried, thirteen years after the trial.

Residual conflicts suggest the extent of the psychological difficulties accompanying a death verdict. Also, we must remember that, at the time of the verdict, jurors are capable of overcoming or suppressing these conflicts, helped by a group process which may reward such suppression with warm and grateful support.

"Automatic Death Penalty People"

Even though they weren't supposed to, there was some angry people in there screaming, "Hang him!" or "Shoot the bastard!" You know?

—*Capital juror*

Since 1990, a wide range of lawyers, sociologists, psychologists, political scientists, and criminologists have participated in the Capital Jury Project, the first major study of this subject. They have now interviewed over 1,000 jurors in nearly a dozen states and have issued some tentative findings—which are, to say the least, troubling. Capital defendants, asserts William Bowers, the head of the project, "are being deprived of an impartial jury. Defendants are not simply facing the unreliability of a crapshoot; they are confronting the bias of dice loaded for death."

Bowers, the principal research scientist at Northeastern University's College of Criminal Justice, is one of America's leading authorities on capital juries. He became interested in the subject after observing that in crucial high court decisions judges repeatedly voiced faith in juries as impartial, fair, and wise arbiters who, essentially, counterbalance most of the inequities elsewhere in the death penalty process. Jurors, in short, tended to check the worst abuses.

"It dawned on me," he told us, "that juries had become a kind of sacred cow. They allow the judges and the lawmakers to report that the public, indeed, plays a central role in the death penalty. It gives the average citizen the sense that it's 'the people,' not the state, that is ordering executions. The illusion that *people* are 'doing it' keeps public support high. Basically, without a jury system, we could not have a death penalty." The jury, in other words, provides an institutional check that supposedly prevents anyone who does not deserve it from being executed.

What are we to make, then, of the recent spate of death row inmates wrongly convicted and released? It's true that prosecutors may have erred in bringing charges, but it was a jury that sent them to death row.

Wendy Kaminer, in her book *It's All the Rage*, points out that trusting a jury to render an unbiased opinion ignores human nature and history (particularly the history of the American South). Juries are made up of people like you and me, no better or worse, and therefore they are fully capable of "arbitrary, irrational, or frightened behavior. They reflect the biases and bad faith of their communities and culture, as well as the goodwill." Yet the notion that juries know best underlies the jury system. "No doubt many jurors vindicate our faith in them," Kaminer writes, "while others do not."

One reason for this, as we've seen, is that they find many ways to distance themselves from the meaning of their verdict. They may decide that they are nothing more than a minor cog in the process, or assume that higher courts will eliminate their verdict if they've done anything wrong, or even assume that if their sentence stands, the prisoner probably won't be executed. And, of course, it's always easy to dehumanize or place full responsibility on the usually unappealing defendant. As a juror in California put it, referring to the killer: "You created your own sentence. We simply carried it out."

One of jurors' most common responses is to invoke "the law" as final arbiter. Jurors may misinterpret the judge's legal instructions and convince themselves that they are merely helping things along to a preordained conclusion, since "the law" seems to dictate the ultimate penalty. This apparently allows the jurors to avoid feeling personally responsible for the sentence. "I think it more or less was a procedure," an Indiana juror explained. "I had a feeling [the judge] was giving us a procedure and we needed to go through these certain steps. And then if all the pieces fit, then you have a responsibility to come back with a death sentence."

Distancing and numbing may be unavoidable human responses, but William Bowers, after much study, feels that one other factor tilts juries in the direction of death—and must be reformed. The fact that jurors must be "death-qualified" to serve helps produce the "expected" result in deliberations, he charges. Although the law instructs that they consider mitigating factors with an open mind, at least half of all capital jurors, in Bowers's research, were *severely* predisposed to a death sentence. He calls this an "egregious tilt," and refers to these jurors at ADPs, for "automatic death penalty" people.

Members of this majority often exert pressure on the holdouts in deliberations, telling them, "You *said* you could impose death, that's how you got on the jury—so what's your problem *now*? Did you mislead the judge? It's time to follow through on what you said." Often at this point the holdouts come to doubt themselves and then reach for a face-saving device, such as finding a supporting statement in the Bible.

In this way, the "automatic death penalty" people on the jury keep the momentum strong and inexorable. Pro-life jurors are an enigma to them; they are seen as shirking their responsibility. Their reluctance to vote for death seems to conflict with being "death-qualified"—that is, it conflicts with the powerful momentum, psychological and moral, of the process. Such a person is looked upon as lacking team spirit, or as a troublemaker.

Capital juries, therefore, can be seen as facilitators of a death sentence. Of course they can decide against execution, but that requires an unusual degree of determined opposition on the part of one or two jurors. It goes against the grain of *collective expectation.* This expectation includes both the guilty verdict and the sentence of death, which are perceived as a reflection of the moral requirements of a larger community, of society itself. Jurors are then caught up in an "energy force" that propels them in the direction of the death penalty.

Bowers does not go as far as Mark Twain, who called the jury system the "most ingenious and infallible agency for defeating justice that human wisdom could contrive." He believes, however, that the overall system isn't working, because too many "automatic death penalty" people are allowed to serve on juries. Not many judges and defense attorneys are schooled in identifying these people and keeping them off juries. Judges often ask potential jurors if they have an "open mind," but how many people, in that setting, are going to respond, "No"?

Life Without Parole

Despite the ADP factor, there is an encouraging counterbalancing trend in capital verdicts. Rising sentiment for life without parole, in place of executions, is already having an impact on jury decisions. In fact, if the trend continues, it has the potential to produce a kind of gradual grassroots abolition of capital punishment in practice, even if courts and legislators refuse to end it in law.

Life sentences have long existed, of course, but usually they didn't mean what they said. Murderers commonly became eligible for parole after eight or eighteen or twenty-eight years, and often were granted it. The public and politicians have long cried out against killers walking the streets after what seem like disturbingly brief prison terms.

In recent years, however, dozens of states have toughened laws and procedures that mandate life sentences with no chance for parole—or at least guarantee that early release will not even be considered for twenty-five years or more. These are no-nonsense provisions, but the public can be forgiven for wanting to see if judges and parole officials really abide by them. So far, they have, and public confidence in them is deepening. Surveys already show (as we will explore later) that a majority of people now say that they prefer "certain" life without parole (LWP) to executions as a penalty for convicted murderers.

This has already had some impact on capital juries. The number of convicted killers given the death sentence recently declined in conservative Georgia, Virginia, and Indiana, for example, after these states instituted LWP as an option. California, one state where life without parole has been widely used for many years, has stuck to the letter of this law, which probably contributes to the fact that prisoners are rarely executed there.

Both research and common sense suggest that many jurors would gravitate to life without parole instead of death if given a clear option. In some states, however, judges are not allowed to tell jurors that LWP is even an option, since this may "prejudice" them against a death verdict. Jurors often ask judges about the likelihood of parole but are usually denied information. This is enormously significant, as research shows that the jurors' life-or-death decision often hinges on fears of early release—and "life" in this context can signal danger.

Many jurors feel that a convicted defendant doesn't quite deserve to die but does merit a "true" life sentence. One juror recalled: "Unanimous(ly), we'd have voted for life without parole but that wasn't an option, and we felt sure that if he was given life, he'd be given parole. . . . We all felt like . . . there wasn't enough evidence to feel like he deserved death." A juror in North Carolina said: "We all had decided if we were absolutely sure that he would never have gotten out of prison we wouldn't have given him the death penalty. But we were not sure of that."

Jurors often impose death "not as the appropriate, but as the least inappropriate, of the available punishment options," William Bowers declares. "In such cases, defendants are sentenced to death and executed because their jurors cannot impose the punishment they deem appropriate"—in his view, life without parole.

Indeed, as more states institute LWP, there is a growing "retributive gap," in Bowers's words. Legislators in some states oppose life without parole because it would weaken support for the death penalty. Indeed, in South Carolina, a group of top state law enforcement officials sent a letter to the legislature, which was considering a proposal for LWP, asserting that passing the bill "will increase the risk of major crime by encouraging juries to refrain from applying the existing death penalty"—that is, undermine the kind of righteous indignation that goes into decisions for death. A legislator warned that if that bill passed they might as well close the South Carolina death house and "transfer the [electric] chair to the state museum."

That fear reveals a sentiment close to love for both death house and electric chair—and profound disrespect for the moral misgivings of jurors.

Judges

If a person who deals with it on a daily basis doesn't call the public's attention to the fact that it's not working, then who will?
—*Gerald Kogan, former chief justice,*
Florida supreme court

IN most states, as we have seen, the decision to send a convicted killer to death row, or spare him that ordeal, rests solely in the hands of juries. The theory is that the defendant must be not only tried but sentenced by a jury of his or her peers—representatives of a large and varied community, seeking justice. At the present time, judges may override a jury's recommendations in only a handful of states, but occasionally an inmate, sentenced to life by a jury, is executed thanks to the judge. Overrides, in fact, are fairly common in Florida. Studies show that in all states judges reverse life sentences much more often than death verdicts.

Some defense attorneys, nevertheless, favor putting the final decision in the judge's hands, and advise their clients to plead guilty, waiving their right to a jury trial. Lawyers feel it's hard for them to win sympathy from jurors—having to plead for mercy after asserting for weeks that the killer was innocent. Their clients have a better chance, they believe, if they stand up and admit they murdered, and then ask a judge for mercy. Perhaps more important, placing the sentencing decision in the hands of one person instead of twelve reduces the chances for psychological distancing. It makes one individual come face to face with the fact of execution, and many judges have a hard time choosing death.

A juror who recently took part in a deadlocked capital trial in California advocated passing the buck directly to judges in all such cases. "There are only two choices," she said, "and why should a jury have to make that choice? It can be very traumatic."

The idea of putting the decision in the hands of a single judge gives that judge absolute life-or-death power. One would expect that many judges would cringe from the awesome power offered to them, but it is also possible that some embrace the omnipotence. The individual judge, in any case, replaces the jury as the bearer of the entire national conflict over the death penalty. Many citizens, of course, would happily go along with that.

In 1995, legislators in Colorado, backed by many prosecutors, passed a law that took the penalty phase away from juries and put it in the hands of three-judge panels (a system then in effect only in Nebraska). Defense attorneys railed against it, arguing that judges, who often must win election to regain their posts, feel tremendous political and public pressure to vote for death. They also alleged that judges feel little compassion for convicted killers, partly because (as one public defender put it) they "live in cloistered communities." The whole point of a jury is that "it will act as the conscience of the community," says David Lane, a defense attorney in Denver. Finally, persuading one of twelve jurors to vote against the death penalty is considerably easier than persuading one of three judges.

Prosecutors in Colorado, long frustrated by 11–1 votes that lead to hung juries or life sentences, exclaimed that it was about time they got a break. The state solicitor general said that jurors "have no context or background in making this kind of decision," claiming further that the new setup would "get rid of the irrationality in the process." Similarly, a district attorney in Colorado explained that juries are overly influenced by emotional appeals from the families of victims and killers alike. "Judges hear that stuff every day," he observed. "Juries don't."

Some prosecutors, however, feared that they would be stymied by the occasional judge who is morally or philosophically opposed to capital punishment. Jurors who feel that way are screened out, but this would not necessarily happen with judges.

In any event, in the first three capital cases decided by the three-judge panel in 1999, the decision went in favor of the defendants—who got life sentences instead of death. In one of the cases, two judges voted for death but the third declined, and the decision must be unanimous. This caused some legislators to consider going back to the old system. They complained that, as with the jury system, one person with qualms about capital punishment can stall the will of the majority. Defenders of the three-judge system replied that its critics simply wanted more executions any way they could get them.

It's a question of who, in the end, will take responsibility for the killing. One is reminded of the Nazi doctor who said that "euthanasia" or mercy killing was all right, but that doctors should not do it. In the case of deciding for the death penalty, there are moments when no one seems to want to do it, which suggests that there is something wrong with "it."

From Halting Executions to Hanging Hard

Although relatively few judges get to decide the fate of convicted killers at trial, others do play a vital role, making crucial, sometimes final, rulings in the appeals process. Some seem predisposed to grant appeals, others appear dead set against it. Like so many in the execution process, a substantial number of judges question the value or ethics of taking a life but claim that duty compels them to allow that to happen.

Rather famous in this regard was Judge Robert S. Vance of the U.S. Court of Appeals for the Eleventh Circuit, which hears cases from three very active death penalty states—Florida, Georgia, and Alabama (it's sometimes referred to as the "death court"). Vance once explained to one of his law clerks that he did not believe in capital punishment: if he were a legislator, he would vote against it; if he were the governor, he would commute death sentences; and if he were on the U.S. Supreme Court he might hold the death penalty unconstitutional. His son later explained that Vance considered death penalty cases "to be almost unbearable."

Still, during his tenure, Vance affirmed a great number of capital convictions because he found that they were the result of proper trials, "and he knew that it was not his role to change that system to suit his personal preferences." In 1989, Judge Vance was killed by a package bomb, and the man charged with the crime, Walter Moody, Jr., would be convicted of capital murder and sent to Alabama's death row—despite pleas from the judge's widow to avoid capital charges.

Other judges who oppose the death penalty on principle find it nearly impossible to implement, as the years pass; they are unable to distance themselves from the results the way most jurors can.

Gerald Kogan, in his final months before stepping down as chief justice of Florida's supreme court, toured the state in 1998 speaking out against capital punishment—which he had administered for decades as both a prosecutor and a judge. During his twelve years on the state supreme court, more than twenty men died in Florida's electric chair and, Kogan now believes, some of them may have been innocent. "There are several cases where I had grave doubts as to the guilt of a particular person [and] other cases where I just felt they were treated unfairly in the system," he explains. In a handful of cases he tried to stop executions but was outvoted by other justices. For years he believed that capital punishment did not deter and that it took up too much of the justices' time, but for him the possibility of making a mistake overrides all else. "To take the life of an innocent person," he declares, "is indeed the most tragic thing that we can do."

Even more striking was the turnabout by a supreme court justice in Ohio, Paul E. Pfeifer, author of the state's death penalty law. He now expresses second thoughts about capital punishment, saying he doubts that society is better off for killing condemned prisoners.

He wonders if the state should be in the business of "ending peo-ple's lives." Like Judge Kogan, he came to see the death penalty as harmful to what might be called the ethical function of his profession.

The federal judge Alex Kozinski, a well-known conservative who has written widely in favor of the death penalty, heartily disagrees with this, however. Some of his colleagues, he complains, take their cue from former Supreme Court Justices Thurgood Marshall and William Brennan and have never voted to uphold a death sentence and doubtless never will, feeling that they are morally justified in undermining capital punishment. Other judges regard this as a "shameful breach of duty," Kozinski declares, a violation of their oath to enforce a valid law.

Some on the bench, on the other hand, are the modern-day equivalent of a "hanging judge." In 1991, Judge William Harmon in Texas told a defendant during a capital trial that he was doing "God's work" by making sure the defendant was executed. Harmon had taped to the bench a photograph of the famous Judge Roy Bean's "hanging saloon." On another occasion, when some-one suggested transporting some death row inmates to court, Judge Harmon commented, "Could we arrange for a van to blow up on the way down here?" In 1992, a Houston Judge, Charles J. Hearn, earned criticism, and praise, when he signed a death war-rant and drew a "happy face" along one side.

Judge Kozinski, in the eyes of some, is another "hang-hard." As with Ron Sievert, the Texas prosecutor, his early doubts about cap-ital punishment were scattered long ago when he started reading case reports. The son of two Holocaust survivors, he frequently asked himself if he would have spared Eichmann's life, and the an-swer was always no, so he knew he supported capital punishment on principle.

Yet Kozinski is no execution automaton. Increasingly, he ex-presses surprising misgivings about both the process and his own role in it. He feels that capital cases "come at you sort of like freight trains." He describes the difficulty, on a sleepless execution night, of chasing from his mind the image of the man whose last-minute stay he has denied, and wondering if has "done the right thing." He compares it to "a nagging sense of unease, something like motion sickness." It's one thing to guide a trial, even give advice to jurors, "and quite another to be the judge signing the order that will lead to the death of another human being—even a very bad one." He's had a hand in more than a dozen executions "and it's never easy. . . . It takes a piece away from you to do that."

Kozinski's qualms go still farther. He fears it's inevitable that innocent men and women will be executed. And he wonders if the death penalty is nothing but an "expensive and distracting sideshow" in the real battle against violent crime, diverting talent and resources from more mundane efforts to lock up a greater number of predators. Yet despite all this, he still comes down on the side of capital punishment—because he has taken an oath, and because he believes that "society is entitled to take the life of those who have shown utter contempt for the lives of others. And because I hear the tortured voices of the victims crying out to me for vindication."

Witness for the Prosecution

With bracing honesty, Judge Kozinski admits that he never wants to witness an execution—he is "afraid" to do that, he says—and he wonders whether "those of us who make life-and-death decisions on a regular basis should not be required to watch as the machinery of death grinds up a human being. I ponder what it says about me that I can, with cool precision, cast votes and write opinions that seal another human being's fate but lack the courage to witness the consequences of my actions."

Kozinski's conflict derives from opening himself painfully to both deaths—that of the killer's victim and that of the killer himself. His recognition of the contradiction between promoting executions and fearing to witness them makes him a strong candidate for eventual opposition to capital punishment—the retirement syndrome in the making.

A former U.S. attorney named Jeremy Epstein proposes requiring judges and juries in capital cases to attend executions—as they were expected to do in New York in the 1840s. It would "focus the attention of those imposing the punishment on the gravity of their act," he points out. Judges and jurors "could not simply depart from the courtroom and leave the state with the unpleasant task of disposing of the defendant." One of the purposes of our penal system, he argues, "is to teach that acts have consequences: crime, in short, leads to punishment. It is no less fitting that judge and jury understand [that] their acts, taken in the isolation of the courtroom, have consequences that reverberate far beyond it."

PART III

THE

REST

OF US

7

WITNESSING

As a punishment of myself—and as a lesson to others—I should now like to tell everything I saw.

—*Ivan Turgenev*

WITNESSING means both being present at an event and taking it in. It means having a responsibility to it, the obligation of telling the tale. It means conveying an event, through one's own experience, to the outside world. Witnessing becomes invaluable for significant events: life-affirming events such as birth and marriage, or events of death, loss, and suffering.

As we have seen, executions in America have always posed a challenge to thoughtful witnessing. The early spectacles were public, communal events in which witnesses were generally protected from painful contemplation by the context of celebration and justification. Our contemporary experience is the seeming opposite—executions hidden away, hurried, often done in the middle of the night, in front of only a select group of witnesses. Recently there has been a trend toward curtailing even this minimal witnessing. Onlookers are admitted for only a brief moment, seeing nothing of the preparations—and are ushered out immediately after the prisoner is declared dead. One might say that this turns witnesses into bystanders.

A notable example occurred in 1998, when ABC's Ted Koppel,

for a prime-time *Nightline* program, attended a lethal injection in
Texas as a heavily promoted act of witness. He emerged, after just
a few minutes, with virtually no feeling at all (he confessed), saying
little more than this: The death of the condemned man was a lot
easier than that of the person he killed. This was undoubtedly true,
but it also suggested that it had been hard—one may say, impossible—for Koppel to take in the death he had just observed.

This is the age of the bystander. We are bystanders in connection
with violence, war, even genocide depicted on our television
screens, and with just about any form of suffering, so readily conveyed to us by our media—whether of starvation in Africa, murder
and rape in Kosovo, or inner-city killings or drug deaths in this
country. Yet some witnesses, attending some executions, do manage to experience the full brunt of what is occurring before their
eyes. A few years ago, three psychiatrists at Stanford completed a
revealing study of media witnesses to the execution of Robert
Alton Harris in 1992 in California's gas chamber. They found that
the witnesses suffered from posttraumatic stress and "experienced
a high prevalence of dissociative symptoms . . . similar to that of
people who endured a natural disaster." One of the psychiatrists
concluded that the witnesses had found that "killing is killing,
whether socially sanctioned or not."

There is something chillingly special about every single execution. "As a killing carried out in all our names, an act of state in
which we by proxy participate," Wendy Lesser has observed, "it is
also the only form of murder that directly implicates even the witnesses." People who witness an execution often say they are
"soiled" or defiled, because they have seen a living person con-
verted into a corpse—a person who was helpless and could put up
no struggle, many years after committing his crime. There is a kind
of unbridgeable gap between the crime and the later execution—
unbridgeable in the psychological sense and, many of us would say,
in the ethical sense as well. And by being there, if one really takes
in the experience, one can readily feel implicated in the state killing,
in the new "murder." The question, then, is what one does with

that sense of self-condemnation, of guilt and shame, and of the taint of death.

It is true that one can, and should, retain a sense of witness and obligation toward the victim of the murder committed by the condemned man. Many take this stance, however, as a means of distancing themselves from the execution—to which one, indeed, becomes not a witness but a bystander.

They Would Have Saved Them If They Could

Around Capital Punishment there lingers a fascination, urging weak and bad people towards it and imparting an interest to details connected with it . . . which even good and well-disposed people cannot withstand.

—*Charles Dickens*

Much has changed in the methods, scope, and hoopla surrounding executions in America since the first years of the nation, when the rituals of killing, often religious in nature, were presented as group theater for the benefit of hundreds or thousands of spectators. Yet, for the witnesses, and society as a whole, one wonders how much has really changed. Describing early executions, the historian Louis P. Masur wrote: "The extent to which spectators internalized, reformulated, rejected, or ignored the intended meaning of the ritual is unclear. What is certain is that hanging day embodied political, theological, and cultural assumptions that mattered dearly to social elites in the early Republic." Just as they do on execution days today.

Each state tightly regulates the number of official witnesses permitted at executions, and that number varies considerably. By law, Pennsylvania and North Carolina allow only six official witnesses, New Hampshire allows twelve, and many other states fall somewhere in between. Many of the laws further require that these citizens be "reputable" or "respectable"—that is, dignified enough to attend an official killing. In addition, the condemned prisoner is generally allowed to invite a handful of family members or supporters, or his attorney and a spiritual adviser. In a recent development in many states, the murder victims' family members are also allowed to attend—and many of them do.

Still, as the pace of executions accelerates, it gets harder and harder to fill the seats with the required number of witnesses. In some states, prison officials have been forced to recruit witnesses by telephone or run solicitations on the Internet. Florida is so desperate for witnesses it no longer asks the reasons a volunteer wants to watch someone die. Such states are grateful for hardened regulars always ready to attend; they have the added value of never fainting at an execution, not an uncommon occurrence.

Unless you have actually witnessed an execution, it is impossible to fully understand what it is like to be one of those spectators. Fortunately, there is a great body of testimony, even literature, based on the accounts of famous writers. The testimony comes from around the world and stretches back centuries, but there is something universal, and timeless, about much of it.

Many writer-witnesses describe their feelings of revulsion, or absence of feeling, or more often a combination of the two. Observing the execution of three men in Rome, Lord Byron wrote: "The first turned me quite hot and thirsty, and made me shake so that I could hardly hold the opera-glass (I was close, but was determined to see, as one should see every thing, once, with attention); the second and third (which shows how dreadfully soon things grow indifferent), I am ashamed to say, had no effect on me as a horror, though I would have saved them if I could."

Such conflicts accompanying the witnessing of executions have been poignantly described by three great Russian novelists.

In 1870, Ivan Turgenev was unexpectedly invited to attend the beheading of a particularly cruel killer in Paris. Awaiting the early-morning event, Turgenev was uneasy about his witness, repeating to himself, "I have no right, I have no right." He came to experience a sense of complicity: "By being present with an air of hypocritical solemnity at the killing of a being like us, we are participating in some kind of lawless detestable farce." After watching the preparations for the killing, and the "composure" of the condemned man, Turgenev decided that there was only one thing he was sure of, "namely that I had no right to be where I was, that no psychological or philosophic considerations excused me."

At the moment of decapitation, Turgenev turned away, and he later observed that "not one of us, *absolutely no one looked like a man who realized that he had been present at the performance of an act of social justice;* everyone tried to turn away in spirit and, as it were, shake off the responsibility for the murder." Turgenev's revulsion never left him, and his only recourse for legitimating his witness was to transform it creatively in his powerful sketch, "The Execution of Tropmann."

Fyodor Dostoevsky was no less repelled by executions, but he was contemptuous of Turgenev's squeamishness. Having been nearly executed himself twenty years earlier, and pardoned at the last moment, his vantage point was that of the prisoner being killed. In his novel *The Idiot*, he asked, "What do you suppose is going on in such a man's soul" when the blade is descending on him? In a letter to a friend he mocked Turgenev for being "fussy to the nth degree—about himself, his integrity, his composure—and all this over a decapitated head." Rather than turn away from the horror, as Turgenev did, he was drawn to witnessing what was most extreme: "Everywhere and in everything I go to the uttermost limits." Dostoevsky insisted that "The attributes of the executioner are to be found in almost every contemporary man."

Leo Tolstoy attended a different execution in Paris and was profoundly disturbed by the "ingenious and elegant machine [with] which they kill a strong, hale, healthy man in an instant," and by the "calm and convenient murder finely worked out." Yet he refused to turn away from the execution, this "loathsome evil," because he felt the need to "test" his own capacity to bear full witness. He drew a further personal moral from it: that all politics are a lie and he would "never go to see such a thing again [and] . . . never serve any government, anywhere."

He too transformed the experience artistically. In his master-work, *War and Peace*, his character Pierre, upon witnessing the "hideous murder" of an execution, undergoes a complete shattering of the self: "It was as if the spring in his soul, by which everything was held together and acquired life, had been suddenly pulled out and all had collapsed into a heap of senseless refuse. Though he did not realize it, his faith in the right ordering of the universe, in humanity, in his own soul and in God, had been destroyed."

Differing greatly as they did in their responses, what these three writers had in common was an insistence upon taking in, bearing full witness to, the act of execution as the methodical killing of another human being. All rejected the role of bystander. A witness is responsible to an event, feels the need to absorb it, in order to carry out his or her moral commitment to testify about it—or *bear* witness to it. A bystander by definition has the opposite inclination—that of distancing the event, remaining numbed toward it, not taking it in, and not being responsible to it.

Mark Twain, like some of the other writers, felt certain he could not observe the hanging "without turning my head at the last moment," but chose nonetheless to witness it fully. In his days as a reporter he attended a hanging in Nevada in 1868, and wrote an article about it for a Chicago newspaper, uncovered only recently. "I can see that stiff straight corpse hanging there yet," he wrote afterward, "with its black pillow-cased head turned rigidly to one side, and the purple streaks creeping through the hands and driving the fleshy hue of life before them." Then he added: "Ugh!"

George Orwell wrote a bit more somberly about witnessing an execution of a Hindu in Burma in his classic "A Hanging." Orwell, watching, realizes for the first time how wrong it is to destroy a healthy human being.

Arthur Koestler, one of the most influential writers on capital punishment, traced his opposition to the death penalty to witnessing executions in 1937 during the Spanish Civil War. Koestler spent three months in Spain under a death sentence as a suspected spy.

He spoke of having a "vested interest" in capital punishment, comparable to that of a man who is cut down after swinging from a noose and survives. "Each time a man's or a woman's neck is broken in this peaceful country [England], memory starts to fester like a badly healed wound," he wrote in his classic *Reflections on Hanging*. "I shall never achieve real peace of mind until hanging is abolished."

Koestler had, in other words, survived his own death, and the survivor mission he took on was to oppose any deaths by execution. He was a gifted, difficult man, who renounced his earlier communist ideology, became a rather outspoken cynic with an attraction to various forms of mysticism, and involved his wife in his eventual suicide. His opposition to the death penalty might have been his most consistent ethical stand over the course of his life.

In the case of Albert Camus, witnessing was transmitted from father to son by his mother, who told him the tale. His father was killed in World War I before Camus's birth and had not been a man who made much of a lasting impression anywhere. The most powerful image Camus received of his father was the story of how he decided to attend the execution of an assassin who had slaughtered a nearby family of farmers. He went there feeling that decapitation was too good for the killer, but returned unable to shake the image of a living body being dumped on a board to have its head removed. Pained by the experience, he could say little and only vomit. Camus later wrote:

> He had just discovered the reality hidden under the noble phrases with which it was masked. . . . When the extreme penalty simply causes vomiting on the part of the respectable citizen it is supposed to protect, how can anyone maintain that it is likely, as it ought to be, to bring more peace and order into the community?

This witness was virtually Camus's only legacy from his father, which made it doubly powerful. With Camus, as with Koestler, rejection of communist killing—of imposing the death penalty broadly and loosely in political contexts—was an important element in opposition to capital punishment in general.

Camus later served as one of the century's preeminent witnesses against the death penalty. He wrote, movingly, on what could be called his philosophy of witnessing: "When the imagination sleeps, words are emptied of their meaning: a deaf population absent-mindedly registers the condemnation of a man. But if people are shown the machine, made to touch the wood and steel and to hear the sound of a head falling, then public imagination, suddenly awakened, will repudiate both the vocabulary and the penalty."

An execution scene burned into many minds is the hanging of Perry Smith and Dick Hickock, as depicted in Truman Capote's *In Cold Blood* (and re-created in the movie of the same name). The scene in the Kansas prison warehouse included these timeless elements: rain falling, a dog wailing in the distance, a dark-eyed executioner pulling the brim of his black hat down low, and two men climbing the stairs of a scaffold to their doom. Only recently have others revealed that Capote ran out of the warehouse after Hickock was hanged, unable to witness the death of Smith, the small, tortured man he had become close to.

Reporters versus the Official Narrative

When executions in America retreated behind prison walls, newspaper reporters were generally included among the handful of inside observers. Allowing reporters to witness hangings was a double-edged sword for the authorities, as we have observed. True, their presence suggested that the executioners had nothing to hide, but they also provided the first accounts of hangings that were not tightly controlled by the upper class, the church or the publishers of gallows literature.

In the earlier pageants, the condemned man usually admitted guilt and repented and so was delivered up to heaven when he died. Reporters became a problem because they broke with the official narrative—that the condemned man had received his just punishment with appropriate religious ritual. Reporters noted that prisoners cried or were sometimes belligerent in proclaiming their innocence. Some hangings were horribly botched.

Many readers, in fact, were horrified by what they learned, and this led to an attempt, at the end of the nineteenth century, to limit or forbid newspaper coverage. The same New York commission that proposed electrocution as a more humane method of killing suggested making it a crime to publish any details of an execution. The press, naturally, rebelled. The state had no right to regulate journalistic "decency" or "good taste," the *New York Times* declared.

Yet when William Kemmler became the first man to die in an electric chair in 1890, no newspaper reporters were present. Reporters were forced to re-create the event by interviewing witnesses, some of whom (as we have seen) called it "death by torture." The New York *Sun* viewed the flouting of the gag order as "one of the most valuable services which a free press ever rendered to the cause of civilization."

Several states passed laws outlawing execution coverage, but prosecutions rarely went forward. Such censorship cut against the American grain—a sense of fairness, openness and morality compelled most people to insist on being allowed to judge a gruesome procedure with all facts at the ready. Yet few publications insisted on being allowed to capture *visual* evidence of what occurred in the death chamber. No photographers were ever allowed inside, which is why the one exception—the fuzzy picture of Ruth Snyder in the electric chair at Sing Sing in 1928, secretly snapped by a New York *Daily News* staffer—has been so widely reproduced. (When the *Daily News*'s decision to publish the Snyder photo in 1928 brought howls of protest from some readers and rival newspapers, its editors replied: "We think that picture took the romance out of murder into every retina which received it. . . . If recollection of that picture shall ever stay a hand raised to commit a murder, then that picture will have done a service.")

Today, reporters are routinely invited to executions, their number ranging from one pool reporter in a few states to upward of twenty-five in California. The presence of journalists supposedly guarantees that prisoners will not be tortured or undergo undue suffering and that the American people, who have sanctioned executions, will learn the details of what they have authorized.

Of course, reporters are human and are often emotionally torn by what they witness in the death chamber, and this can be reflected in what they write or say. A reporter for the San Francisco *Examiner*, after witnessing the oft-delayed gassing of Barbara Graham in California in the 1950s, began her article, "Barbara Graham was tortured to death by the sovereign state of California yesterday." Before publication, her editor, respecting the official narrative, deleted "tortured" and replaced it with "put."

Occasionally, reporters unwittingly change execution policy, or at least the method. Not long ago, Lynn Ford, who wrote light lifestyle features for his paper in Indianapolis, reluctantly granted a condemned man's plea that he attend his execution; the prisoner simply liked Ford's writing. Ford found himself hoping the governor would call it off, but when he didn't, the reporter wrote a vivid account—describing an orange halo, the smell of burning flesh— that is credited with persuading the state legislature to replace the electric chair with lethal injection. Certainly in Florida the press reports of botched electrocutions spurred the state's recent shift to lethal injections. In fact, it's probably fair to say that electrocution might remain the execution method of choice in most states if reporters had been barred from the death chamber.

Recently, the writer Susan Blaustein recounted her experience witnessing with trepidation the execution of Anthony Cook by lethal injection in Huntsville, Texas: "I'd never even seen anyone die, and here I was, about to witness a man's death, to observe it without objection. Already I felt sullied, voyeuristic. Yet this is the law, I told myself. . . . I kept up this interior debate until it was time to report [to the administration building]. . . . We were then marched single file to the death house. The other woman reporter must have seen the fearful look in my eyes. She told me that she couldn't sleep for three nights after her first execution. 'Just attend to the business at hand,' she advised. . . . We got our signal and were abruptly herded into the carpeted witness room." Her more experienced colleague was telling her to treat the matter as a professional task.

A reporter who might be described as the world's leading expert in viewing executions takes a more hardened view. He is Michael Graczyk, who has attended well over 150 of them (he has lost count) in Texas. Graczyk has worked out of the Associated Press bureau in Houston since 1983. Hanging on the wall of his office is a framed certificate from public information officials at Huntsville Prison, which refers to him as "a.k.a. Dr. Death" and thanks him tongue-in-cheek for his "undying devotion to death row dregs, and criminal composition of death-less prose." He speaks unemotionally about executions, referring those who question his devotion to this matter to the case files of the murderers. "Go and pull the file of a murder case and look at the crime scene photographs," he advises, "just the human carnage and terror that these people went through when they died. The look of terror that is frozen forever on them is something you don't forget. Watching the killer die can be easier than interviewing a murder victim's relative." One suspects that Graczyk keeps his feelings in check by making himself a continuous witness to the original crime.

Graczyk claims that covering executions has not yet become mundane, and he compares them to baseball games. "There's a certain similarity to every game," he explains, "but no two are the same." When people say that executions have become "routine," he objects, because "you never know what's going to happen, and that's what makes it a good news story." One inmate forever ruined "Silent Night" for Graczyk by singing the song as his "final words." Some inmates die quietly, others have violent spasms or writhe; some relatives sit impassively, others beat on the walls or windows or beg to be let out of the witness room. Yet, by the time Graczyk drives home to his wife and children he has put the death scene out of his mind, or so he claims. "I don't know these people [the killers], they're not my colleagues, my family," he explains. "I don't want to sound cold, but I don't know them."

His wife, Mary, works as an intensive care nurse who struggles to keep people alive, utilizing one of the same family of drugs used in lethal injections. She is not convinced that her husband is as numbed as he seems, and says that this apparent lack of emotion may be "his own protective mechanism in distancing himself" from these executions.

Timing Is Everything

In England and France, executions were commonly set for just after daybreak or at midday. Until recently, however, modern-day executions in the United States usually took place during the dead of night. Between 1977 and 1995 more than 80 percent occurred between 11 P.M. and 7 A.M., with half of these occurring between midnight and 1 A.M. Reporters stationed outside often described prison lights flickering in the night sky at the moment of electrocution. Inside, inmates were said to be terrified by the dimming lights.

Many explanations have been put forward for the timing of death in America. Execution warrants commonly set a specific date, and scheduling the killing close to midnight gives the state nearly twenty-four hours to do the job, allowing for malfunctioning equipment or last-minute stays. Irrespective of this, however, many state laws require executions in the middle of the night—for example, between midnight and 3 A.M. in Delaware and Louisiana, and between 12:01 and 6 A.M. in South Dakota. Indiana, Wyoming, and Kentucky, among others, insist that executions occur "before sunrise."

It is hard to fully explain the reasons for this particular demand, although it may be rooted in a belief that the condemned prisoner should not live to "see another dawn." There is, as well, a special aura to an execution that takes place under cover of darkness. After an unprecedented 1 A.M. hanging in Connecticut in 1894, the

Hartford Courant observed, "To hang a man one hour after midnight may not be, to the person chiefly concerned, a highly important difference as compared with the customary daylight hour for such performances. . . . But to the general public the idea of a midnight execution probably adds a little to the horror of the experience."

More practical reasons are offered for nighttime executions in modern times. Fellow inmates, often upset or angered by an execution, are more likely to be asleep. Journalists and other witnesses are less likely to attend, and the execution can take place after the eleven o'clock TV news and past the deadline for the morning newspapers. Protesters are much less likely to show up outside the prison at late hours.

In recent years, however, as the pace of executions picked up, some states, including Texas and Virginia (both very active), started moving away from after-midnight executions. Texas, for example, now schedules lethal injections for 6 P.M. This is meant to accommodate more easily the schedules of prison personnel, judges and attorneys, witnesses and journalists alike—and cut down on overtime pay for guards and other members of the execution team. A spokesman for a prison in Texas put it this way: "It was just a strain on everyone to be up to all hours in the morning trying to make clearheaded decisions."

In 1996, after an execution in Arizona that took place at 3 A.M. following a flurry of last-minute appeals, Supreme Court Justice Sandra Day O'Connor complained that dispensing justice at that hour of the morning "is difficult to say the least, and we [the justices] have an obligation . . . to give our best efforts in every one of these instances." Arizona subsequently switched its killing time to the afternoon, causing the attorney for a recently executed prisoner to comment, sardonically: "About the only difference with 5 P.M. is, once the flurry is over, the restaurants are still open."

What this time shift may also signal is that executions have now become so routine in certain states, and meet so little public protest, that prison officials have little reason to hide, or appear to hide, them in the middle of the night. The columnist Molly Ivins, of Texas, recently observed, "We are dead-beddin' folks down here so fast and so often, you can't get people to raise an eyebrow over it, no matter what the specifics of the case are." But the move to 6:00 P.M. executions in Texas, writes John Bessler in his book *Death in the Dark*, "hardly signals a new openness insofar as execution proceedings are concerned; it merely represents the voices of lawyers and judges who do not want to stay up late or be awakened in the middle of the night to decide a convicted murderer's fate. Throughout America, executions remain private affairs, and the public continues to be kept in the dark about the nature of executions"—another way of saying that executions are increasingly constructed in ways that curtail genuine witness.

Limiting Witness

Reporters, indeed, are allowed to write anything they like, but controversy remains over new limits on what they are permitted to observe and hence describe firsthand.

After Oregon's first execution in thirty-four years, in 1997, state correction officials proposed curtailing the media's right to attend executions—changing rules that stated that they "shall" be present to they "may" attend. A state ACLU director commented, "It's clear that the corrections department would just as soon not have anybody there." An official at the Potosi Correctional Center in Missouri admitted that the prison would like to "avoid" having to deal with reporters at all, "but they're not going to go away. The key is knowing how we can handle the press in an effective way that will be to our benefit." Customs have changed since Gary Gilmore's execution in 1977, when reporters were allowed to approach the chair where he had sat facing the firing squad, "and rubbed our fingers around, feeling for ourselves how deep and wide the death holes were," as the columnist Bob Greene observed.

In many states, witnesses are ushered to their seats just moments before killing time, a curtain is hastily opened, and they see the prisoner already strapped into an electric chair or on a gurney, with plungers ready to be pushed or switches thrown. "I mean, newspaper reporters or the public or whoever gets to witness an execution should not believe that they have seen much of what was done to the person if they witnessed only the last five minutes," complains the well-known attorney David Bruck, who has defended many on death row. "It's so quick and antiseptic."

When lethal injections are botched, curtains are immediately drawn, leaving witnesses in the dark. This happened in Texas in 1988, when the IV in Raymond Landry's arm broke loose, spewing the fluids around the chamber. The curtain remained closed for fourteen minutes, then reopened, and soon enough Landry was dead. Several dozen reporters were invited to witness the execution of William Bonin, California's first lethal injection. Bonin, however, was hidden behind a sheet for almost the entire procedure, until just seconds before the lethal substances started flowing. The scribes also had their wristwatches confiscated, apparently so they could not time how long it took Bonin to die. This caused media organizations to sue for greater access, and led to protests that continue to this day in California.

Officials explain that they are just considering the privacy and dignity of the condemned, and attempting to protect the anonymity of members of the execution team. They argue further that the preparations for a killing are no different from the routine insertion of IVs in a hospital—further testimony to the medicalization of the procedures. The media feel that these are phony excuses, arguing that there is no evidence that a single guard has ever been threatened for taking part in an execution, and that in any case the public is entitled to know exactly how the death penalty is implemented.

In 1997 a federal judge in California ruled in the media's favor, declaring that the public must "have sufficient access to the execution . . . so it can understand and appreciate the nature and quality of the event." He called capital punishment "the ultimate exercise of state power" short of war. But the following year, an appeals court overturned that ruling, asserting that the media had at most a "severely limited" constitutional right to view executions; in fact, reporters had no greater right of access than the general public.

States have attempted to restrict not only what journalists see but what condemned prisoners say. In many states, prisoners are no longer allowed to make a spontaneous final statement just before dying, or are allowed to do so only within strict parameters.

In the distant past, at large spectacles and at small private executions as well, the prisoner was made a part of the ritual by being offered an opportunity to deliver his final words. But as executions have become more mechanized and orderly, that privilege has been gradually withdrawn—there is a fear that he will say something nasty that will disrupt the proceedings. So in some cases he is only permitted to write out, not speak, his last words. Written or stated, they tend to be something like, "I'm going to a better place." This phrase has become almost a cliché, but it does mean something, as many of the prisoners have undergone spiritual counseling and are desperate to find some means of transcendence in their otherwise hopeless fate.

When a prisoner says he's going to meet God, everyone's role in the execution can be somewhat eased, even affirmed. This is most directly true in the case of the prosecutor and representatives of the state; it is also true for the prisoner himself (to the extent that he means what he says), and his family and attorneys. There is a sense of such scenarios still being scripted, so they take on some of the ritual of the executions of earlier centuries.

Yet the ritual has become increasingly empty. The last words are no longer a significant part of the ceremony. In Ohio, for example, the condemned man's written statement is subject to editing by prison officials, and it is not released until after he has died (i.e., he speaks from the grave)—or it is not released at all if the warden objects to its contents. This policy was adopted to spare victims' family and friends from potentially profane or abusive remarks by the inmate, a spokesman for the Ohio prison system explained. Being allowed to offer his "last words" was a privilege, not a right, for a condemned man, he added. Critics argue that the state was afraid the prisoner might spark the public conscience with a powerful statement. An ACLU attorney in Toledo called the move unconstitutional "censorship" and, with telling psychological accuracy, said that the prison was trying to "pretty up the whole process, sanitizing the execution to distance all of us from it. It dehumanizes even further the person you are executing."

Conflicts in Witnessing—and "Voyeur's Guilt"

Among the most affecting commentary by witnesses comes from the family members of murder victims, who have the opportunity (as many demand) to stare the killer in the face and then watch those features freeze up in fear or go blank in the moments before and after life ebbs from his body. Often they try to make some emotional sense out of the prisoner's final words, as the condemned man meekly asks for forgiveness, proclaims his innocence, or arrogantly chastises the family members for lobbying for his death.

These families have much more complex feelings than is generally recognized (as we explore in Chapter 8). Typically, they attend an execution, leave the chamber, and tell reporters at a press conference that while they were not happy to see another human being die, it was quite deserved, and they hope the death will bring "closure" to their long and painful struggle for justice. Their survivor mission is resoundingly clear in its quest for justice, but not without ambivalence in its quest for revenge.

It is hard for anyone to contest their views, or to be certain that one would not feel exactly the same way in their position. Yet there are people in much the same position—family members of other murder victims—who nevertheless oppose the death penalty. What unites all types of witnesses, however, is a profound sense of unease, no matter how much they may have wished for this moment to arrive. In his book *Among the Lowest of the Dead*, David von Drehle observed:

> Most execution witnesses have never met the man they are watching die, and for them these few moments when the prisoner studies the room are often the hardest. They feel a pang of voyeur's guilt. Strangers in the audience often secretly hope the prisoner's gaze will not settle on them; they dread being caught watching the utter humiliation of another human. They dread questions in the prisoner's eyes: Who are you, and why have you come? The nakedness and shame of a man [in this position] is far more profound than mere nakedness of the flesh—his sins, his brokenness, his fear, his helplessness, all these are laid bare before the watching eyes of strangers.

A Virginia prisoner in 1998, asked if he had a final statement, replied, "Personally, yeah. Why was all them sick people looking at me through that glass?"

This "voyeur's guilt," which we observed earlier in Turgenev and Tolstoy, contains a painful question: Do I, or does anyone, have the right to watch the killing of a helpless human being? Even a murder victim's family cannot fully avoid that inner question.

Richard Moran, a professor of sociology, who witnessed the execution of Thomas Barefoot in Huntsville, Texas, later disclosed, "The condemned man looked right at me. Only a few feet separated us. I was afraid he would try to touch me. . . . I was ashamed—ashamed of being there and afraid that he would ask something of me. I was an intruder, the only member of the public who had trespassed on his private moment of anguish. In my face he could see the horror of his own death."

Occasionally, strong opponents of capital punishment choose to attend an execution, even while denouncing executions, in order to better understand what they protest. Invariably, they emerge more committed than ever to abolishing the practice. Christopher Hitchens, after writing many articles against the death penalty, witnessed Samuel Lee McDonald being "snuffed, choked off and put down" by lethal injection in Missouri, and then wrote:

> In my time, I have seen people die and be killed, in sickness and in warfare. . . . It's all, in a manner of speaking, part of life. But I feel permanently degraded and somewhat unmanned by the small part I played, as a complicit spectator, in the dank and dingy little ritual that was enacted in that state prison cellar in Missouri. The medical butchery of a helpless and once demented loser . . . made neither society nor any individual safer. It canceled no moral debt. It was a creepy, furtive, and shameful affair, in which the participants could not decently show their faces or quite meet one another's eye. I don't know that I shall ever quite excuse myself, even as a reporter and writer who's supposed to scrutinize everything, for my share in the proceedings. But I am clear on one thing. Death requires no advocates. It is superfluous to volunteer for its service.

David Bruck, attorney for Terry Roach, whom he watched die in the electric chair in South Carolina, later declared that everything that happened "made you think we ought not to be doing it. It's an ugly, very ugly ritual." He elaborated:

> I suppose it would be better to say that the actual killing was incredibly disgusting, painful, gruesome, and gory. . . . But, to me, the truth is, it was not as bad as that, and at the same time it was much worse. It was as easy as shutting a drawer or snapping one's fingers. To me, what it said was that they take a living person, who took twenty-five years to create, and within just a few seconds they converted him into a piece of junk to be wrestled out on a stretcher and carted away. To me, the message was that human beings are junk and if you don't believe it—watch this. It is a completely incomprehensible miracle how a human being comes into this world . . . but to snuff one out, it is nothing. It is the easiest thing. Murderers can do it, anyone can do it. We can

do it. Watch this! It was banal. It was dehumanizing. Not only to him. It was a ritual which denied the importance and uniqueness of any of us.

Posttraumatic Shock

Among this small community of anti–death penalty witnesses, Richard Stetler, chief investigator for the Capital Defenders' Office in New York, is almost unique. He is one of the few Americans who have ever been allowed (indeed, ordered) to film an execution, and his memories of the experience still devastate him.

It was 1992, and Stetler, a native of Philadelphia then living in California, was assisting the defense team for Robert Alton Harris, who had killed two high school students in San Diego in 1978 and was slated to become the first person executed by California since the late 1960s. Judge Marilyn Patel had stayed the execution, ruling that the gas chamber inflicted cruel and unusual punishment. When another judge overruled this decision, Patel ordered someone associated with Harris's legal team to videotape the execution, to provide evidence for future appeals; she would keep the tape tightly sealed until it was needed. The someone directed to shoot the tape was Richard Stetler. He had never witnessed an execution before, and he had not planned to attend this one.

When he arrived at San Quentin on April 20, 1992, the night of the execution, he noticed a change in the air. He had visited the prison, as part of his defense work, almost weekly for months and had always been treated cordially, but this evening prison personnel greeted him with hostility (he later told us) and even subjected him to a strip search. Overall, this was a "traumatic" experience. "They were treating me like the enemy, like a terrorist or at least someone out to thwart the execution," he reports. Of course, he *had* been trying to thwart it, through legal channels, for a long time—but a camera seemed to make him more dangerous. As he set up the video equipment, an officer started yelling at him, claiming that he was deliberately delaying the procedure while they wanted to "get on with it—that is, kill someone," as Stetler later put it. He was perceived as an enemy of the process.

Close to 4 A.M., Harris was hustled into the room, seemingly relaxed and ready to meet his fate, and inserted in the gas chamber, which struck Stetler as some kind of "science fiction device." San Quentin has an unusually large viewing area, with banked seating, and about fifty witnesses waited there. Harris was quickly strapped into the seat. Two minutes later, seconds before the poison tablets were to be dropped into the sulfuric acid, the phone rang—just like the movies—and he was soon, surreally, escorted from the chamber, under his own power. A U.S. Court of Appeals judge had granted another stay.

"It was, to say the least, an unusual experience," Stetler told us, "seeing a man about to be deliberately killed, then not." Perhaps the guards were right, after all: Stetler's fumbling with the video equipment may have saved Harris's life. Stetler felt elated, but the execution had only been delayed, not canceled. Awaiting the outcome, Stetler spent a few quiet moments with prison guards who had been ordered to keep an eye on him. He came to feel a strange bond with these men, sensing that none of them really wanted to be there either.

A couple of hours later, his final appeal denied, Harris was guided back into the gas chamber—now a broken man—and strapped in the seat once more. He mouthed his last words, "I'm sorry," in the direction of the father of one of his victims. This time the poison pellets were dropped, and Stetler was forced to watch as he videotaped Harris fighting for breath, lapsing out of and into consciousness, an artery in his forehead practically exploding. "It was hard to watch him struggling for air, for life," according to Stetler, "so you want the suffering to be over—that is, you want him to be dead." Still, a kind of "slow-motion effect" made the process seem to go on forever, although only minutes had passed. Stetler not only wanted the man's suffering to end, but also wanted his own pain in watching the suffering to stop.

Then it was over, Harris was declared dead, and the witnesses filed out. Only Stetler remained, for he had been ordered to tape the aftermath as well. He waited in the room as the guards vented the deadly fumes from the gas chamber into the outside air. Harris, meanwhile, remained strapped into his death seat, his head slumped on his chest—a piece of meat, bizarrely frozen in time, as if in a diorama or wax museum, Stetler felt. One of the guards informed him that the fumes remaining in a prisoner's lungs were still lethal. When the chamber door was opened, the guard walked up to the dead man and unceremoniously gave his chest a hard poke with the end of a mop handle, forcing out some of the poison. By this point, the morning shift at San Quentin had arrived and some of the guards were making macabre jokes.

"I suppose I could have feigned illness and left," Stetler says. "One of my friends had witnessed an execution and told me he threw up uncontrollably afterward. But I felt it was my job to be there, collecting important evidence. At the same time, however, I felt utter despair and a sense of failure, on multiple levels."

Stetler was even less prepared for what followed. Although he had long opposed the death penalty, he was surprised at how much that feeling was deepened by actually witnessing an execution. "I had opposed it mainly intellectually and philosophically and in the abstract," he explains. "I wasn't prepared for how horrific it was, my raw, emotional response. I went home feeling soiled."

For months Stetler suffered nightmares. When we spoke with him, more than six years after Harris's execution, he said the memories were no longer so "intrusive" but could still be triggered when he reads something about one of his current cases that reminds him of Harris or his family background. "Talking with my colleagues [in death penalty work] helps a lot, but it's sort of like those who survive combat," he explains. "You feel you can only talk to someone else who has witnessed an execution; no one else really knows what it's like. The gas chamber 'visuals' may be particularly bad—it's what they call in veterinary ethics the 'aesthetics' of euthanizing animals. But even talking to people who have witnessed lethal injections, the impact is still tremendous." Stetler retains a survivor's indelible image—an image of ultimate horror, in this case, a man gasping for breath, a blood vessel in his forehead seemingly about to explode.

Still, for Stetler, there was this positive result: the execution had the animating effect of making clear to him the terrible fact that one of his clients could be killed, that death is not abstract, and that at the end of a seemingly endless legal struggle a lifeless corpse awaits.

The Camera as Witness—Live from the Death Chamber

The debate over televising executions began in the 1950s, with proponents including death penalty advocates and abolitionists alike. They argue that transmitting the event over the visual medium, the main entertainment and information outlet for most Americans, would reveal to a wide audience the profound truth about executions (though they differ about what that lesson would be). Skeptics charge that it would trivialize or sensationalize the killing process, and brutalize a society already in many ways inured to pain and suffering.

While in no way resolved, this debate tells us much about the broader issues surrounding the witnessing of executions.

Decades ago, the debate centered on the medium of radio. Lewis Lawes, the warden at Sing Sing who was opposed to capital punishment, advocated "bringing home, in the most vivid manner not only the news of the accomplished fact of an execution, but also the actual procedure followed in carrying out the death sentence." In his famous book *20,000 Years in Sing Sing*, Lawes predicted what such a broadcast would be like and how listeners might react. He imagined, for example, a tired businessman observing, "They do these things quickly nowadays," and a teenage boy feeling sympathy for the condemned man as "a brave fellow, all right."

Years later, early in the television age, Norman Mailer, tongue in cheek, took the idea a step further, calling for an end to capital punishment except in states that agreed to allow the condemned man and his executioner to hold a fight to the finish on national

television, like gladiators of old. "Since nothing is worse for a country than repressed sadism," he observed, "this method of execution
would offer ventilation for the more cancerous emotions of the
American public."

Soon after the Supreme Court cleared the way for executions to
resume in the mid-1970s, a television reporter in Dallas sued the
state for the right to film them. The Newspaper Guild and other
press associations filed briefs on the reporter's behalf, arguing that
television "conveys more of the content or reality of the experience
than a written or spoken description can." A federal judge ruled
that officials could not declare executions unfit to be seen, since
they are sanctioned and paid for by the public. But the U.S.
Supreme Court subsequently ruled otherwise, on grounds that the
public could be fully informed about the event without televised
images. A Harris survey found 86 percent of the public against
cameras in the death chamber.

Phil Donahue tried unsuccessfully to televise an execution in
North Carolina on his talk show in 1994, with the cooperation of
the condemned man, for the benefit of 20 million viewers. Donahue, an opponent of the death penalty, wanted to test both the deterrence theory (allowing people to "watch these people fry right
here on television") and the First Amendment, but a federal court
dismissed his suit.

The debate over cameras in the death chamber has simmered
ever since, with officials and judges routinely rejecting requests for
live or taped coverage by reporters who argue that if advocates are
so sure executions act as a deterrent, they should be happy to stage
them for millions to view. Senator Mark Hatfield, an opponent of
capital punishment, introduced a bill to *require* TV coverage of
federal executions. A measure promoting televised executions in
California gained strong support in the state legislature before ultimately failing. (Some Democrats feared that it might encourage
more executions.) In 1994 a district court judge in Ohio ordered
an execution televised on the basis that "we have everything else on
TV [so] let this be shown so the public can see there is swift and

certain punishment." That year, NBC aired a TV movie, *Witness to the Execution*, which concerned a fictional (but all too plausible) pay-per-view event.

Indeed, some tough-minded prosecutors, such as Harry Connick, the district attorney of New Orleans, favor televising executions to bolster the deterrence argument. Dana Rinehart, mayor of Columbus, Ohio, once predicted that "you'd have an overnight reduction in homicides" following the first televised execution. Other supporters for this idea, however, come from surprising corners. Sister Helen Prejean, author of *Dead Man Walking*, is convinced that "if executions were made public, the torture and violence would be unmasked, and we would be shamed into abolishing executions." Inmates occasionally ask that their deaths be taped to prove (after the fact) that the killing represented cruel and unusual punishment. This had a startling result in Maryland in 1993, when a U.S. District Court judge approved the filming of Donald Thomas in the gas chamber—inspiring the state legislature to pass an emergency bill approving lethal injection as an alternative to gassing.

After fading from the headlines, the idea of "prime-time execution" gained national prominence again when Timothy McVeigh was sentenced to death. Phil Donahue sparked the discussion once more, pointing out that television routinely airs videotapes of robbers holding up convenience stores and that these holdups sometimes end in shootings and death. He also mentioned the film of President Kennedy's assassination, and dead bodies created by plane crashes, earthquakes, and terrorist bombings. "Why the piety when it comes to the state's taking of a human life?" Donahue asked. And why the double standard that allows print journalists, but not other media, to cover the execution?

Mike Wallace of *60 Minutes* took a similar approach ("I would watch it, I would broadcast it"), denouncing the hypocrisy of showing so much gore on television but not airing "clean" lethal injections. If capital punishment is a deterrent, he insisted, let's show McVeigh's passing to millions and see what happens. CNN's

Greta Van Susteren endorsed this idea, calling executions "a barbaric procedure" which should not be hidden; if televised they might change people's views and the death penalty "might go out of existence."

But Mike Wallace's boss, Don Hewitt, disagreed, saying he did not hunger for ratings that badly and the whole idea was "in terrible taste." Cokie Roberts of ABC, who describes herself as against the death penalty, declared that society "is barbarous enough" without adding to it visual images of actual executions, which would only encourage voyeurism of a sadistic kind. Geraldo Rivera also attacked the idea. Ernest van den Haag, a relentless advocate of capital punishment, warned that televised executions would take the focus off the murder victim and shift sympathy to the inmate's "pitiable fear" in facing cold, certain death. Polls seem to show steady public opposition to the idea. A Time/CNN poll found that 80 percent of Americans opposed airing McVeigh's execution.

The debate over televising McVeigh's demise soon faded, but this notion, once considered extremist, continues to gain serious attention, as broadcast organizations in several states frequently petition for the right to cover executions, up close and personal, as the saying goes. A lawmaker in Louisiana in the spring of 1999 renewed the call for televised executions, to show potential murderers the consequences of their actions—explaining that this is the only way to re-create the days of hangings on the courthouse steps.

The KQED Case—Murder, Theater, and "the Sleaze Factor"

The fullest and most revealing struggle over televising executions emerged not from the sound bites surrounding McVeigh's execution but from a lawsuit in California. The case of public television station KQED versus San Quentin's warden Daniel Vasquez "points up the crucial connection between murder and theater—between death imposed on a human being by another human being, and dramatic spectacle," Wendy Lesser wrote.

Robert Alton Harris's execution in 1992 drew unusual attention. KQED, a public television station in San Francisco, sued Warden Vasquez for the right to bring a camera into the execution chamber, arguing the media's right to use all the "tools of its trade"—whether notebooks or television equipment. As Wendy Lesser has noted, the case was explicitly about the First Amendment but implicitly about much more—our feelings about the death penalty, about violence on television, about the difference between real and stylized killing, publicity versus privacy, "spectacle versus procedure." It combined "everything from bad taste to moral depravity, from empathetic concern to sentimental illusion, from fear and disgust to curiosity and hilarity; and it did so in a way that had no easy answers."

A KQED director argued that what people found most disturbing was not the "sleaze" factor but the camera's ability to make plain that "it's our government carrying out the executions, and the only reason our government does it is, we vote for it, so at some level we all carry the responsibility for it."

Both sides in the KQED affair took the moral high ground, stressing the seriousness of "taking the life of another human being," as Warden Vasquez said. From one perspective, this required full coverage; from the other, it meant (in the words of Vasquez) that executions be carried out with "tactfulness and precision." KQED based its case largely on recent Supreme Court rulings permitting cameras in courtrooms. The state responded by claiming that televising the event would violate the condemned man's right to privacy, would inflame inmates and possibly cause rioting, and might unmask the executioners. (KQED offered to electronically obscure the faces of all participants.)

These arguments aside, what the case really came down to was its impact on the death penalty itself. Supporters of the death penalty mainly opposed the idea, although some endorsed it on grounds that it would deter future murders. Abolitionists, overall, seemed to favor TV coverage. KQED's attorney William Bennett Turner acknowledged that television coverage would indeed be "degrading in some way for all," but for him "the evil is the death penalty. . . . The only thing worse than having executions and watching them is having executions and having our government prohibit us from watching them."

Anthony Lewis, the *New York Times* columnist, on the other hand, argued that television would not make the killings real for a viewer but would trivialize them—reduce them to the level of entertainment "to be clicked on and off." He was afraid that people would "invite friends over for beer, pretzels and death." A *San Francisco Examiner* journalist said that by the time the tape was shown over and over on news programs, and made its way onto music videos on MTV, "it will lose its power to scare us and stop us and make us think about, hey, we're killing a guy today."

KQED argued that killings were nothing new for television, listing examples ranging from reenactments in dramas such as *L.A. Law* to the occasional suicides and murders on live TV. But the comparison was, to say the least, disingenuous, since what gives executions in America their troubling singularity is that they are the only killing occasions that are both real and scheduled.

At the heart of the matter was what sort of "witness" a camera would make. Would it be neutral or interpretative? Thorough or highly selective? The attorney David Bruck opposed KQED, arguing against the distortions of the camera. The few seconds of the inmate's death that the public would see are "almost no part of the death penalty," he argued. Capital punishment was mainly the process of an inmate waiting for death for years; and the suffering of his family. "None of that would be on TV," Bruck complained. "The truth of the matter is that the public's imagination of what this must be like is much truer than what they would see on TV."

Finally, the judge ruled against KQED's right to videotape Harris's execution. The media, he decided, had a right to attend an execution but "no *special* access," and he agreed with the state's justifications. Richard Stetler, as we've seen, was later ordered to videotape this execution; but that was on different grounds (to illustrate possible cruel and unusual punishment), and the tape was never shown and in fact was soon destroyed. Ironically, the media covered Harris's last gasps in the gas chamber so thoroughly and explicitly, even without the aid of cameras, that many observers complained that it frightened and appalled men, women, and children. There was a panel discussion on television afterward about whether in the end Harris *jerked* or merely *twitched*, whether he lowered his head once or in agony moved it right (or was it left?). A videotape might have settled these debates—as if they mattered. David Bruck was undoubtedly right: the death penalty is not about those final twitchings.

Tabloid TV or Moral Drama?

Many foes of the death penalty do not believe that televising executions would rally the public against the procedure. Richard Dieter, director of the Death Penalty Information Center, predicts that it would bring no lasting change. "There would be a big tabloid-TV splash the first time," he observes, "but the shock value would quickly fade. It, too, would become ordinary."

As ever, Phil Donahue remains an angry advocate for televised executions. He renewed the call as recently as November 1999 in an appearance on *Larry King Live*. He believes it's a First Amendment issue, and he calls executions "the people's business"—arguing the media should have "team coverage of what's happening in the thirty-eight states in our union that now promote the death penalty" rather than allowing the killings to proceed "in the middle of the night when nobody is watching."

He claims that many in the media supported CBS's *60 Minutes* when, with great fanfare near the end of 1998, it broadcast its now-famous tape of Jack Kevorkian injecting a dying man with chemicals—killing him on camera. Some critics claimed that the program was in it only for the shock value—that is, for ratings—but, in a sense, *60 Minutes* seemed to make too *little* of this groundbreaking event. It scarcely filled one of its regular fifteen-minute segments, and then CBS cut to a commercial and on to Andy Rooney. What was most surprising, and troubling, was how dull and methodical and unaffecting the death—from lethal injection—appeared on the screen, and how quickly it was forgotten by commentators and, one suspects, by viewers as well.

At the close of *Pictures at an Execution*, her study of the KQED case, Wendy Lesser predicted that someday a television station would be allowed to televise an execution, but she comes down against the idea. Few viewers, she explains, would be willing to put themselves at moral risk and implicate themselves; instead, they would interpret the execution in a "false" or "merely sentimental" way. The problem is, "we do not have enough self available to risk, to implicate, in a theater of actual murder. . . . We cannot afford to risk what that kind of theater would cost us." She is saying that we lack the psychological capacity to witness executions in that fashion—implying that it would make us into numbed bystanders because we would protect ourselves extravagantly, rather than truly grappling with what is at stake: killing, and our relationship to it.

In the end, the debate over cameras in the death chamber is essentially a diversion from the real issue. The camera can be nothing more than a limited and unreliable witness, for the death chamber contains images and truths that are unmanageable, and unpredictable, in their human impact.

8

MURDER VICTIMS' FAMILIES

And if you wrong us, shall we not revenge?
—The Merchant of Venice, *Act III, Scene 1*

WHEN someone is murdered, he or she inevitably leaves behind shocked, angry family members who take a profound interest in the identity of the murderer and what happens to him once he is apprehended, incarcerated, and convicted. In most cases, family members attend the trial. In the penalty phase, prosecutors often urge them to testify in favor of the death penalty for the defendant. Usually, family members comply and later repeat their anguished, moving pleas to journalists.

After a jury orders an execution, family members then begin a kind of deathwatch, though not always a passive one, which can stretch for years, even decades. Many keep close tabs on the appeals process and do everything they can (usually not very much) to speed it along, protesting at courthouses and in the media when the system perversely seems to postpone or deny what they consider ultimate justice. Finally, at the end of the long, dark road, an execution date may be set. Many of the family members elect to attend the execution ceremony, to which they often respond with public expressions of satisfaction or relief.

This reflects the typical family experience surrounding the death penalty in America, but increasingly other voices are being heard.

Throughout our history, some murder victims' families have called for sparing the life of a murderer, although such pleas generally were ignored. Today, more of these families are speaking out, even campaigning against all executions, and getting more attention from the media and the public.

Those close to a murder victim, especially family members, are survivors desperately seeking some kind of meaning for what has been a morally unacceptable and psychologically unmanageable encounter with death, loss, and cruelty. In a sense they are forced to do the "survivor work" of the entire society. They have to decide whether or not to view the killer as the embodiment of evil—or to experience him as a human being who performed a very evil act. The former stance is more self-protective, but it can be difficult to maintain, especially as an execution approaches. The latter stance, considering the whole person, can be more painful and more confusing, as it often inspires pity for the murderer or the tragedy of his life—and his possible death.

Those family members who speak out for sparing the murderer are entering into a survivor mission of commitment to life and opposition to killing of any kind. They feel a need to restore a moral universe, as a first step toward their own healing.

"I'll Give Him the Lethal Injection Myself"

Survivors who favor capital punishment are hardly monolithic. Some attend executions, others do not. Some speak to reporters, even seek them out; others refuse all comment. Some express the wish that they could kill the condemned man themselves; others express some sympathy for the killer and claim no satisfaction in knowing that he has breathed his last. Many of these differences are dictated by how strongly the family members hold on to their understandable feelings of anger and their need for revenge.

Before Hammurabi's Code, a victim's family would punish the perpetrator themselves, and often the punishment was disproportionate to the offense. Even today, some family survivors say they would volunteer for the post of executioner. A mother in Ohio who has waited fifteen years for the killer of her two daughters to die claims that she would have "no problem injecting him myself. I could lie down and have a good night's sleep, knowing that justice had been done." The brother of a young black man beaten, stabbed, and strangled by a white racist attended the perpetrator's electrocution in Alabama in 1997, yet still felt justice was not done. "I would rather have had [him] in a ring one-on-one for fifteen rounds," he comments, "and whipped him the way he whipped my brother." The father of a young man murdered in Boston laments that Massachusetts does not have the death penalty, adding, "I'd be the first one to pull the switch. I'm sorry. Some may disagree with me, that's perfectly your right. But I've lost a son I can't replace." The widow of Dr. Barnett Slepian, the abortion doctor slain in Buffalo in 1998, said of the sniper, "If I have anything to say about it, I'll give him the lethal injection myself." One of her sons, she added, felt lethal injection was too good; he wanted to see the man "tortured."

A survivor of the terror attack in Oklahoma City said that he wished the authorities would amputate one of Timothy McVeigh's legs and then suspend him over sharpened, growing bamboo shoots which would slowly penetrate his body. Rick Bragg, covering McVeigh's trial for the *New York Times*, described the families' hatred as being "like a laser, glowing, steady, narrow." In talking to the press, many of them claimed, however, that they were looking not for revenge but for justice.

Responses to watching the actual execution vary. The twin brother of a murdered woman in Florida, witnessing the killer expire in the electric chair, murmured "Yes . . . yes" as the 2,300 volts of electricity made his body snap back in the chair, and he thought to himself, *Die, you monster.* After watching the man who killed her daughter die in Texas, the mother told reporters, "I feel happy, I feel wonderful. I want you all to know I'm very glad." The sister of a murder victim in Texas carried two framed photographs into the witness area of the execution chamber in 1997, saying that she wanted her sister's face to be "the last thing he saw, because we all know he was the last thing she saw."

Family members often complain, however, that the prisoner's passing is far more peaceful and dignified than the death of the person he killed. When they attend lethal injections, they wonder why they aren't allowed to see the prisoner brought into the room and strapped down, terror presumably etched on his face. "You stand there and you watch a man take two gasps and it's over," a mother of a murder victim complained.

In an unusual case, the son of a murder victim in Oklahoma complained when the killer said he wished to forsake his appeals and be swiftly executed. He wanted the prisoner to suffer through years behind bars anticipating his death. "He's almost robbed us of the punishment," he explained.

Vengeance Is Mine

> Since murder is the worst of all crimes in this nation, this needs the worst of punishment. It is not murder, it is punishment, it is justice.
>
> —*Fred Goldman, murder victim's father*

Much can be said about the families' need for vengeance. The word revenge is related to *vindicate, judge,* and *vendetta.* Rather than renounce one's anger, as in forgiveness, one pours that anger into action, or desired action, against the sinner. The goal is a moral and emotional balance. When family members speak of direct palpable revenge—the wish to pull the switch themselves—they seek to impose on the murderer a death in some way equivalent to that of his victim. A young man who had lost his mother in a murder in Texas said, as the killer neared his execution date in 1998, "It sounds really mean, but I'd almost like to see him beg for his life."

There is a distinction, however, between *revenge* (a visceral, personal desire to hurt the wrongdoer) and *retribution* (a deep-felt desire to uphold society's values), although they are psychologically related. Retribution derives from the Latin *retribuere*, which means "to pay back." It means punishment that is deserved and appropriate to the crime. Revenge combines retribution with the infliction of an extreme punishment. It requires that the murderer truly suffer for his evil act, which could extend to a painful and violent death (hanging or electrocution). The lethal injection confuses everything, because it seems to snuff a life out so gently that nothing much has happened.

Both retribution and revenge are closely related to *vindication*. Survivors of Auschwitz who had experienced the cruelty of Dr. Josef Mengele wanted him brought into the dock so that they—and the court system—could confront him, and make what he had done officially known. Whether or not they held vengeful fantasies of watching him killed or tortured (most apparently did not), they wanted public acknowledgment that they had suffered, and they wanted their rights and needs respected. Family members of murder victims require similar vindication—recognition by society of their loss and their pain—whatever form of justice they seek.

The power of this constellation of retribution, vengeance, and vindication must be recognized by any student of the death penalty. And one must imagine one's own feelings following the brutal murder of a wife or husband, a child or parent. Speaking subjectively, we believe our own reactions would include an impulse to kill the murderer, literally tear him apart, along with wanting to subject him to every kind of extreme legal punishment, including a cruel form of death. We believe we would then step back from these feelings and take a stand against execution—but can we be certain that we would be able to tame the emotional need for vengeance?

Feelings of vengeance can play an important psychological role in the survivor's healing process. These emotions can be channeled into trials and other legal procedures in ways that help survivors deal with their pain and loss. Bringing the victim's picture to the execution, as some families do, makes it explicit that revenge has been achieved and justice has been done.

But those who nurse feelings of vengeance for years as appeals drag on may be unable to carry out the necessary psychological work of mourning. Other emotions, such as so-called "survivor guilt" (for having outlived the victim or having failed to protect him) may contribute to a need to cling to vengeance. Healing is never complete, but as it progresses, the quest for justice often depends less and less on feelings of vengeance.

The Elusive Search for "Closure"

Some family members, while supporting the death penalty, do not campaign for it or celebrate when it is carried out. They balance their anger with sad resignation. The mother of a young man slain in Texas said, after the execution of his killer in 1977, that she was "glad it is over," but she added, "I doubt I will feel better." The brother of a murder victim in Nevada explained that he would attend the execution, but "it's not anything I look forward to." He simply wanted to bring "closure" by being able to tell the rest of the family that the execution "really did happen." An Arkansas woman told a state prison board in 1998 that she did not want to attend the electrocution of her mother's killer, but she hoped to be in the building "and watch the lights flicker. It would say, 'The end. It's closure.' "

Betty Slusher refused to attend the execution of the killers of her husband in South Carolina in 1998. "I thought when this day came that I wouldn't be sad, that I would be happy, but I am sad," she revealed. "Let's face it, we're taking two men's lives." While she declined to witness the execution, she planned to stand vigil outside—saying that she wouldn't let anyone curse the killers or make a spectacle of their deaths. "My husband," she explained, "would want those men to go out with dignity."

At the end of this process, family members hope to be released from their nightmare. That is what they mean by "closure." A victims' advocate in California who has counseled many families explains that some put their entire lives on hold awaiting resolution.

A mother in Texas still awaiting the execution of the man who killed her son in 1976 says, "Most of my life it seems like I've been in the justice system. I can't go on with my life. I can't close that chapter until he's put to sleep. It's been twenty-two years." The sister of a California murder victim explains, "It is a sad and sick situation. You want to throw yourself across the bar [in the courtroom]. But you don't know who to choke first." They hope the execution will enable them to go on with the rest of their lives.

But punishment does not necessarily bring peace. The mother of the dead baby girl who became a symbol of the Oklahoma City tragedy—after a photograph of her in a firefighter's arms appeared around the world—applauded the death penalty for Timothy McVeigh, calling it "an eye for an eye," but confessed, "I don't think there will ever be closure."

Some family members, however, view the very existence of the death penalty as the reason for this extended agony. In this view, capital punishment makes closure more difficult, not less so. The brother of a murdered Texas man explained, "From the trial, which would be brief and simple without the ancillary issues raised by the death penalty, through the years of appeals, the death verdict forces the survivors to relive the experience. It hangs over the heads of the survivors as well as the killer, albeit in different ways." Prosecutors, he complained, "simultaneously tell the survivors that they are not responsible for seeking the death penalty and that their support is necessary to obtain it."

The respected authority on the death penalty, Hugo Bedau, describes another problem with closure by execution. He tells the story of a man who called for the execution of his son's murderer, in the name of closure, but afterward discovered that he wanted the killer back—for he no longer had anyone to project his anger toward, and now he internalized it all. Ironically, the execution had ended the killer's suffering but not this survivor's. When deprived of anger (after the killer has been executed), one may feel still greater confusion and helplessness.

Psychologically speaking, "closure" is an illusion. Family members' sense of horror, pain, and loss may gradually diminish over time, but no outcome can enable them to be free of such feelings. They remain death-haunted survivors throughout their lives.

Perhaps that's why the father of a murder victim in Virginia, preparing to attend the execution of the killer, barked at a reporter who had asked him if he sought closure. "Don't use that word with me," he said. "I hate that word. I don't know who made that word up. There is no closure. So many people don't seem to understand that. There is no closure."

Getting Off the "Train of Hatred"

Recognizing that closure, in these cases, is impossible, some family members come to oppose executions. They may also feel that taking the life of the perpetrator—even if it roughly balances the scales of moral justice—does not undo the past and creates even more grieving family members. The mother of a young girl murdered in Pennsylvania expressed all these sentiments when she said, "The gaping wound will never heal. And it is because of this intense pain that I have come to know that I would not, and could not, inflict it on another mother. . . . Justice would only be served if, in taking his life, Aimee could come back to life, and that is impossible."

These feelings cause some of the families to resist, even resent, the usual pressure from prosecutors to speak out against the perpetrator. The daughter of a woman slain in Michigan observed, "I know that wanting revenge can be a normal, initial response to a terrible crime. Society seems to say if we loved our family member, we need to kill to prove it. Too often families are swayed by prosecutors to want the death penalty to avenge our loved ones. The law should not use our grief at such a vulnerable time to further such an agenda." The daughter of a murdered Texas woman revealed that the more the prosecutors fed her "anger and hatred," the more it intensified "the pain in my heart."

Some even intervene on behalf of the killer. In November 1999, the father of Matthew Shepherd, the young gay man murdered in

Colorado, appeared at the sentencing of the convicted murderer in Denver and said that although he was not opposed to capital punishment, and would "like nothing better" than to see the perpetrator die, he believed it was "time to begin the healing process, to show mercy to someone who refused to show any mercy." The prisoner was then given a life sentence instead of the death penalty. Addressing the killer, the father, Dennis Shepherd, said, "May you live a long life and may you thank Matthew every day for it."

Occasionally, members of a family are split over the death penalty for the person who took away a loved one. This played out most publicly in the case of Karla Faye Tucker in 1998. Two of the relatives of the murder victims in that case attended the execution and appeared on national television afterward, with sharply different emotions, one applauding Tucker's death, the other decrying it. The media circus surrounding the event tended to obscure the family drama.

Another case later that year revealed the same conflict, in a much quieter setting. In Virginia in 1989, a man named Dennis Wayne Eaton had gone on a killing spree, and his fourth and final victim was a state trooper named Jerry Hines, who had pulled him over on Interstate 81 for a traffic violation. Surrounded by police, Eaton turned the gun on himself, but survived a head wound. He was convicted of murdering the policeman and sentenced to die.

Hines's widow, Carol, the mother of his three children, called for an execution, and then waited impatiently for it. She said she believed in an "eye for an eye" and hoped it might bring "closure" for herself and her children. As a firm execution date for Eaton approached in June 1998, Carol Hines decided she would attend the ceremony, with her oldest son, Justin. But the murder of Jerry Hines not only ended his life, it divided his family. For his sister, Maria Hines, came not only to oppose his killer's execution, she forgave him, and even offered to serve as his spiritual adviser in his final moments.

Maria Hines is a former nun and retired mental health professional in Louisville, Kentucky, now in her mid-sixties. She considers the two most difficult decisions in her life her decision to leave the convent and "deciding to go public on the death penalty," especially since other family members didn't agree with her and could not "understand my position." Maria Hines says she has always opposed the death penalty, but can't quite explain what her opposition stems from, explaining that she received no particular direction during her Catholic upbringing. After her brother was killed and Dennis Eaton was convicted, she did some soul-searching, questioning her principles. She felt bad for Eaton's family, for they would "have to go through what I was going through." Confused, she said little publicly.

Finally, in 1996, she saw the movie *Dead Man Walking*, and its graphic execution scene made her sob and realize "the depths of my feelings. I thought, 'I've got to do something.' " The next day she joined a local abolition group. The following year, she decided she would contact Eaton personally and tell him she had forgiven him, and that "forgiveness is not in the heart, it's person to person if that's at all possible." In her first letter to him she explained that "forgiving you is not only for you but also for me—and what it would do to my own soul if I refused to forgive."

The killer and the survivor started corresponding, and Eaton eventually asked her to visit him. About a month before his scheduled date with death in June 1998, the two met for six hours. Eaton expressed remorse but claimed that he had been "saved" by God and that the person who killed several people was "gone."

When Dennis Eaton's execution finally arrived, on June 18, 1998, Maria was not there to witness it. Her request to serve as Eaton's spiritual adviser was turned down by the state, with a spokesman explaining that officials feared she had an "ulterior motive" and might try to disrupt the lethal injection. On the night of the execution she stood outside the prison at a prayer vigil with about twenty others, and she helped form an "honor guard" as Eaton's body was taken from the prison. The next night she took part in a memorial service. After Eaton died, other family members again expressed confidence this would produce closure. For Maria, however, a sense of "indescribable peace" could come only through "forgiveness."

A quite different case, ending in a similar result, revolves around one of the condemned murderers, Robert Lee Willie, featured in Sister Helen Prejean's book, *Dead Man Walking* (and the model for the Sean Penn character in the film based on it). Debbie Morris, a woman he raped and nearly murdered when she was sixteen, eventually came to write a book called *Forgiving the Dead Man Walking*.

After barely surviving her ordeal, this young woman felt betrayed by God and turned to drink. She hoped the cloud would lift after Willie's execution, but instead her anger, drinking, and panic attacks continued. Later, however, through her experiences teaching children with behavioral disorders, she began to feel compassion for Willie because of his troubled background. She came across a book called *Forgive and Forget* by Lewis Smedes in which he observes that if we don't forgive the "monsters" among us, we give them a power they should not have—"to keep their evil alive in the hearts of those who have suffered most." Like Maria Hines, Debbie Morris felt that her refusal to forgive "meant that I held on to my pain, my shame, my self-pity."

Now in her mid-thirties, married and with two children, she explains, "Justice didn't do a thing to heal me. Forgiveness did. . . . I've seen mankind's idea of ultimate justice. I have more faith in God's." Morris believes that the evil she experienced would never lose its grip on her until she forgave Willie. "I want people to know," she insists, "that our only hope for healing is not in the legal system."

Debbie Morris and Maria Hines represent a version of Christian forgiveness which is almost the reverse of a survivor mission of revenge. It embraces the principle of love as a basis for forgiveness. In forgiving the murderer, one seeks forgiveness for one's own sins. But forgiveness is difficult to achieve and sustain, particularly when the original act of murder is so egregious. We suspect that Maria

Hines and Debbie Morris must frequently fend off feelings of anger and revenge. For them too, closure is probably illusory, at least in pure form, but they have achieved through forgiveness a measure of psychological comfort.

The psychology of Christian forgiveness is complex. There is the phrase from the Book of Common Prayer: "And forgive us our trespasses, As we forgive those who trespass against us." In that sense there is a direct, even numerical, equation between forgiving others and having others forgive you, with the implication that everyone is part of a vast psychological and moral equilibrium.

Then, in the gospel of John: "Father, forgive them; for they know not what they do." Sin or evil becomes a form of moral ignorance. By asking God to forgive, the implication is that one has no such power oneself. But what one can do is to "give up" or "give away" one's anger or judgment of others. James Hilton, the British novelist who imagined Shangri-La, clarifies one of the difficulties: "If you forgive people enough you belong to them, and they to you, whether either person likes it or not." So much continuous psychological work is required on both sides that the sinner and the forgiver become locked in a lifelong bond.

Like Maria Hines and Debbie Morris, many of those shaken by murder who come to oppose capital punishment do not take what could be called a "political" stand or even denounce the death penalty in all cases. They simply express a personal view and sometimes briefly gain prominence in the media. As Timothy McVeigh awaited sentencing for the Oklahoma City bombing, for example, Bud Welch was selected by reporters as an earthy representative for the view that McVeigh's life should be spared. In truth, they didn't have much choice: among the victims' families, there appeared to be few others willing to express that sentiment, at least publicly.

For the first few months after his daughter was killed, Welch had favored death for McVeigh. But then he recalled his daughter telling him that she opposed the death penalty, since it "doesn't teach us anything but hate." He also came to believe in the

Catholic teaching that everyone has a soul and can be forgiven, and though he hadn't yet forgiven McVeigh, he wanted to at least make that struggle—and he couldn't do that if the man was dead. After all, he observed, "hate and vengeance" caused the terrorist bombing in the first place. Besides, Welch believed in the sanctity of life even for "mass murderers." Killing McVeigh would not bring his daughter back, and parents of other murder victims had told him that their grief did not end with the execution of the killer.

Welch, the owner of a service station in Oklahoma City, called for others to "get off the train of hatred." Only a few additional family members seemed to take his side, but because of his own loss and his gentle approach, Welch did not stir up much anger. Then, remarkably, Welch traveled to upstate New York to meet Timothy McVeigh's father after seeing him on television and recognizing the "extreme pain" in his eyes. After visiting with him at his home, Welch said that Bill McVeigh was an even greater victim of the bombing; while Welch can talk about what a wonderful daughter he lost, McVeigh must "live in shame."

Hatred is a difficult emotion to live with, but it may be less painful than confusion, meaninglessness, or guilt, and it may be seized upon, individually or collectively, to avoid those other emotions. Hatred can be a means of reestablishing meaning through angry or violent impulses directed at the murderer, or sometimes at defense lawyers or judges or those who advocate abolishing the death penalty. The difficulty is that hatred is unreliable for *maintaining* psychological or moral equilibrium.

That is why some family survivors want to "get off the train of hatred" and replace it with alternative meanings and practical actions. Gail Willard, mother of a college student raped and murdered in Pennsylvania in 1996, has directed her anger not toward revenge or seeking execution but toward campaigning for parole reform (the killer in her case had served only twelve years of a previous life sentence). This is how she "fights despair," she explains.

A state representative in New Hampshire recalls, "Prior to my father's murder I had evolved a personal set of values that included a respect for life and an opposition to the death penalty. For me to change my beliefs because my father was murdered would only give over more power to the killers, for they would take not just my father's life, but my values. The same is true for society. If we let those who murder turn us to murder, it gives over more power to those who do evil. We become what we say we abhor."

The Abolitionists

Other survivors, however, have universalized their personal reaction against a specific execution, and taken it into the political arena.

The groundbreaker was Marie Deans. She has been compared to a character out of classic southern fiction, a slim, gray-haired, compassionate but tough-talking woman from Louisiana who gave the authorities hell in Virginia. Her life in the abolition movement began after her mother-in-law was murdered. The killer was not given the death sentence, but the murder inspired Deans to learn more about capital punishment, and when she did, she founded Murder Victims' Families for Reconciliation (MVFR). They act not only as a support group for relatives of both the slayers and the slain, but as grassroots activists against the death penalty in America. Later she became a paralegal and director of the Virginia Coalition on Jails and Prisons, and served as legal or spiritual adviser to thirty inmates on death row. Asked to explain why she remained committed to this work for so long, she replies, "I have the need to understand why we are so good at passing on violence and so poor at passing on love." She thus connects her abolitionist advocacy with the continuity of human life and the flow of generations.

Dozens of survivors of homicide soon joined Deans's group, which now claims 3,000 members, and some of them (including Bud Welch) speak at rallies and meetings around the country and appear on national television. Every year the group sponsors a Journey of Hope, an intensive speaking tour in a particularly execution-prone state, such as Texas, California, or Florida. In the political struggle against capital punishment, survivors like Marie Deans play a vital—perhaps *the* vital—role. Advocates of executions often challenge their opponents on grounds that they simply don't know what it's like to lose a loved one to murder. MVFR members do know what it's like.

Occasionally, personal conflict erupts between victims' families. Advocates of the death penalty sometimes charge that Marie Deans lacks credibility because she did not lose a blood relative, only a mother-in-law; or they charge that MVFR members do not love their slain family member enough, or at least aren't proving it. MVFR stalwarts like Bill Pelke really make them shake their heads. He has exchanged more than 200 letters with the young woman who, at the age of 16, murdered his grandmother, and helped get her death sentence commuted to sixty years in prison.

Norman Felton, a TV writer, director, and producer best known for the series *The Man from U.N.C.L.E.* and *Dr. Kildare*, has campaigned against the death penalty in California for years. His activities began after the savage murder of his daughter, her husband, and the couple's nine-month-old daughter. Felton somehow found sympathy for the drug-addled, impoverished killers in this case, and for others like them who, he said, have no reason to live and no place to turn for help—for whom "inhumanity" becomes the norm.

Then there is, perhaps most dramatically, SueZann Bosler. As a young woman she watched a man, high on drugs, named James Campbell stab her father, a minister, thirty-six times, in Carol City, Florida, then turn the knife on her, an attack she barely survived (she still wears two plastic plates in her skull). Bitter and angry at first, she had come to forgive Campbell by the time of his sentencing. She asked the jurors to spare his life, and they did. She recalled that her father had once told her, "If anyone ever were to murder me I still wouldn't want him to get the death penalty." Now she looked right into Campbell's eyes and told him, "Your life is as valuable to God as anyone's"—a painfully straightforward rejection of any doctrine of life unworthy of life.

Later, however, he was resentenced to die in the electric chair. Bosler declared that if the state killed him "we become murderers, too. We become just like him. I don't want to be like him. I don't want his blood on my hands." Bosler persistently pushed her views into court, as Campbell's case came up on appeal or resentencing. In 1997, at another hearing, when it appeared she would not be allowed to speak, she hired a victims' rights lawyer to defend her right to appear. The prosecutor responded, "This is not an individual decision for SueZann to make. This is a societal decision, and society has spoken in this case."

Bosler won the right to testify, however, and though she was prohibited from speaking directly for mercy, her demeanor on the witness stand spoke volumes. Campbell was then sentenced to life without parole. Even that outcome did not resolve the tensions between Campbell and Bosler. He was grateful, but he made no effort to thank her, and he refused her requests for a meeting. This must have wounded her, and she insisted she still wanted to learn from his own lips why he had killed her father. But in a twist on the familiar argument, she said that sparing, not taking, the life of the killer would finally bring her peace.

9

PUBLIC OPINION,
PRIVATE DOUBTS

PUBLIC opinion drives the death penalty in America more than it does virtually any other issue. Legislators and candidates for office embrace capital punishment, convinced that it would be political suicide to act otherwise. Even Supreme Court justices have cited polls in ruling that the electric chair and gas chamber do not represent cruel and unusual punishment.

Understanding what the public actually believes about the death penalty is obviously critical, for any dwindling of public support endangers the entire process. Support for capital punishment (as we have observed) has quietly declined in recent years, falling to 66 percent in a Gallup poll of February 2000—down from 80 percent six years earlier. A poll for ABC News in January 2000 pegged support for executions at 64 percent (with 27 percent opposing and 9 percent undecided). Yet despite this trend, and despite the extensive evidence of ambivalence that we have uncovered, there remains a mythology of decisive, unyielding support.

Why is public acceptance—and the myths surrounding it—more crucial to this matter than to almost any other legal or political issue? Perhaps it's because the death penalty exists uneasily in any contemporary democracy. Emerging democratic attitudes, over centuries, mostly militate against state killing. Politicians sense this, even if they do not articulate it. On other issues they are more willing to do the unpopular or expedient thing, but they are reluctant to carry on their own shoulders the ethical and psychological burden of state killing. They require that the wider public share the burden.

Killing by the state has become part of a social routine in recent years. It is what America does—what all of us are part of. The various components of the execution machinery have found a functional equilibrium, what physicists call a "steady state." The politicians, the prosecutors, the wardens, and their staffs have all converged in a continuing killing project. There may be a lull in executions, or a sudden rash of them, but this collective entity is always in place, always at the ready.

The execution protocol is so impressive that it tends to obscure the underlying conflicts and confusion. There are few other issues about which one can find such a gap between prevailing assumptions and actual public feelings. One reason for this may be the totalistic aspect of the execution itself. That is, in order to justify so absolute an act there is a need for an exaggerated claim of public support.

Consider the declaration by the California pollster Mervin Field, who could find no issue "where the public opinion is so fixed and hardened as it is in favor of the death penalty now. The idea of not wanting to convict an innocent person has gone by the wayside, and now the public wants an eye for an eye." An article in *The New York Times Book Review* recently began, "Americans want capital punishment, and they want it now." But is this really what the public wants? If so, is the support as overwhelming as politicians and journalists seem to believe? Or is this, indeed, a tragic American myth—with deathly consequences?

False Assumptions

The death penalty has been around since this country's founding, and has often been the subject of withering debate, so one would expect a long record of intense probing of public opinion. But this has rarely been the case. As we have seen, some states abolished capital punishment, or reinstated it, on the basis of perceived public sentiment, but these were highly speculative and politicized readings, not based on actual studies. Focus groups, where analysts study the views of a small sample of citizens, are almost unheard of in this area.

That leaves scattered public opinion surveys, dating back to 1936. The first poll followed the execution of Bruno Richard Hauptman, convicted killer of the Lindbergh baby, which came on the heels of sensational Depression-era cases involving the outlaws John Dillinger, Bonnie and Clyde, and Pretty Boy Floyd. Gallup found that Americans favored death for murder by a surprisingly modest 61 percent to 39 percent. It took another poll a year later, then ignored the question for sixteen years. When it returned to the subject in 1953 (at the time of the Rosenberg spy case), support had jumped to 70 percent. But then support started falling, at least partly because of controversies such as the Caryl Chessman case, reaching a historic low point of 42 percent in 1966.

Two years later, in considering whether citizens who opposed executions could serve on capital juries, Justice Potter Stewart observed that a panel consisting solely of supporters of capital punishment would "speak only for a distinct and dwindling minority." As opposition to executions, revealed by opinion polls, grew throughout the 1960s, state and federal courts ruled time after time in favor of prisoners' appeals. The path to *Furman* was set, and in 1972 the Supreme Court temporarily halted all executions. All the justices endorsed the view that the legality of capital punishment hinges on its acceptability under "contemporary standards."

Four years later the Court changed direction and the death penalty was reinstated. By then, polls were showing that support for capital punishment—after years of rising crime rates—had risen from 42 percent to about 60 percent, a sea change in just ten years. Writing for three of the judges, Justice Stewart again cited public opinion in affirming that the Eighth Amendment (rejecting cruel and unusual punishment) must draw its meaning from the "evolving standards of decency that mark the progress of a maturing society." And how was one to judge that? Among the "objective indicia": public opinion polls. Stewart, in fact, mentioned recent Harris and Gallup surveys to support his conclusion that "a large proportion of American society continues to regard [the death penalty] as an appropriate and necessary criminal sanction."

What was surprising was not that the Court could be influenced by public opinion, but that justices would explicitly cite polls, and even rely partly on them, in a profoundly important decision. Apparently the ultimate arbiters of legal principle are uneasy about taking substantial responsibility for the ultimate penalty. "We have been told," the death penalty scholar Hugo Bedau observed, "that the justices of the Supreme Court, like the rest of us, read the headlines; but it is rare for the Court to trot them out so blatantly as it did here."

In the following years, with polls finding public support for executions creeping upward to 70 percent and beyond, the Court reaffirmed the death penalty and continued to cite opinion polls as a factor. It's possible that referring to polls comes not only from a wish to share the burden of killing but also from a calculation of what a "healthy" society collectively "needs" in the way of retribution. Such estimates, whether or not articulated, are partly drawn from polls. Even then, evaluations of social health can be no more than suppositions. The "objective indicia" are hardly objective.

And what if the results of polls, in any case, are misleading—ambiguous and open to critical interpretation? What if support for capital punishment is a mile wide and an inch thick? And what if the overall poll numbers showing support for the death penalty continue to decline, or even plunge dramatically? Might the Supreme Court, as in *Furman*, respond to public trends and halt executions again even before state legislatures seriously discuss the subject?

Gaps

To begin to understand what surveys already suggest, below the surface, one must study the smaller print. Opinion analysts, for example, have pointed out that national polls on this subject reveal an unusually large number of "undecideds," an average of about 9 percent per poll over the years, indicating that large numbers remain either highly conflicted or distanced from the issue.

One obstacle in looking beneath the superficial raw numbers in surveys is that Americans have not often been asked to rank the *salience* of the death penalty as an issue. Recent election polls that bothered to probe this question, however, invariably failed to find the death penalty near the top of voters' concerns. A close study of the survey results reveals several other fascinating patterns.

Race. The biggest gap in surveys divides African-Americans and whites. Whites who support executions far outdistance blacks in every poll. In January 2000 a survey for ABC News found a difference of 31 percentage points: 69 percent of whites but only 38 percent of blacks favored the death penalty. Analysts have attributed this gap to the disproportionate application of the death penalty to blacks, and to the liberal views of many African-Americans. We also suspect a deep-seated distrust of white authority—especially of whites' "ownership" of blacks' deaths.

Income. Another partial explanation for the "race gap" can be found in the fact that those in high- and middle-income brackets are much more likely to support the death penalty than those in lower-income groups, although the poor still support executions by a narrow margin. The analyst T. W. Smith attributes the economic gap to "a greater interest in order" by financially secure groups and a belief among the poor that there are "class inequities in the judicial system in general, and the punishment of capital crimes in particular."

Gender. There's always been a gender gap on this issue, but until recently it was rather slight. In fact, the narrowness of the gap was a little surprising. If, as some claim, the persistence of the death penalty stems from residual, frontier-related machismo, one would expect a great disparity between men and women. And there tends to be a very large gender gap on most issues of "violence" or "war-peace" and related matters. Perhaps the death penalty, as compared with these questions, has more to do with a kind of primal, retributive anger that has little gender distinction. But what was once a narrow divide is now growing. That same ABC News poll found male support at 73 percent, female at 56 percent.

Political Party. Since the mid-1980s the divide between Republicans and Democrats on this issue, once narrow, has widened considerably, to the region of 20 percent—greater than any gap except the racial one. Still, Democrats back executions by better than 5–4.

What can be said, then, in summary, is that blacks, the poor, women, and Democrats are much more likely than others to oppose the death penalty. And even among the majority that continues to back executions, as we'll soon learn, nearly half actually prefer another form of maximum punishment.

Pro and Con

> Revenge, nobody wanted to use the word revenge for years. I mean, how can you suggest civilized folk would want to take revenge? What's wrong with revenge? It's that anger that makes a society.
>
> —*Bill Kunkle, prosecutor in Illinois*

Beyond endorsing or opposing capital punishment, how do people explain their position to researchers? Deterrence was once the factor cited most often by proponents of the death penalty, but lately they have abandoned this approach almost entirely. And no wonder: in 1995 a poll of police chiefs found that even they did not think the death penalty deters homicide.

Indeed, since 1981, surveys show that Americans now cite retribution (or "a life for a life") as the main reason for supporting state killings—by a strikingly wide margin over every other explanation.

The Gallup poll of February 2000 found 46 percent citing this; 12 percent stated that it "saves the taxpayer money," and only 8 percent mentioned deterrence. Vengeance or retribution, in fact, may have always been the main motive; perhaps, in talking to pollsters in the past, supporters found it socially correct, or less embarrassing, to emphasize deterrence. More recently, norms have changed, and retribution is now more socially acceptable. Unfortunately, few polls have probed deeply behind the "life for a life" argument, although one survey found that 34 percent admitted that the execution of a murderer could give them "a sense of personal satisfaction."

Why do others, that growing minority of about 25 to 30 percent, say they clearly oppose the death penalty? Surprisingly, many do not quickly mention its unfair or arbitrary application, or the possibility of executing innocent men and women. Most often they simply tell interviewers: it is wrong. They say that it is "wrong to take a life" or that "taking a life solves nothing," or they explicitly mention a religious motive, typically that "punishment should be left to God." Polls find that about two-thirds of the opponents would still oppose the death penalty even if it were shown conclusively that it was a deterrent; the concept of taking one life to save others does not sway them.

So by the 1990s a true impasse had been reached, with both sides seeing the issue in terms of right and wrong. Two researchers who have studied this issue deeply, Phoebe C. Ellsworth and Samuel R. Gross, describe it this way: "For both proponents and opponents, their preferred rationale is moral and absolute; they are taking a stand that brooks no argument and suggests little differentiation. Such attitudes," they add, "are unlikely to be swayed by arguments based on factual information."

We cannot be surprised that some form of "moral absolute" readily forms around the death penalty, given the totalistic nature of executing a human being. What may happen is that advocates divest the death penalty of its extremity by separating the *principle* from the *actual killing*. From a distance one can maintain the luxury of absolute advocacy without taking in the absolute consequences of that advocacy.

The McVeigh Exception

If not McVeigh, who? If not now, when?

—Newsweek

The trial of Timothy McVeigh for the Oklahoma City bombing brought such advocacy of the death penalty into stark relief.

After McVeigh's conviction in June 1997 a brief national debate on whether he deserved the death penalty ensued. It was rather one-sided, of course, but the poll results were intriguing. Here was a case involving a mass murderer, a domestic terrorist, a slayer of 168 people (including fifteen children) who showed no remorse. He was an easy target for proponents of capital punishment. Thus the polls would finally reveal exactly how many Americans truly oppose the death penalty *on principle* and in all cases—for if you could not endorse executing McVeigh, who could you imagine killing? "It's like asking those of us who oppose the death penalty, what about Adolf Eichmann or Adolf Hitler?" Hugo Bedau observed. "This is the kind of case where people who oppose the death penalty are willing to make an exception or are troubled by their inability to explain why they're unwilling to make an exception."

Bedau surprisingly revealed that he is one of those willing to make such an exception—with a certain condition. "Speaking personally," he said, "I'll let the criminal justice system execute all the McVeighs they can capture provided they sentence to prison [not death] all the people who are not like McVeigh. That would cover 99.9 percent of the people on death row."

So what did polls about McVeigh consistently find? A little less than 20 percent of the various samples opposed sending McVeigh to his death (with women only slightly more likely to take this position). This, then, seems to be the "moral floor" for capital punishment in America.

The McVeigh case, indeed, tests everyone's beliefs concerning the death penalty, but if one opposes the death penalty in general as inhumane, one must oppose its use with even the worst among us (e.g., McVeigh). And to be consistent, one would also have to oppose the execution of a Hitler or an Eichmann—no matter how evil or genocidal his actions. Yet when Hugo Bedau, so prominent a voice in opposition to the death penalty, tells us that he would let the system execute the McVeighs if it would refrain from executing others, we must take that stance seriously. He is in effect making a deal with society: ban executions in general and I will give you a few mass murderers as occasional exceptions.

Then there is Norman Mailer's argument to the effect that society may *need* to execute people who have committed the most extreme crimes in order to give expression to passions of retribution, and thereby maintain its own broad equilibrium between retribution and compassion. As Mailer puts it:

Living amid all the blank walls of technology, we require a death now and again, we need to stir that foul pot. Needless to ask why we must learn over and over again that execution by the state looses a stench deeper than murder on the street. As the Greeks taught us, a country without a theater that dares to be profound is a weak society. . . . Maybe a little capital punishment is better for society than a lot of repressed insanity.

Bedau may also be saying that his own inner balance—and that of many people who oppose the death penalty—could be enhanced by allowing for such exceptions. In that way, such people are no longer held to the kind of tyrannical moral principle that would not permit them to execute even Hitler, and they are relieved of their self-condemnation for holding fast to this principle. McVeigh's crime was so evil that activists in Italy, usually the most vociferous concerning American capital verdicts, were silent. Indeed, McVeigh is an ultimate test of anyone's psychological capacity to oppose execution.

Chaos and Control

Beyond a doubt, a large number of Americans support the notion of capital punishment, but do they really know what they are endorsing?

When he concurred in the *Furman* opinion in 1972, halting executions temporarily, Justice Thurgood Marshall offered two serious critiques often quoted since. He charged that the American public was woefully ignorant about certain "facts" about capital punishment—that the death penalty does not deter and that it is administered in a racially discriminatory way. He also held that *if* these facts were widely known, "the great mass of citizens . . . would conclude that the death penalty is immoral and therefore unconstitutional."

Nearly three decades later, large numbers of people freely admit (to pollsters) that the death penalty fails to deter and often discriminates against the poor and minorities. Yet they have not responded in the way Thurgood Marshall imagined. They still support capital punishment.

The explanation may be that, starting in the 1970s, vast numbers of Americans became angry about high crime rates, the threat of violence, and the rise of youth gangs. They grew tired of waiting for someone to do something about the problem and therefore embraced the ultimate penalty for such behavior as a kind of grim compensation. "It is not hard to understand why many people support capital punishment even though they believe it does not deter crime and is not fair," Ellsworth and Gross observed. "The death penalty is concrete, it is forceful, and it is final (which nothing else seems to be); it is *something*, and being for it means that you insist that *something* be done."

So much so, that people may suppress their belief that the death penalty is unfair or ineffective. This view of executions places them in a larger social trend toward absolute but edgy solutions that eliminate uncertainty, hesitation, and above all ambiguity.

Cultural common sense, what some call "folk wisdom," holds that criminals are not punished severely enough and are released from prison far too soon because the criminal justice system is overly concerned with defendants' rights and not concerned enough about victims' rights and crime in general. Why the swing to punitiveness? A beginning answer takes us once more to a desperate longing for *control*—to a fear that not only crime but just about everything else in one's life may be *out* of control.

When everything feels out of control, punishment of others can have special appeal as a clear-cut, hard-hitting solution that seems to put society back together. You may correspondingly feel that you can better hold yourself together. Life without parole is appealing because it, too, can convey a sense of control while stopping short of killing. But for many, such a resolution lacks the power of an actual execution for combating what is perceived as chaos. Or, to put the matter another way, chaos—the absence of control—is perceived as so advanced that only a decision for death can stem it.

Bolstering this view, media coverage dwells on the nightmare cases of parolees who murder again and ignores statistical evidence that those cases are rare. This encourages politicians to take a get-tough posture on crime and the death penalty in their election campaigns, even as the murder rate declines in many parts of the country. This played out most dramatically in the Willie Horton case during the presidential campaign of 1988. Focus group data at the time suggested that the Horton episode tapped into a broadly shared culture of mistrust on issues of crime and punishment. This distrust does not depend on accurate knowledge, or even on any awareness of policies leading to a parolee's early release from prison. Instead, it settles on the message that dangerous criminals are simply not being treated harshly enough.

It will be interesting to see whether the recent plunge in the murder rate in many parts of the country leads to diminishing support for capital punishment—or whether support for executions will grow if many feel that the death penalty itself was one of the *reasons* for that decline, even if no evidence supports that association.

Contradiction and Hypocrisy

We often hear the blanket assertion that "overwhelming numbers of Americans favor capital punishment." More accurately, they favor it for some crimes but not others. Indeed, a recent *Newsweek* poll found the usual high percentage favoring capital punishment but discovered that nearly half want to reserve it only for the most brutal murders. Most advocates of the death penalty strongly favor discretion. Americans want judges or juries to be able to make exceptions and spare many murderers the ultimate sentence.

Still, that leaves the question of which crimes should be classified as capital. There is murder—and there is *murder*. Different degrees of murder, calling for penalties of varying harshness, have always existed in America. Executing those who slay policemen or prison guards has always ranked high, but support has grown for the notion of killing those who commit murder during rapes, hijackings, and terrorist acts or while sexually molesting a child or dealing drugs. But the percentage of support for executions in each of these cases still varies widely, and there is no general agreement on which crimes deserve death.

The public also differentiates between categories of people who commit murder, but interestingly, in some cases, prosecutors and judges seem not to be listening. Support for executing mentally retarded prisoners has always been relatively low—21 percent in 1987, for example—but this has not prevented the execution of many brain-impaired inmates, and the Supreme Court ruled in 1989 that this does not offend public standards of morality. Concerning female killers, surveys find little sentiment for a double standard, but judges and juries rarely sentence women to death. The strong sympathy expressed for Karla Faye Tucker can't be attributed solely to her religious conversion and her likability—these qualities are shared by many condemned males who draw little compassion.

Amid all the ambivalence, ambiguity, and contradiction of the many poll findings, one result is particularly telling: polls consistently show that people are much more likely to support the death penalty in general than when it is applied to a specific case (except for archvillains such as McVeigh). This is not surprising. It is always easier to justify the *idea* of executions than to kill a specific human being. (Nazi doctors in Auschwitz could support killing Jews but would frequently protect Jewish doctors whom they had come to know.) This has to do with the hierarchy we described earlier: the contrast between theoretical decision-makers who put the death penalty in place and the hands-on executioners (broadly defined) who undergo its psychological and moral consequences.

The level of support often dips still further where a local case is involved, or where one has some tangential connection with a defendant, as we observed when a hometown jury refused to sentence Susan Smith to death for drowning her two children. As we have seen, unwavering views suddenly become unpredictable when an average citizen is asked as a juror to mete out the supreme penalty—that is, to become a vital cog in the death machine. "Americans seem guilty of vast hypocrisy," a writer for *Newsweek* observed after the local jury failed to send Susan Smith to death row. The justice system promises the death penalty but rarely delivers it. Citizens support capital punishment, he noted, "but frequently refuse to apply it when they are confronted with a face, a name and human frailties that, however lurid, bear at least some resemblance to their own."

The Alternative—Life Without Parole

As we've seen, a still strong majority of Americans endorse the idea of executions, and many of them embrace the idea ardently. But does this mean that they *prefer* executions over other ways to punish or control a convicted murderer? Recent polls provide valuable insight into this crucial question. One might expect that few advocates of executions would be open to alternatives, since, in the view of many, moral "justice" (or simply an eye for an eye) requires the death of the prisoner. Polls increasingly find, however, that a majority of Americans accept or even favor life in prison without parole as an alternative to execution.

Until recently, in most states, there was no such thing as life without parole. Life sentences rarely meant life, even for convicted murderers, who often served twenty or more years but eventually emerged from prison. The public has always known this. If anything, people have known it too well, often getting the impression (from the media or politicians) that most murderers are walking around free again a few years after their conviction. Although this does happen, it is rare in the case of first-degree murder. But because of well publicized (and well manipulated) episodes such as the Willie Horton case, the public, understandably, did not consider life in prison as a valid alternative to execution.

In recent years, however, more than two-thirds of the states have enacted procedures for sentencing murderers to life without parole—meaning exactly what it says, with no chance that the convict will ever get out. (The killer of Bill Cosby's son received this sentence.) At the same time, pollsters began listing life without parole as an alternative to executions in their surveys, and coming up with interesting results. In many surveys, support for executions as the preferred choice for punishing those convicted of capital crimes suddenly dropped below 50 percent.

That ABC News poll of January 2000 that found support for the death penalty at 64 percent showed it falling off to 48 percent when life without parole was an option. These numbers are in line with Gallup surveys and local polls in New Jersey, North Carolina, Virginia, Ohio, California, and other states. A survey conducted by a research center at Southwest Missouri State University in November 1999 found that in Missouri—which has one of the nation's most active death chambers—support for executions dropped from 78 percent to 47 percent when life without parole was added to the equation. A poll by the *Chicago Tribune* in March 2000 found virtually an even split in Illinois—43 percent backing executions, 41 percent life without parole.

Most damaging to the myth of "overwhelming support" for capital punishment was the ABC poll, which found several large segments of society showing strong preference for life without parole over executions. Democrats chose "life" over death by 53 percent to 37 percent, women by 50 percent to 39 percent, blacks by a lopsided 67 percent to 26 percent. In these groups, that is, latent opposition to the death penalty could be brought forth by the suggestion of a plausible alternative.

What's striking about these results is that they come at a time when many Americans still have little confidence in life without parole. The trend to life without parole is only a few years old, few know about it, and it will take many more years before most of the public believes that it is binding. Nevertheless, polls suggest that about one-third of those who support the death penalty already prefer life without parole as an alternative.

The Beginning of the End?

Rising sentiment for life without parole is already having an impact on capital verdicts, as we saw in Chapter 6. In fact, if the trend continues, it has the potential to produce a kind of grassroots abolition of capital punishment in practice even if courts and legislators refuse to end it in law.

Why do a growing number of citizens and jurors in capital trials seem to favor an alternative to executions? A recent *Newsweek* survey found that 73 percent of death penalty advocates worry about wrongful convictions, and 67 percent agree that poor people are more likely to be executed than others. In another poll, roughly half the sample decried the high costs of implementing the death penalty.

The analysts Ellsworth and Gross believe that a key reason for rising support for life without parole is that (like the death penalty) it embodies both incapacitation and a form of retribution. People want to be absolutely sure that murderers will never have a chance to victimize anyone else—or to lead a normal life. The recourse to life without parole suggests that it may serve as a kind of psychological bridge between opponents and advocates of the death penalty. One can embrace life without parole as a moral equivalent of execution. It is a severe punishment (if not extreme vengeance) and a guarantee of safety.

Yet there can be psychological difficulties with life without parole on both sides of the death penalty debate. For some advocates of executions it fails to provide a visceral sense of retribution. For some opponents it is too absolute, a punishment that permits no redemption. Many abolitionists, in fact, consider it no less cruel than execution, and therefore oppose life without parole—despite its political usefulness for them. Some warn that the policy of locking the door and throwing away the key could become all too popular, and impossible to reverse—because there are no dead bodies hauled out of execution chambers for Americans to feel guilty or uncomfortable about.

Nevertheless, the growing support for life without parole signals, we believe, the beginning of the end for capital punishment in our society. Consider the most recent survey in the enormous, and pivotal, state of California—which, as we have observed, is one of the few states that already has a fairly long track record with life without parole.

This survey of more than 2,000 citizens, conducted by the nonpartisan Public Policy Institute of California, found that, asked to choose between execution or life without parole for those convicted for first-degree murder, 49 percent picked death and 47 percent life. This in a state where, as we observed earlier, a leading pollster had recently declared that high support for the death penalty was "fixed" and the public "wants an eye for an eye." The poll director of the Public Policy Institute said that one poll does not prove a significant shift, but it does suggest that "opinions are not as hard on this issue as we might have thought they were."

The lesson for state lawmakers may be clearer, however. The message, according to Sherry Bebitch Jeffe, a well-known political analyst at the Claremont graduate school, is that elected officials "need not be so rigid in their stance—and their perception of the public's stance—on the use of the death penalty."

PART

IV

WHO

OWNS

DEATH?

10

THE END OF EXECUTIONS

A man who seeks revenge digs two graves.

—*Proverb*

CAPITAL punishment is a form of killing. However quick and efficient, an execution is a violent act that turns a human being into a corpse. Executions make use of a technical apparatus constructed solely for the purpose of killing an immobilized person. Behind that technical apparatus, and inseparable from it, is a bureaucratic apparatus that includes politicians and prosecutors, judges and juries, and wardens and prison guards, among others. The entire system, as we have seen, is geared to soften or eliminate the harsh truth of the killing. Nevertheless, we have found doubts and contradictions within all groups of individuals bound up with bringing about executions, caused by their unease with what we call *ownership of death.*

Such ownership is widely perceived as illegitimate by many of those involved in executions and has a corrupting effect on all who act on its behalf. It also contributes to an expanding dynamic of killing and then more killing, furthering a long-standing American habit of violence. Yet the strains in the whole system are now so great that we believe that, before long, the death penalty apparatus in our country will collapse under its own moral, psychological, and eventually political weight.

Uneasy Ownership

The assertion of death ownership by the death penalty bureaucracy is made on behalf of the state. Hence the condemned man, when ill or suicidal, is given medical or spiritual treatment to keep him alive until the state, and only the state, can kill him. Ownership of death is a form of entitlement to violence and killing. A similar claim has existed in a wide array of religious and political movements, in revolutionary organizations, and in warring states and ethnic antagonists. These groups, such as extreme American paramilitary units or Japan's fanatical Aum Shinrikyō cult, have killed on behalf of the "higher purpose" of their own belief systems.

In the United States we may say that the claimed ownership of death by the overall capital punishment apparatus creates a corner of *totalism*—claims of omniscient judgment—in a democratic society that prides itself on its openness. In that corner, the prevention of suicide prior to execution becomes a suppression of protest. On the other hand, authorities look more kindly upon the suicidal tendencies of condemned prisoners—most famously, Gary Gilmore—who drop their appeals and seek their own execution, becoming what are known as "volunteers," because they reaffirm the state's ownership of death and its entitlement to kill.

Defense lawyers who oppose the death penalty call into question that ownership and entitlement. In defending death row inmates, they are insisting that their client's death is not owned by any governing body. Some of them tell us of the anguish they experience over the possibility that insufficient energy or professional skill on their part could cost the life of a person who has become completely dependent on them for survival; who, whatever his heinous acts, has emerged as a human being with whom they have formed a bond. In that way the lawyer shares in the death encounter and its potential for guilt, as well as its potential for transcendent achievement when an execution is prevented or an innocent man is freed, an experience that one former death row lawyer described as "terrifying and stressful and beautiful." The beauty lies in the effort to reclaim a life.

From the other side, prosecutors reassert the state's dominion over death. They often see themselves as leading a crusade against evil, as "the avenging voice of the community." Yet, as we have seen, they distance themselves from the death they "own" and advocate in order to avoid discomfort and doubt. Judges, similarly, never claim full ownership of the decision, for that, they say, belongs to the jurors. Yet they must invoke at least partial psychic numbing, for they are painfully aware (in Judge Kozinski's words) that "signing the order will lead to the death of another human being—even a bad one."

Not surprisingly, the idea of being conduits of killing rests uneasily on the minds of most jurors, as expressed in the comment: "We felt the weight of just the word 'death.' " Jurors, like others in the execution sequence, can experience a desperate need to invoke a higher power, so that God and not the individual juror can bear the ownership of death, and perhaps the guilt for the legal killing. Hence the observation that a particular juror was incapable of uttering the word "death."

Virtually everyone involved at one time or another senses that there is something absurd about submitting the question of whether to put someone to death to the often nasty adversarial combat of the American legal process. The adversary system in general is a reasonable one and probably provides most citizens with as much justice as any other legal system. But it is a kind of game, a hard-fought contest—with its own rules, gambits, and tricks—which a lawyer or a prosecutor either wins or loses.

Judges and jurors can come to feel that this legal game, whose outcome depends greatly on the skill of the players, is a profoundly inadequate venue when it comes to deciding death—all the more so when defendants are assigned incompetent attorneys. Paradoxically, those who sit in judgment often immerse themselves energetically in the elaborate details of the game as a means of fending off awareness of what the game is really about.

To regain such awareness, a former prosecutor suggested that judges and juries be required to attend executions in order to focus their attention "on the gravity of their act." In the same spirit, Alex Kozinski, the conservative judge, criticized himself for his capacity to write opinions that "seal another human being's fate" while lacking "the courage to witness the consequences of my actions." Both men were insisting that all of us, particularly those who claim ownership of death, need to experience killing as the essential truth of executions—as opposed to a mere ritual at the end of a legal contest. In several states, in fact, the death certificate for the condemned prisoner lists the cause of death as "homicide."

Corruptions

There exists, as we have seen, a bureaucratic momentum toward execution. Though much in the process is highly random—according to region, race, class, and especially the quality of defense lawyers—political pressures and legal maneuvers may render it irreversible. The attorney Michael Mello refers to that kind of situation in describing his sense of desperation when preparing an appeal for a death row client before the Florida Supreme Court: "The justices are honorable people, but the system of capital punishment impelled them to kill an innocent man."

His only means of saving the man's life was to enlist the local media (thereby violating a court order) to reveal both the man's innocence and the corruption of the legal machinery. Other defense lawyers in capital cases tell of feeling tainted or dirtied by a system that is so random about killing people and can invoke all the tricks of legal advocacy to do so.

Mello goes further, calling defense lawyers like himself "complicit" because "The participation of good defense lawyers in the capital punishment process *does* make the system, legal and beyond, feel more comfortable about executions." He goes so far as to experience himself as "the executioner's mask." Devoted defense lawyers save a few lives by struggling to combat a killing system from within, but by doing that provide the system with a false aura—even an illusion—of legal and moral compassion. And the defense lawyers experience their own death-haunted terror of the consequences of failure. "We're only lawyers," Mello wrote. "We make mistakes. Those mistakes ought not to kill people. But they do."

The killing machinery itself corrupts all the professionals it enlists. The prosecutor who responded uneasily to the accusation of being akin to "a Nazi taking orders" must also fend off an element of self-accusation to that effect, even as she continues to carry out her professional duties. Something in her knows that in capital cases she functions as a *killing professional*.

A particularly dramatic example of these corrupting tendencies, as we've seen, can be found in prosecutors who morally oppose capital punishment and must grope for a rationale for their participation in it, such as a district attorney's claim that he could enhance his influence as an *opponent* of executions by prosecuting death penalty cases. An equally corrupting rationale is the claim of a governor who has the power of clemency but chooses to leave the whole matter to a "higher power," thereby making God, and not himself, responsible for the death that he could have prevented. What this claim inadvertently suggests is that human beings lack the moral authority to make judgments that kill their fellows.

Most directly corrupted is the medical profession in relation to lethal injections. Not only do healers become killers but, perhaps even more important, a healing profession lends its knowledge and practice to obscuring the fact of killing. The situation is structured so that even when doctors themselves refuse to take part, their professional authority is claimed by technicians (themselves medically trained) who carry out the injections. With this diffusion of responsibility, the corruption also becomes amorphous. More than just individual doctors, medical practice in general becomes tainted and corrupted in the extreme.

A key to capital punishment, as we have seen, is that no one feels responsible for the killing. Decision makers (prosecutors, judges, jurors, governors), remain aloof from the execution itself as they ambivalently contemplate legal arguments or make judgments from afar while hands-on executioners simply "do their job." The Supreme Court has further diffused responsibility by citing public opinion polls in its arguments. No wonder Camus could declare: "A law is applied without being thought out and the condemned die in the name of a theory in which the executioners do not believe."

Executions are bad for our minds because of their effect on our violent and vengeful impulses. All of us possess such impulses, so much so that they are considered "natural" in family members of murder victims, but prevailing social practices and ideologies can have much to do with whether they are kept in check. Capital vengeance, the principle of "a death for a death," sustains and legitimates those violent impulses. It encourages us to remain "stuck" in them rather than transforming them into constructive advocacies and actions.

The Killing Dynamic

For some prosecutors, judges, and jurors, vengeance becomes the equivalent of a "just war." And the power and rectitude of that mission can readily take precedence over moral and psychological compunctions about legal killing. What can result is a killing dynamic: the prisoner killed and did so brutally, so *we* must kill *him*. This may, in turn, stimulate further killing in the society.

The pattern can be observed in the martyrology fostered by groups on the violent American right. The Oklahoma City bombing in 1995 was timed to occur on the third anniversary of the ill-advised government attack on the Branch Davidians in Waco, and possibly timed as well to take place on the exact day of the execution of Richard Wayne Snell in Arkansas for murders he had committed. Snell and the dead Branch Davidians remain martyrs for the radical right, as does Timothy McVeigh in the anticipation of *his* execution.

Even without such clear martyrology, executions can set off violent impulses in ways that are difficult to detect. Killers can readily assume a sense of "righteous slaughter" when they can view their act as appropriate revenge for some prior killing, including an execution. What emerges is a self-propelling dynamic, a vicious circle: from criminal murder to legal killing inspiring further criminal murder and then more legal killing, *ad infinitum*.

Moreover, that vengeful mind-set can extend to larger arenas. It is consistent, for instance, with embracing almost any level of violence, including "ethnic cleansing" or even genocide. "A death for a death" can become thousands of deaths for a death. In that way habits of killing can be sustained and infinitely expanded. The death penalty is hardly in itself the cause of such large-scale killing, but it does (in Mario Cuomo's words) "configure our souls" in that direction.

The American Habit of Violence

However one feels about capital punishment, one must admit that it is almost uniquely ours. The writer David Rieff recently observed that the death penalty is "one of those peculiar American institutions that make citizens of the other developed countries shake their heads with wonder." Indeed, it is so widely disowned that international tribunals seeking to bring the perpetrators of genocide in Bosnia and Rwanda to justice cannot even consider it as an option. Henry LeClerc, president of the Human Rights League in Paris, has said, "For us, what the Americans are doing is completely incomprehensible, that such an advanced country can be involved in such an act of barbarism." The United States is the only nation in the world since 1997 known to have executed inmates who committed crimes while under the age of 18. Even Iran, Nigeria, Pakistan, Saudi Arabia, and Yemen have apparently stopped doing this.

There is no simple answer to the vexing question of why, among western democracies, only America retains the ultimate ownership of death. One could fill many volumes with a consideration of all the relevant factors—historical, psychological, and racial—and still be left with much uncertainty.

We choose here to emphasize one overriding theme, what we call the American habit of violence, as it overlaps with a second important pattern, the sustained polarization of good and evil. America is by no means the only nation of settlers with a history of extreme violence toward the native population; nor are we the only society guilty of centuries of black slavery. But America is special in creating so extreme and long-standing a practice of gun-centered killing, along with a reverence for the gun that has rendered it a sacred object. The overall ideological phenomenon can be given an awkward but revealing name, "gunism." Nothing symbolizes control or ownership of death better than the gun. By holding a loaded gun in one's hand, one takes possession of life and death.

Violence is at the heart of our creation myth. The cultural historian Richard Slotkin tells us that in American mythology the founding fathers were not "those eighteenth-century gentlemen who composed a nation at Philadelphia" but rather "the rogues, the adventurers, and land-boomers; the Indian fighters, traders, missionaries, explorers, and hunters who killed and were killed until they had mastered the wilderness." The mythology was enormously enhanced by romanticized visions of citizens' militias during the American Revolution, and it was racialized from the beginning, bound up with the slaughter by guns of native Americans and with the gun-power that created and sustained the institution of black slavery. It was greatly elaborated in the frontier narratives of Daniel Boone and Davy Crockett, and the flintlock rifle and the Colt .45 revolver were especially sacralized. Both weapons have been lovingly portrayed in generations of western films whose heroes, with only their horses and weapons, create or defend their version of a just society.

Through the flux of people and ideas in our always fragile society, the gun remained entrenched as an essential aspect of our identity—the icon of freedom, power, and the rights of the individual.

In that way, the gun has filled some of the psychological vacuum created by the relative absence of traditional American culture. Looked upon as an "equalizer," it became an important vehicle for our sense of creating a new, egalitarian people. The American reverence for guns became (as a leading proponent put it) "one of the great religions of the world." This suggests how close we have come to being a "gunocracy."

This gunocracy always claimed a religious component, and it came to be bound up with absolutized American visions of good and evil. The gun could be embraced as part of the godly forces of light in the struggle against satanic forces of darkness. Even though the gun, over the years, has been the agent of millions of homicides, we tend to focus more on punishing the gunman (often by sending him to death row) than combating the gun.

Of course, many murders are committed with other weapons, or with bare hands. But the gun, by making murder easy, has had much to do with our astonishing homicide statistics and our large number of convicted killers—and therefore with the widespread American sense of social evil. An early American answer to all such evil was the near-instant death penalty imposed by "frontier justice," whether by means of the gun or by hanging. Evil was to be eliminated by killing. While subsequent forms of execution became more structured and medicalized, the death penalty became an ultimate weapon in this continuing crusade to destroy or "murder" evil.

Executions also became part of a "pornography" of violence and death—a prurient display of grotesque forms of killing and dying. A historian describes a nineteenth-century "taste for body-horror," as displayed in many executions and in most lynchings, as "illicit" and "titillating." In the twentieth century a broader pornography of death (according to the respected anthropologist Geoffrey Gorer) has taken the form of lurid, highly exploitative renditions in the mass media of every variety of killing. Our newest pornography, at the beginning of the twenty-first century, lies in the seemingly opposite direction, a muting of killing—through lethal injections—

so that death becomes a "nonevent," deemed necessary for the moral health of American society.

More generally, our many-sided habit of violence feeds our fascination with the death penalty. We can take steps to redirect our imaginations into healthier forms of expression only if we confront that long-standing "habit" which so distorts them.

False Witness

By maintaining the death penalty, we institutionalize our habit of violence. Americans have only now begun to grasp the psychological and moral consequences of this structured state killing which, overtly or indirectly, reverberate throughout our society.

We have seen capital punishment as society's attempt to bear witness to acts of brutal individual murder, but it turns out to be an expression of *false witness*. Other than revenge, it fails to carry out commitments made on behalf of murder victims—to provide solace and "closure" to their families and to the rest of society, to deter other potential murderers, and to diminish homicidal violence in general. And by implementing the death penalty the state assumes ownership of death and thereby claims an ultimate form of omniscience, "the authority of perfect knowledge in final things," as John Leonard put it. That is what Norman Mailer means when he speaks of the prosecutor in capital cases as "an avenging angel" and the judge as "a god."

In that and other ways, the death penalty violates democratic standards. Indeed, the prolonged and excruciating litigation surrounding capital cases can be understood as the desperate efforts of a democracy to deal with a totalistic policy. The huge costs of that litigation to the state—far exceeding, as many have pointed out, the costs of lifelong imprisonment—have to do with the insistence, within a democracy, upon a detailed search for every possible factor that might prevent what is surely the most extreme abuse of state power: the execution of an innocent man or woman (and by extension, of *any* man or woman). But the overall problem remains the existence in a democratic society of the most antidemocratic of institutions.

To put things differently, by arrogating to itself the ownership of death the state threatens its very democratic structure.

The End of Executions

That institution, however, will not last much longer in America. About half of all Americans, as we've seen, now say they favor an alternative to executions, and we believe that very soon this will become a clear majority, as life without parole, now in wide practice, proves loophole-free and gains credibility. We predict that the number of those opposed, "undecided," or ambivalent about executions will grow so large that the U.S. Supreme Court, or dozens of state legislatures, will move against executions.

Steven Hawkins, longtime director of the National Coalition to Abolish the Death Penalty, recently told us that when capital punishment is abolished in America it will come about "not through one action, but many, over time." In a very real sense, this process, we believe, is already under way.

The year 1999, as we have observed, was a turning point, with a sharp rise in the number of executions forcing the public, the media and religious figures to confront the issue. New opposition from the pope and from Catholic bishops in America provoked debate across the religious and political spectrum, while energizing abolition activists. They held national conferences, circulated petitions, and raised money for full-page ads in the *New York Times*—all aimed at what was politically feasible (a moratorium) over what was, for now, still unlikely (abolition). At the same time, the media widely covered the many emerging cases of innocent men freed from death row (partly because of the rising use of DNA evidence). Finally, late in the year, another botched execution by electric chair in Florida forced an unprecedented outcry in that state, leading to its adoption of lethal injection.

Perhaps the most significant moment of all came on January 31,

2000, when Governor George Ryan of Illinois, a moderate Republican, halted all executions in that state, the first such moratorium in the country. He acted after the *Chicago Tribune* documented the cases of thirteen exonerated prisoners released from death row in the state since 1977 and found, further, that of 260 death sentences appealed in Illinois in recent years, fully half had been reversed (in more than thirty cases, death row inmates had been represented by lawyers who were later disbarred or suspended from practice). "I cannot support a system which, in its administration, has proven so fraught with error, and has come so close to the ultimate nightmare, the state's taking of innocent life," Ryan declared.

Ryan revealed that "the most anguishing period of my life" had occurred the first time he considered, then denied, a stay for a convicted killer, who then went to his death. While remaining a proponent of capital punishment, he clearly felt uncomfortable presiding over such a flawed system, observing, "I am ultimately responsible" and "There is no margin for error when it comes to putting a person to death." Referring to critics of his moratorium, he said, "I'd like to see those people sit in that chair and make the decisions I have to make." He appointed a panel to study the apparatus that enabled so many flawed convictions, saying, "I believe that a public dialogue must begin on the question of fairness of the application of the death penalty in Illinois."

His action was extremely significant, for it is officials like Ryan—tough-minded but extremely troubled by their personal responsibility—who will ultimately bring an end to executions in this country, much as they did throughout Europe.

And, crucially, Ryan's move met with little public or political opposition. The *Chicago Tribune* poll found that support for the death penalty had fallen off to 58 percent from 76 percent five years earlier, and that two of three Illinoisans supported the moratorium. A Republican state representative named Jim Durkin put it, "Even the most conservative individuals realize that there's a problem."

Later, in an interview, Ryan explained, "When you're the fellow that says, 'We're going to inject this person and put him to death,' you have to be able to live with yourself." Four months after declaring the moratorium, Ryan started sounding like an abolitionist. He said he strongly doubted any inmate would be put to death while he remained governor, unless the panel he appointed gave him "a 100 percent guarantee" against any mistaken convictions (which, of course, is impossible). "I don't know if we'll ever go back to the death penalty as we knew it as long as I am governor," Ryan advised.

As opponents of the death penalty are quick to point out, the possible execution of the innocent is not confined to Illinois. In recent years, over eighty-seven such cases are on record, including nineteen near-misses in Florida alone. In fact, a recent Columbia University study of 4,578 death sentence appeals from 1973 to 1995 found that *two-thirds* were successful in state or federal court, largely due to errors by incompetent defense lawyers or overzealous police and prosecutors who withheld evidence. And in 75 percent of the retrials the defendants were handed sentences less than death. "It's not one state, it's almost all the states," declared James Liebman, the lead author of the June 2000 report. He added that the capital punishment system seemed to be "collapsing under the weight of its own mistakes."

Governor Ryan's widely publicized moratorium marked the zenith of a year of new national soul-searching over the issue, and it set in motion a critical period of political and moral debate. The Roman Catholic archbishop of Los Angeles, for example, has called on the state's Catholic governor, Gray Davis, to impose a moratorium. Richard Dieter, director of the Death Penalty Information Center, said, "It's like snowflakes adding up on the branch may cause the branch to break at some point." Sisten Helen Prejean observed that, at last, she sensed "the waters moving" on this issue. The European Union called on America's other thirty-seven death penalty states to follow the lead of Illinois.

Related actions occurred in many states. Bills to enact statewide moratoriums were introduced by legislators in twelve states, including Oklahoma, Maryland, Alabama, and Kentucky. The state legislature in New Hampshire surprisingly voted to abolish the death penalty, as several conservative lawmakers switched sides expressing concerns about faulty convictions or said they had come to recognize that there was something "unseemly about the state being in the position of executing people," as one senator put it. (The governor later vetoed the bill.)

The Philadelphia city council called for a moratorium in the state until a study could determine that the death penalty was being applied fairly. In Oregon, forces led by former senator Mark Hatfield moved to put a "life for life" measure on the ballot that would end executions and instead provide for sentences of life without parole. Senator Patrick Leahy, declaring a "growing national crisis in the administration of capital punishment," introduced in Congress a package of death penalty reforms called the Innocence Protection Act. "There hasn't been this kind of discussion questioning the death penalty in decades," U.S. Senator Russ Feingold asserted. "I think you're at the beginning of the wave of public sentiment against the death penalty."

The *St. Petersburg Times, Gainesville Sun*, and *Miami Herald* called for a moratorium in conservative Florida. A wide range of other major newspapers in Maryland, California, Pennsylvania, and Texas demanded halts to (or outright bans on) executions in their states. The *New York Times* called for the abolition of the death penalty *everywhere*, recalling Justice Harry Blackmun's declaration that he wished to dismantle the "machinery of death." The American Bar Association released a report called "A Gathering Momentum," referring to the drive for moratoriums, an idea it had proposed in 1997.

There have been other developments pointing to a profound reconsideration of the entire question of state killings. Shortly after protests caused Florida to practically put its electric chair in mothballs, the U.S. Supreme Court halted an execution by electrocution in Alabama and hinted that the justices might use this opportunity to debate the constitutionality of the method. Meanwhile, Barry

Scheck and other attorneys spearheaded a new nationwide drive to study the claims of innocence of hundreds of prisoners on death row, often relying on new DNA results. Indeed, the expanded use of DNA testing dramatically increases the chances of establishing, scientifically, the occurrence of wrongful executions.

Popular culture can be a partial barometer of public and political opinion, and we find it significant that there has been a sharp swing in the number of anti–death penalty dramas on television (even on daytime soap operas) and in movie theaters. The popular film *The Green Mile*, for example, despite its somewhat muddled moral message, exposed millions of Americans to several graphic execution scenes.

Within a few days in February 2000 this sequence of events took place: Senator Feingold, along with the National Conference of Catholic Bishops, called for President Clinton to suspend federal executions (twenty-one prisoners sat on federal death row, including Timothy McVeigh); at a church service attended by Clinton, the president's pastor in Washington called for a "serious reexamination" of capital punishment; Attorney General Reno ordered a new study to determine if racial disparities exist in federal capital cases; and the NBC television program *West Wing* depicted a president agonizing over a federal execution, and after allowing it to proceed, getting down on his knees in the Oval Office, praying, "Forgive me, God, for I have sinned."

In real life, President Clinton ultimately refused to initiate a federal moratorium, but he did voice support for Governor Ryan's "courageous" stand in Illinois and promised to tighten up procedures to decrease the chance of wrongful convictions. Clearly, the image of an innocent man or woman going to the death chamber had put advocates of the death penalty on the defensive, for this is the ultimate denigration of the democratic process Americans revere.

This has caused an increasing number of nationally known conservatives—ranging from Oliver North and Pat Robertson to George Will and William F. Buckley Jr.—to question capital punishment. "The political climate is shifting," Ted Lynch, an authority on criminal justice at the Cato Institute, said recently, adding: "When you consider the foul-ups and mix-ups and incompetence that you often find in government work it gets scary. You realize that the institution that puts people to death is the same one that delivers the mail to the wrong people." Indeed, many longtime anti–death penalty activists now emphasize issues of fairness and innocence, not moral principle. They have discovered that most people "are not going to be opposed to the death penalty just because a few people say they should," Richard Dieter of the Death Penalty Information Center observed.

In addition, some anti-abortion activists are now speaking up against the death penalty, claiming a desire to be "consistent."

Polls continue to drift in the direction of opposition to the death penalty. One of the most interesting came out of Missouri, one of the nation's most active execution states. A poll of 1,000 state residents conducted by the Center for Social Sciences and Public Policy Research of Southwest Missouri State University in November 1999 found that 56 percent said they would support a moratorium on executions for three years to allow a study of sentencing practices. And, equally significantly, only 35 percent said they would be less likely to vote for a legislator if he came out against the death penalty. Indeed, Ron Tabak, a leading anti–death penalty attorney in New York, believes that more politicians will begin speaking out against executions "as they see it no longer means political death to do so."

Indeed, every case of an innocent man freed from death row drives another stake into the heart of capital punishment. The Gallup poll of February 2000 found, rather surprisingly, that the average American estimates that about 10 percent of people sentenced to death "are really innocent." At about the same time, a statewide poll in Connecticut found that 30 percent of the public believed it likely that the state would execute someone later found to be innocent.

While opposition to the death penalty is growing, it is also true that surveys continue to show that most Americans are not philosophi-

cally opposed to the notion of state killings. But does that necessarily mean that executions cannot be outlawed in America any-
time soon?

Few people know that at the moment when many western nations, such as France and England, abolished the death penalty,
polls showed strong public support for capital punishment. In
many of these countries, surveys *continue* to find significant support. Yet executions were banned (sometimes quite suddenly) and
continue to be outlawed without much protest. In fact, Peter
Hodgkinson, director of the Centre for Capital Punishment Studies in London, once said he knew of no country which had abolished executions with clear majority support from its citizens.
Today, in Canada, our relatively peaceful neighbor to the north,
polls have consistently revealed that three out of four citizens support the death penalty for the most heinous crimes. Yet capital punishment was outlawed in Canada long ago, and there is no strong
movement to restore it.

In the final years of "Saint Guillotine" in France, in the 1960s
and 1970s, polls showed strong support for the principle of capital
punishment, yet little clamor for its widespread use. Many candidates who ran for the National Assembly spoke out against the
death penalty and found that this did not prevent their election
(the public ranked this issue relatively low in import). Significantly,
legislators in France (and England too) tend to claim that they lead
public opinion and do not necessarily follow it, unlike their counterparts in America.

In France, the turning point came in 1981, with the election of
Francois Mitterand as president. He named as minister of justice a
criminal attorney and longtime foe of the death penalty. During his
first year in office, riding a wave of popularity, Mitterand endorsed
abolition, the assembly complied, and after more than 200 years of
decapitations, the reign of the guillotine was over. Although polls
show that close to half of the French people support capital punishment, few have pressed for its return.

In England, a long tradition of hangings was challenged repeat-

edly starting in the 1950s, following a number of controversial
cases, including the executions of an innocent man (Timothy
Evans), a woman (Ruth Ellis), and a mentally impaired teenager
(Derek Bentley). Parliament split on abolition, but in 1965, Prime
Minister Harold Wilson freed his Labour party supporters in the
House of Commons to vote their conscience on the issue—ex-
plaining that while citizens might not like what you stand for, they
tend to respect conscience.

This led to two months of Parliamentary debate, culminating in
the passage of a bill mandating a five-year moratorium, while the
issue was studied further. When the murder rate did not soar, the
legislators did away with the hangman permanently in 1969, without much protest from the public, which by then had grown
accustomed to the absence of hangings and perhaps felt relief in
losing that burden. Since then, bills calling for the return of capital
punishment have often been proposed, and they gained some support after IRA terrorist attacks in London. But even the efforts of
Prime Minister Margaret Thatcher—and support in the polls—
failed to bring back the hangman.

Some of the trends that led these two countries to abolition are
already occurring in America: outrage over the possible execution
of the innocent; a growing number of legislators speaking their
conscience; the imposition of moratoriums. Meanwhile, recognition of the merits and credibility of life without parole expands
every year. It became clear in Europe and Canada that most people
did not care passionately about this issue; in fact, they felt so ambivalent, even tortured, when the state killed a prisoner that they
would just as soon see the practice stopped entirely, and eventually
it was. This surely intersects with current attitudes and emotions in
our country.

Indeed, William Bowers, the research scientist who has spent
years studying attitudes of the public and jurors toward the death
penalty, calls capital punishment "a hollow symbol to most who say
they favor it." Support, he adds, is abstract, ideological, and non-
empirical. The death penalty, he told us, "holds appeal as an ex-

pressive symbol, not as a policy preference. It has become a self-perpetuating political myth."

The U.S. Supreme Court could reverse course and, as in the *Furman* case in the early 1970s, suddenly and unexpectedly declare a moratorium—perhaps a lasting one—on executions. This might happen if the Court became persuaded that it is mistaken about the public's view of capital punishment. The tide could turn because, as Bowers declares, "the Eighth Amendment requires the Court to act on its most enlightened interpretation of contemporary values." As Richard Dieter, director of the Death Penalty Information Center, put it, "There are a lot of reasons why the Supreme Court could find that capital punishment is still arbitrary and freakish."

If polls continue to show majority support for life without parole as a preferred alternative to executions, it could change the way judges, lawmakers, and the media respond to this issue on every important level, especially as new cases of innocent men and women on death row emerge, perhaps proliferate in the coming months (as we expect they will). Large numbers of Americans, we feel, will come to believe that if—as nearly everyone agrees—the justice system can never be 100 percent right, then how can it administer punishment that's 100 percent irreversible?

As the *Christian Science Monitor* recently put it, "The best way to resolve the controversy would be to put this form of punishment on the shelf of history, as most other modern democracies have. State-sanctioned killing is at odds with the need to reduce the level of violence in society." America would then join most of the modern industrial world, which has abandoned capital punishment "out of some embarrassed sense that it is a barbaric vestige of an archaic culture," as the writer Russell Baker recently observed.

We believe the day will soon come when a clear public desire for an alternative to the death penalty will prompt legislators to convert this preference into law—or they will be replaced by those who will.

Rick Halperin, a historian and director of Amnesty International's Death Penalty Project in Texas, tells us that now, even from the execution capital of the world, he can "clearly see the end of capital punishment in sight. I am much more optimistic now than in recent years. I know we are going to lose many more individuals before it is abolished; but," he adds, "we are reaching the point where abolition is obtainable."

Overcoming Illusions

As always, we have choices. Top officials sometimes find it easier to change their minds later in their careers. This late-life turnabout—what we have called a "retirement syndrome"—exists, as we have seen, among people who have spent much of their careers advocating and carrying out the death penalty. Upon leaving or planning to leave their involvement in that work, they call forth long-suppressed doubts by giving voice to the negative pole of their ambivalence.

Many examples have been mentioned in this book. Governor Pat Brown's switch late in his final term is a particularly poignant case in point. He went from a deepening doubt to an unsuccessful campaign as an opponent of the death penalty, then wrote a memoir decades later in which he expressed his sense of profound personal cost, of guilt and regret, at having been given such "awesome, ultimate power over the lives of others."

In these ways the "retirement syndrome" permits one to state, and act upon, what one has always known in a part of one's mind: that executions are wrong and profoundly harmful to everyone. But can we, as a society, afford to wait for such retirement wisdom?

A condemned man can be criminally guilty and at the same time an object of human sacrifice. He becomes a target not only for society's justified anger at his crime but for the pain, guilt, and rage having to do with *all* crime—and beyond that, for the overall violence in our society. In the process we fail to confront the broader social conditions that are conducive to destructive behavior of every kind. We also foster the illusion that we are taking bold steps to combat evil.

The death penalty is both a concrete policy—something we can *do* about killing and sin—and a highly abstract symbol. Behind it lies a mystical vision of total evil that can be extirpated to achieve total virtue. Our illusion becomes not only that of controlling crime and killing, but of controlling death itself. We resort to "the most premeditated of murders," as Camus wrote, in order to convert our moral and psychological confusion into an illusory certainty.

In this book we have explored a constellation of confusion: high support for the death penalty, indifference to having it carried out, and discomfort with actual executions. There appears to be a psychological need to keep capital punishment in place, for now. Doing so provides a collective vision of toughness and revenge, along with an all-pervasive illusion of control. People can feel that this is the right thing for true justice—until they are exposed to the fact of actual executions and, currently, the alarming rise in the number of executions.

We have seen the widespread moral and psychological ambivalence in prosecutors and all others who implement the death penalty, including judges, jurors, wardens, prison guards, doctors, technicians, and state governors. All make use of distancing mechanisms—forms of psychic numbing—to enable them to carry out their professional duties. Some may embrace the death penalty with particular fierceness as a means of overcoming that ambivalence and of suppressing feelings of guilt. While dealing with the transgressions of convicted murderers, all struggle to fend off a sense of their *own* transgression in assuming the godlike stance of determining whether another human being will live or die. It seems that no one involved can be comfortable with capital punishment.

And what of the ordinary Americans who have nothing to do with actual executions? They may want the death penalty on the books, yet they rarely seem enraged that the vast majority of convicted murderers escape with less than the ultimate penalty. (If they thoroughly believed in violent revenge, they would have to demand thousands of executions every year.) And little widespread celebration greets the instances when the state actually executes someone.

What does this mean? Hugo Bedau wrote a few years ago: "One might hazard the hypothesis that the average person seems convinced the death penalty is an important legal threat, abstractly desirable as part of society's permanent bulwark against crime, but that he or she is relatively indifferent to whether a given convict is executed on a given date as scheduled, or is indeed ever executed." That is, people embrace the principle as a psychological source of security—which turns out to be fragile because it is readily threatened by whatever reminds them that execution is a form of killing.

That fragility has been made clear by the increasing number of Americans—now believed to be a majority—who surrender their support for the death penalty when given the alternative of life without parole. The shift suggests that political support for the death penalty is grounded not in bedrock, as often asserted, but in sand.

Why is that so? We have observed that human beings are constituted so as to resist face-to-face killing of another human being, especially if he is immobilized—a psychological barrier that has to be overcome to carry out the killing. We recall Turgenev's observation at the execution in Paris in 1870 that "not one of us, absolutely no one looked like a man who realized he had been present at the performance of an act of social justice; everyone tried to turn away in spirit and, as it were, shake off the responsibility for the murder." Even those of us far away from an execution can feel glimmers of that disjunction and self-condemnation, whether in connection with the guillotine or the IV drip of the lethal injection. Executioners and bystanders alike have become psychologically vulnerable to the reverberations of the killing many of them endorse—because they feel it to be so deeply wrong.

The Survivor Mission

As we have seen, feelings of vengeance in response to horrible murders are widespread and, in part, understandable. Yet we have observed how such vengeance fails to relieve the terrible pain of grief and loss. At the other end of the continuum we find increasing numbers of Americans who seek to break out of that killing dynamic by rejecting vengeance and by advocating social policies geared to prevent or minimize violence in general.

For this survivor mission on behalf of all society to have genuine power, however, it must also include a visceral sense of the horror of the original crime. That recognition, along with feelings of anger and vengeance, can then be transmuted into an ethos of enhancing human life. In that way we reject all claims to owning the death of anyone else.

Are we capable of holding a compassionate perception of both the horror of the original murder and the wrongness of legal killing in capital cases? Such an inclusive response requires us to confront rather than fend off difficult issues of death and killing, but this is by no means beyond our psychological capacity. Indeed, we see more and more examples of it occurring today. By sanitizing executions and limiting genuine witness, the state seeks to overcome our inherent revulsion to killing, but that revulsion needs, instead, to be nurtured and mobilized. We can then bear witness to human cruelty in ways that enhance the entire flow of human life.

Notes

1: The Pope's Travel Plans

7　*"I guess timing is everything"*: *New York Times*, January 31, 1999.
　　"God works": *St. Louis Post-Dispatch*, January 28, 1999.
　　"If we can't execute": *St. Louis Post-Dispatch*, January 30, 1999.
　　Polls showed that: *New York Times*, May 9, 1999.
　　"should have received": *St. Louis Post-Dispatch*, January 30, 1999.

8　*"I think that if"*: *Boston Globe*, January 31, 1999.
　　"I knew as soon as": *St. Louis Post-Dispatch*, January 31, 1999.

9　*"That kind of discrepancy"*: *Kansas City Star*, March 10, 1999.
　　"courage": *New York Times*, March 9, 1999.
　　"pope's travel schedule": *Washington Post*, March 21, 1999.

10　*"a relic of barbarism"*: *Cincinnati Post*, February 18, 1999.
　　"The taking of human life": *Richmond Times-Dispatch*, March 22, 1999.
　　"killing people to show": *St. Petersburg Times*, July 1, 1999.

11　*"The pope is the leader"*: *Lincoln Journal Star*, January 29, 1999.
　　"There's a change": *New York Times*, May 21, 1999.

13　*"The teachings of the church"*: *Boston Globe*, March 20, 1999.
　　Cardinal Law and Susan Gove: *Boston Globe*, March 20–23, 1999.

14　*"If you take"*: *San Francisco Examiner*, May 1, 1999.

16　*"failed completely"*: *New York Times*, April 26, 1999.
　　"Babbitt sounds": *Boston Herald*, April 28, 1999.

17　*"They're sane enough"*: *New York Times*, April 26, 1999.
　　"strong commitment": *Associated Press*, May 2, 1999.
　　"died as a result": *Sacramento Bee*, May 5, 1999.

18　*"We definitely have the potential"*: Authors' interview.
　　"He has to have several": *New York Times*, May 9, 1999.

2: Executions in America

Much of the death penalty history material in this chapter and later is
drawn from the following books: Cesare Beccaria, *On Crimes and*

Punishments (New York: Marsilio Publishers, 1996); Walter Berns, *For Capital Punishment* (New York: Basic Books, 1981); John Bessler, *Death in the Dark* (Boston: Northeastern University Press, 1998); Jan Gorecki, *Capital Punishment: Criminal Law and Social Evolution* (New York: Columbia University Press, 1983); Jesse Jackson, *Legal Lynching: Racism, Injustice and the Death Penalty* (New York: Marlowe, 1996); John Laurence, *The History of Capital Punishment* (New York: Citadel Publishing, 1960); James W. Marquart, Sheldon Ekland-Olson, and Jonathan R. Sorensen, *The Rope, the Chair, and the Needle: Capital Punishment in Texas* (Austin: University of Texas Press, 1991); Louis P. Masur, *Rites of Execution: Capital Punishment and the Transformation of American Culture, 1776–1865.* (New York: Oxford University Press, 1989); James J. Megivern, *The Death Penalty: An Historical and Theological Survey* (Mahwah, N.J.: Paulist Press, 1997).

23   *"I think there's some idea"*: *Nightline*, April 20, 1998.
25   *"launched into eternity"*: In this way those who carry out the execution can see themselves as benefiting the condemned man by conferring immortality upon him. This is a form of what Lifton calls "altruistic killing" in Robert Jay Lifton, *Destroying the World to Save It: Aum Shinrikyō, Apocalyptic Violence and the New Global Terrorism* (New York: Metropolitan Books, 1999), 65–70.
29   *They learn it from*: Quoted in Masur, *Rites of Execution*, 65.
       psychic numbing: This is explored in Robert Jay Lifton, *Death in Life: Survivors of Hiroshima* (Chapel Hill: University of North Carolina Press, 1968, 1991).
37   *Abraham Lincoln once told*: William J. Buchanan, *Execution Eve* (New York: New Horizon Press, 1993), 76.
       Mainly in the South: Jackson, *Legal Lynching*.
       "So much for deterrence": Ibid.
       By the 1920s: Marquart, et al., *The Rope*.
39   *"perhaps the saddest aspect"*: Arthur Koestler, *Reflections on Hanging* (New York: AMS Press, 1957), 61.

3: Methods of Execution

43   *G. W. Peck*: Louis P. Masur, *Rites of Execution: Capital Punishment and the Transformation of American Culture, 1776–1865* (New York: Oxford University Press 1989), 20–22.
44   *"For all the fervor"*: *New York Review of Books*, January 20, 2000.
45   *"They're keeping their tradition"*: Stephen Trombley, *The Execution Protocol: Inside America's Capital Punishment Industry* (New York: Crown, 1992), 41.
46   *"until his flesh rots"*: *Wheeling Countryside* (West Virginia), October 7, 1998.
       A survey of thirty-nine: Mark Costanzo, *Just Revenge: Costs and Consequences of the Death Penalty* (New York: St. Martin's Press, 1998), 54.
48   *"This is the greatest thing"*: David McCullough, *Truman* (New York: Simon & Schuster, 1992), 454.

52 *"the body screams"*: David von Drehle, *Among the Lowest of the Dead: The Culture of Death Row* (New York: Times Books, 1995), 399.

53 *The prison installed a headrest*: Donald A. Cabana, *Death at Midnight: The Confession of an Executioner* (Boston: Northeastern University Press, 1996), 8.
    "not pleasant to watch": Associated Press, June 4, 1998.

54 *"a form of torture"*: Costanzo, *Just Revenge*, 55.

55 Medina execution and aftermath: Based on several dozen clippings from Florida newspapers and the *New York Times* from January 1997 to the end of the year.

58 *"warped sense of humor"*: Associated Press, September 9, 1998.
    Nazi "euthanasia" and Karl Brandt: Robert Jay Lifton, *The Nazi Doctors: Medical Killing and the Psychology of Genocide* (New York: Basic Books, 1986), 45–133.
    "as heart-wrenching a prospect": St. Petersburg Times, August 30, 1998.

59 Davis execution: Based on articles from Florida newspapers, principally the *St. Petersburg Times* and the *New York Times* from July 1999 to the end of the year.

63 *"is supposed to be"*: Christopher Hitchens, "Scenes from an Execution," *Vanity Fair*, January 1998.
    "The use of a well-known": Jerome Gorman essay in Shirley Dicks, ed., *Congregation of the Condemned* (New York: Prometheus, 1991), 210–12.

64 *Nazi medicalization of killing*: See Lifton, *Nazi Doctors*.

65 *"creepy that we pervert"*: *The New Yorker*, February 10, 1997, 53.

66 Cannon execution: *Dallas Morning News*, April 22, 1998.

67 Stewart execution: *Richmond Times-Dispatch*, September 22, 1998.
    "wanted to die clean" . . . *"shithouse and all the shit"*: Robert Jay Lifton, *Home from the War: Vietnam Veterans—Neither Victims Nor Executioners* (New York: Simon & Schuster, 1973), 222–23.

4: Wardens and Guards, Chaplains and Doctors

73 *"without looking sadistic"*: Norman Mailer, "Until Dead," *Parade*, February 6, 1981.

74 *Peter Matos*: Beverly Gage, "The Executioner's Song," *Fairfield County Weekly*, October 24, 1996.

77 *"doubling"*: Robert Jay Lifton, *The Nazi Doctors: Medical Killing and the Psychology of Genocide* (New York: Basic Books, 1986), 418–65.

78 *"decent Nazi"*: Ibid., 114–19.

79 *"much more stress"*: Stephen Trombley, *The Execution Protocol: Inside America's Capital Punishment Industry* (New York: Crown, 1992), 205.
    Bill Armontrout: Ibid., 100.

80 *"Yes, but I refuse"*: Arthur Koestler, *Reflections on Hanging* (New York: AMS Press, 1957), 5.
    "sacred executioner": Hyam Maccoby, *The Sacred Executioner* (London: Thames and Hudson, 1982), 7.

82   *"deathwatch"*: Mark Costanzo, *Just Revenge: Costs and Consequences of the Death Penalty* (New York: St. Martin's Press), 65.
     "task-oriented": Trombley, *Execution Protocol*, 250.
     "Our executioner is a team": *Esquire*, August 1995.
     "knew...what job": Trombley, *Execution Protocol*, 216.
     groups in the past designated as outcasts: Robert Jay Lifton, *The Broken Connection: On Death and the Continuity of Life* (New York: American Psychiatric Press, 1979, 1996), 302–34.
83   *"Don't let them do this"*: From documentary film *Texas and the Death Penalty*, directed by Tassos Rigopoulos.
84   *highly visible model*: Helen Prejean, *Dead Man Walking* (New York: Random House, 1993).
86   *Don Roper*: Trombley, *Execution Protocol*, 146.
87   *One official in Missouri*: Ibid., 153.
88   *"You won't be seeing him"*: *Esquire*, August 1995.
89   *"for the conscience"*: *USA Today*, January 25, 1996.
     "give the firing squad": *New York Times*, December 11, 1995.
     Donald Hocutt and his dreams: *Esquire*, August 1995.
90   *Men will kill*: Quoted in Dave Grossman, *On Killing: The Psychological Cost of Learning to Kill in War and Society* (Boston: Little, Brown, 1995), 30.
91   *"the simple and demonstrable fact"*: Ibid., 4.
     "When one looks": Ibid., 118.
     "this is not like defending yourself": *Sioux City Journal*, February 17, 1998.
92   *"when the face cannot be seen"*. . . . *"and refuse to kill"*: Grossman, *On Killing*, 142–45, 234.
     A soldier at My Lai: Robert Jay Lifton, *Home from the War: Vietnam Veterans—Neither Victims Nor Executioners* (New York: Simon & Schuster, 1973), 36–71,
93   *"In combat, each man"*: Grossman, *On Killing*, 191.
     "zero-degree-torture": Quoted in Daniel Arasse, *The Guillotine and the Terror* (London: Thames and Hudson, 1994), 13.
     Dr. Guillotin came to regret: Ibid., 23.
95   *"Not only is this unethical"*: *Chicago Tribune*, December 12, 1982.
96   *"By using medical knowledge"*: Alexander Capros, quoted in *Washington Post*, December 6, 1984.
     "The syringe belongs" . . . *"it is a putting-to-sleep"*: Lifton, *Nazi Doctors*, 57, 71.
98   *"I knew he was dead"*: Gary E. Goldhammer, *Dead End* (Brunswick, Maine: Biddle Publishing, 1994), 132.
99   *Fred Leuchter*: Execution Protocol, Trombley, *Execution Protocol*, 88.
101 *Lewis E. Lawes*: Lewis E. Lawes, *Life and Death in Sing Sing* (Garden City, N.Y.: Garden City Publications, 1928).
102 *reminiscent of Eduard Wirths*: Lifton, *Nazi Doctors*, 384–414.
103 *William Leeke*: Ian Gray and Moira Stanley, *A Punishment in Search of a Crime* (New York: Avon, 1989), 109–18.
     James W. L. Park: Ibid., 125–32.

104 *Donald Cabana*: Donald A. Cabana, *Confession of an Executioner* (Boston: Northeastern University Press, 1996).

5: Prosecutors and Governors

108 *Brandon Hornsby*: Atlanta *Journal-Constitution*, July 4, 1998.
110 *improper comments*: Atlanta *Journal-Constitution*, March 12, 2000.
never attends an execution: Associated Press, August 29, 1998.
"Everyone who got death": John Bessler, *Death in the Dark* (Boston: Northeastern University Press, 1998), 99.
111 *"crying at night"*: Associated Press, November 16, 1999.
"Since the first day": Wendy Kaminer, *It's All the Rage: Crime and Culture* (Addison-Wesley, 1995), 164.
"deep moral ambivalence": Authors' interview with Kevin Doyle.
Norman Mailer claims: Parade, February 8, 1981.
112 *Ron Sievert*: Authors' interview. Also, Ronald J. Sievert, "Capital Murder: A Prosecutor's Personal Observations on the Prosecution of Capital Cases," *American Journal of Criminal Law* 27 (Fall 1999) no. 1, 105–16.
118 *"retirement syndrome"*: Robert Jay Lifton, *The Future of Immortality* (New York: Basic Books, 1987), 25–26. Lifton equates retirement syndrome with wisdom.
Janet Reno: USA Today, June 17, 1999.
Charles Tetzlaff: Associated Press, March 29, 1998.
119 *Charles Hynes*: From numerous *New York Times* articles, including September 25, 1996, and February 20, 1998.
120 Governor George Pataki and Robert Johnson: From numerous *New York Times* articles from March 17 to March 24, 1996, and December 4, 1996.
122 *Robert Morgenthau*: Based on numerous *New York Times* articles in 1996 and 1997, and James Traub, "The D.A. Dilemma," *The New Yorker*, July 28, 1997.
123 *1999 study*: Associated Press, January 2, 1999.
126 *Richard Blecker*: San Francisco Examiner, November 29, 1998.
"exercise of executive clemency": Bessler, *Death in the Dark*, 144.
127 *"The whole idea of clemency"*: San Francisco Examiner, November 29, 1998.
129 *"we have not executed"*: New York Times, January 7, 2000.
130 *relative altitudes of aircraft*: Robert Jay Lifton, *Home from the War: Vietnam Veterans—Neither Victims Nor Executioners* (New York: Simon & Schuster, 1973), 349.
"I think that's": Pittsburgh Post-Gazette, February 28, 2000.
Parris Glendening: Baltimore Sun, July 6, 1997.
132 *Daniel Kobil*: New York Times, February 4, 1998.
133 *Edmund G. "Pat" Brown*: Edmund G. (Pat) Brown with Dick Adler, *Public Justice, Private Mercy: A Governor's Education on Death Row* (New York: Grove Press, 1989).
135 *"You can't punish people enough"*: Sacramento Bee, August 29, 1998.
"thumbs up they live": Quoted in Ian Gray and Moira Stanley, *A Punishment in Search of a Crime* (New York: Avon, 1989), 326.

136   Mario Cuomo: From his essay in Shirley Dicks, ed., *Congregation of the Condemned* (New York: Prometheus, 1991), 259–63.

137   Cuomo and the Declaration of Life: *Boston Globe*, July 24, 1998.

6: Jurors and Judges

140   *A prosecutor in Macon, Georgia*: Associated Press, September 3, 1998.

141   *"It's a big decision"*: *New York Times*, April 10, 1998.

143   Darrel K. Harris case: From various *New York Times* articles, including March 9, 1998, and June 11, 1998.

145   *A decade ago*: Laurence Tribe, op. ed., *New York Times*, June 9, 1997.

147   *A prosecutor countered*: *New York Times*, June 13, 1997.
      "Were they men or": Robert Jay Lifton, *The Nazi Doctors: Medical Killing and the Psychology of Genocide* (New York: Basic Books, 1986), 4–5.
      One juror later spoke: *New York Times*, June 15, 1997.

148   *Capital punishment inspires*: *Parade*, February 8, 1981.
      It is one thing: Ibid.

149   *"death could not come out"*: *Baton Rouge Advocate*, September 26, 1998.
      "scary but not": Authors' interview with Kevin Doyle.

150   William Bowers and North Carolina quotes: From William J. Bowers, Marla Sandys, and Benjamin D. Steiner, "Foreclosing Impartiality in Capital Sentencing," unpublished draft paper.

151   *In a recent case in Virginia*: *Washington Post*, October 12, 1998.
      In February 1999: *Arkansas Democrat-Gazette*, February 2, 1999.
      "just wrecks": Ian Gray and Moira Stanley, *A Punishment in Search of a Crime* (New York: Avon, 1989), 202–7.

152   *Bowers, the principal research scientist*: Authors' interview with William Bowers.

154   *"most ingenious"*: Quoted in Wendy Kaminer, *It's All the Rage: Crime and Culture* (Addison-Wesley, 1995), 133.

156   Bowers discussion: William J. Bowers and Benjamin D. Steiner, "Death by Default," paper distributed by the Capital Jury Project, Northeastern University, Boston, 121.

158   *"There are only two choices"*: *Los Angeles Times*, April 13, 1998.
      "it will act": *Christian Science Monitor*, December 1, 1998.

159   Judge Robert S. Vance profile: Michael Mello, *Dead Wrong: A Death Row Lawyer Speaks Out Against Capital Punishment* (Madison: University of Wisconsin Press, 1998), 46.

160   *Gerald Kogan*: *Miami Herald*, January 2, 1999.

161   *Alex Kozinski*: *The New Yorker*, February 10, 1997, and *Nightline*, April 20, 1998.

7: Witnessing

168   *three psychiatrists at Stanford*: John Bessler, *Death in the Dark* (Boston: Northeastern University Press, 1998), 121.

Lesser discussion: Wendy Lesser, *Pictures at an Execution* (Cambridge: Harvard University Press, 1994), 4.

169   *Around Capital Punishment*: Quoted in Arthur Koestler, *Reflections on Hanging* (New York: AMS Press, 1957), 167.
laws on witnessing: Bessler, *Death in the Dark*, 72–73.

170   *three great Russian novelists . . . "had been destroyed"*: Robert Louis Jackson, *Dialogues with Dostoevsky* (Palo Alto: Stanford University Press, 1993), 5, 29–82, 307–8.

172   *Mark Twain, like some*: Quoted in Associated Press, October 1, 1999.

173   *He had just discovered . . . "the vocabulary and the penalty"*: Albert Camus, "Reflections on the Guillotine," in *Resistance, Rebellion and Death* (London: Hamish Hamilton, 1960), 127–28. In Camus's autobiographical novel, *The First Man* (New York: Knopf, 1995), the protagonist refers (in the third person) to this story of his father as "the one circumstance that had made such an impression on him as a child, had pursued him throughout his life and even into his dreams," so that "the same dread that so distressed his father and that he had left to his son as his only clear and certain legacy . . . a mysterious bond that connected him to the dead stranger" (81–82).

175   Kemmler execution: From Bessler, *Death in the Dark*, 49–51.

176   *Barbara Graham*: From Lesser, *Pictures*, 257.
Lynn Ford: *Editor and Publisher*, October 9, 1999.

177   *Michael Graczyk*: Bessler, *Death in the Dark*, 59.

180   *"We are dead-beddin' folks"*: Molly Ivins, syndicated column, June 18, 1997.

181   *"the ultimate exercise"*: *Sacramento Bee*, May 9, 1998.

183   *"pretty up"*: United Press, July 5, 1999.

184   *"Personally, yeah"*: Associated Press, December 3, 1998.

185   *In my time*: Christopher Hitchens, "Scenes from an Execution," *Vanity Fair*, January 1998.
David Bruck quotes: Ian Gray and Moira Stanley, *A Punishment in Search of a Crime* (New York: Avon, 1989), 79–86.

186   *Richard Stetler*: Authors' interview.

191   *Harry Connick/Dana Rinehart/Sister Helen Prejean*: Bessler, *Death in the Dark*.

192   *Don Hewitt/Cokie Roberts/Geraldo Rivera/Ernest van den Haag*: Ibid.

193   *As Wendy Lesser has noted*: Much of this section and quotes are drawn from Lesser, *Pictures*.

195   *"There would be a"*: Associated Press, May 15, 1998.

8: Murder Victims' Families

199   *"I would rather have had"*: *Time*, June 16, 1997.
see the man "tortured": *New York Times*, October 30, 1998.
"like a laser": *New York Times*, June 3, 1997.
"I feel happy": Associated Press, November 17, 1998.

200   *Since murder is*: Associated Press, January 13, 1999.

201   *Dr. Josef Mengele . . . needs respected*: Robert Jay Lifton, *The Nazi Doctors:
        Medical Killing and the Psychology of Genocide* (New York: Basic Books,
        1986), 382–83.
202   *brother of a murder victim in Nevada*: *Las Vegas Sun*, June 8, 1998.
        "My husband": *Augusta Chronicle*, November 28, 1998.
203   *A mother in Texas*: *Dallas Morning News*, April 19, 1998.
        "It is a sad": *Sacramento Bee*, April 19, 1998.
        "an eye for an eye": *New York Times*, June 3, 1997.
204   *"Don't use that word"*: *Richmond Times-Dispatch*, January 18, 1999.
208   Timothy McVeigh and Bud Welch discussion: *Colorado Daily*, November
        20, 1999.
209   *"fights despair"*: Associated Press, September 13, 1998.
        "Prior to my father's": Remarks by Representative Robert Cushing in New
        Hampshire legislature, March 12, 1998.
210   Marie Deans: Authors' interview, and Ian Gray and Moira Stanley, *A
        Punishment in Search of a Crime* (New York: Avon, 1989), 71–78.
211   *Norman Felton*: Gray and Stanley, *A Punishment*, 63–70.
        SueZann Bosler: From various sources, including Knight-Ridder article
        November 1, 1998, and Bosler's *Ladies' Home Journal* piece, October 1998.

9: Public Opinion, Private Doubts

215   *public opinion surveys*: Historical poll data from Robert M. Bohm,
        "American Death Penalty Opinion, 1936–1986," published in Robert
        Bohm, ed., *The Death Penalty in America: Current Research* (New York:
        Anderson Publishing, 1991), 113–43.
216   *Gaps*: This section is mainly from Bohm.
218   *Revenge, nobody*: *Nightline*, April 20, 1998.
        in 1995 a poll: *Time*, June 15, 1997.
219   *"a sense of personal satisfaction"*: Phoebe C. Ellsworth and Samuel R.
        Gross, "Hardening of the Attitudes: America's Views on the Death
        Penalty," *The Journal of Social Issues* 50 (1994), no. 2, 19–52.
        Polls find: Ibid.
220   *Hugo Bedau*: *Boston Globe*, June 4, 1997.
222   *"It is not hard"*: Ellsworth and Gross, 109.
223   *Focus group data*: Benjamin D. Steiner, William J. Bowers, and Austin
        Sarat, "Folk Knowledge as Legal Action," unpublished draft paper.
226   *A poll by*: *Chicago Tribune*, March 7, 2000.
227   *A recent* Newsweek *survey*: *Newsweek*, June 16, 1997.
228   *"need not be so rigid"*: *Sacramento Bee*, January 18, 2000.

10: The End of Executions

231   ownership of death: Robert Jay Lifton, *Destroying the World to Save It:
        Aum Shinrikyō, Apocalyptic Violence and the New Global Terrorism* (New
        York: Metropolitan Books, 1999), 210–13.

232 *"higher purpose" of their own belief systems:* Ibid.

233 *"terrifying and stressful and beautiful":* Michael Mello, *Dead Wrong: A Death Row Lawyer Speaks Out Against Capital Punishment* (Madison: University of Wisconsin Press, 1998), 126.

234 *"The justices are honorable people"* . . . *"ought not to kill people. But they do":* Ibid., 6, 218, 263, 270.

236 *"A law is applied":* Albert Camus, Resistance, *Rebellion and Death* (London: Hamish Hamilton, 1960), 134.
martyrology fostered by groups: Lifton, *Destroying the World,* 328–32.

237 *"one of those peculiar":* **Los Angeles Times**, January 13, 2000.
Henry LeClerc: **New York Times**, January 25, 2000.
the only nation in the world: U.S. News, January 17, 2000.

238 *American habit of violence* . . . *destroy or "murder" evil:* See Lifton, *Destroying the World,* 327–28; Robert Jay Lifton, *The Protean Self: Human Resilience in an Age of Fragmentation* (University of Chicago Press, 1993, 1999), 34–36; Lifton, *Home from the War,* 137–59; and "The psyche of a 'gunocracy,' " *Newsweek,* August 23, 1999.
"the rogues, the adventurers, and land-boomers": Richard Slotkin, *Regeneration Through Violence: The Mythology of the American Frontier, 1600–1860:* (Wesleyan, Conn.: Wesleyan University Press, 1973), 83–84.

239 *"taste for body-horror"/"illicit"/"titillating":* Karen Halttunen, *Murder Most Foul: The Killer and the American Gothic Imagination* (Cambridge: Harvard University Press, 1998), 60–90.
pornography of death: Geoffrey Gorer, "The Pornography of Death," in *Death, Grief, and Mourning* (New York: Doubleday, 1965).

240 false witness: For concept, see Lifton, *Home from the War,* 392–93.
"the authority of perfect knowledge and final things": John Leonard quoted in Mello, *Dead Wrong,* 44.

242 *"I'd like to see those people":* Chicago Tribune, February 19, 2000.
The Chicago Tribune *poll:* Reported in *Chicago Tribune,* March 7, 2000.

245 *the president's pastor:* Reuters, February 15, 2000.

246 Ron Tabak: Associated Press, February 14, 2000.
poll in Connecticut: The Economist, May 15, 1999.

247 *Today, in Canada:* Montreal Gazette, December 31, 1998.

249 *"There are a lot":* USA Today, November 14, 1999.
"The best way to resolve": Christian Science Monitor, November 17, 1999.
"out of some embarrassed": From *New York Review of Books,* January 20, 2000.

250 *"retirement syndrome":* Pattern discussed in Robert Jay Lifton, "Nuclear Fundamentalism," in Robert Jay Lifton and Richard Falk, *Indefensible Weapons* (New York: Basic Books, 1982), 96–99.

251 *"the most premeditated of murders":* Camus, *Resistance, Rebellion and Death,* 143.

Index